FEELING PERSECUTED

Feeling Persecuted

Christians, Jews and Images of Violence
in the Middle Ages

Anthony Bale

REAKTION BOOKS

For Tim and Percy, with love

Published by
REAKTION BOOKS LTD
33 Great Sutton Street
London EC1V 0DX, UK

www.reaktionbooks.co.uk

First published 2010

Printed and bound in Great Britain by CPI/Antony Rowe, Chippenham, Wiltshire

British Library Cataloguing in Publication Data
Bale, Anthony Paul, 1975–
Feeling persecuted: christians, jews and
images of violence in the middle ages
1. Christianity and other religions – Judaism – History – To 1500.
2. Judaism – Relations – Christianity – History – To 1500.
3. Jews – Persecutions – Europe – History – To – 1500.
4. Violence – Religious aspects – Judaism – History – To 1500.
5. Violence – Religious aspects – Christianity – History – To 1500.
I. Title
261.2'6'094'0902-DC22

ISBN: 9 781 86189 761 9

Contents

1 'He Who is in Pain is Alive' 7

2 The Violence of Memory: Seven Kinds of
'Jewish' Torture 30

3 The Jewish Profile and the History of Ugliness 65

4 The Jew's Hand and the Virgin's Bier:
Tangible Interruption 90

5 Visiting Calvary: Contrition, Intimacy
and Virtual Persecution 118

6 Making Calvary 142

7 Cultures in Pain 168

CONVENTIONS & ABBREVIATIONS 191
REFERENCES 193
SELECT BIBLIOGRAPHY 239
ACKNOWLEDGEMENTS 245
PHOTO ACKNOWLEDGEMENTS 247
INDEX 249

CHAPTER 1

'He Who is in Pain is Alive'

How can we remember pain? What would an image of it be like?
Augustine thought it absurd to assume that when we think about
sadness or fear, we experience grief or terror. The problem is that
if the image of pain is not painful, how can it resemble pain?
It seems that Augustine did not have a good answer. He says that
we remember the affections of the soul by having 'notions' of them.
—Simo Knuuttila, *Emotions in Ancient and Medieval Philosophy*[1]

An Art of Intimate Terror

A study of the Christian representation of Jews might fittingly open
with a fairy-tale, a seemingly domestic but emphatically grisly fiction.
The Grimm brothers' 'The Boy Who Had to Learn Fear', written
down in the early nineteenth century but based on medieval folktales,
describes two sons. The elder son, though 'smart and sensible', is
afraid: of dark places, of the graveyard, of night-time, of any 'dismal'
place, which make him 'shudder'.[2] The younger son, who is 'stupid',
knows no fear and cannot shudder: 'That, too, must be an art of
which I understand nothing'. The younger son perceives his lack of
shuddering fear to be a kind of knowledge he has not yet acquired.
His brother's maturity is marked by his performance of fear: once
'fear' is known and understood, it is no longer terrifying, but recreational and useful.

The boys' father is concerned at his younger son's lack of fear, con-
vinced that he will never get on in life, so he commissions a sexton to
teach the boy how to 'shudder' in fear. The sexton pretends to be a
ghost, and meets the boy by night at the top of a belfry: the boy is
unafraid and merely pushes the 'ghost' down the stairs. Disgraced, the
boy is given fifty *talers* by his father and told to leave town: he goes on
his way, exclaiming to himself 'If I could but shudder! If I could but
shudder!' A passing man hears him saying this to himself and tells the
boy to spend the night sitting by the gallows where seven corpses are
hanging. But the hanged men cannot scare the boy; he merely feels
cold, stokes his fire, and takes down the bodies because he pities them.

A passing waggoner tells the boy that whoever can free a haunted
castle from evil spirits will marry the king's daughter, 'the most

beautiful maiden the sun shone on'. So the boy goes to the haunted castle, where strange things happen: terrifying animals prowl about, a bed moves of its own accord, a hideous old man appears with bones and skulls (which the boy simply turns on his lathe and makes into skittles).

For the next few nights similar things happen, but the boy remains unafraid. When six men appear with a coffin containing the cold body of the boy's dead cousin, the boy tries to revive the corpse, thinking to himself, 'When two people lie in bed together, they warm each other': he takes his dead cousin to bed, lies with him, soon the cousin revives, only to say 'Now I will strangle you!'

After the third night, the king sees that the boy has survived and driven away the evil spirits, and gives him his daughter's hand in marriage; thus the boy becomes king. The boy says 'That is all very well . . . but still I do not know what it is to shudder!'

The wedding between the princess and the boy is celebrated, but the boy is still muttering to himself 'If I could but shudder!' The princess grows angry, and tells her waiting-maid to gather a bucket of fish:

> At night when the young King was sleeping, his wife was to draw the clothes off him and empty the bucketful of cold water with the gudgeons in it over him, so that the little fishes would sprawl about him. Then he woke up and cried: 'Oh what makes me shudder so? – what makes me shudder so, dear wife? Ah! now I know what it is to shudder!'

The boy has been taught how to shudder, in pleasurable fear, the *art* of fear: he's not really afraid, but he can perform fearful shuddering correctly.

The Grimms' story seems ripe for Freudian analysis, the setting in the haunted house the epitome of the *unheimlich*, the uncanny. The story gathers images of obviously psychosexual neuroses and desires: the rejection by the father, the homoerotic, incestuous and morbid encounter with the dead cousin, the crazy bed with a life of its own, the boy's masturbatory nocturnal turning of his lathe, the fishy conjunction of sex and terror in the final scene of the wriggling gudgeons in the marital bed. Freudian horror is inherently sexual; Freud described emotions, like fear and terror, as a chain of repressions, displacements and negations, interrelating pleasure and pain. The Grimms' story is exactly about what Freud called 'that species of the frightening that goes back to what was once well known and had long been familiar'.[3]

Such a Freudian reading, though illuminating, has its limits, and would certainly fail to do justice to the story's complicated notion of edifying 'fear'. This fear is socially and culturally determined; it is a key part of 'becoming' a civilized adult; fear has its own pleasures, fear itself being precious and wished for; acquiring fear is what makes the protagonist of the story heroic; and fear is itself a learned *art*, a performance of shuddering, to use the boy's own terms, not the eruption of a thing repressed. Between learned fear and learned pleasure is an intimate and personally involved place, but it is also culturally constructed and socially contingent; the boy cannot perceive fear or terror, because these things do not inhere in, for instance, a black cat or an old castle – he must learn how to read with fear, to imagine terror, and to enjoy this painful kind of interpretation.

The thing that finally makes the boy shudder turns out to be a thinly veiled metaphor for sex, feminine intelligence and masculine vulnerability: the fishy slithering concocted by his wife and her maid, in bed, when he is naked. As he becomes king and becomes a man, the boy finally learns what it is to shudder. This is also a metaphor for pleasure, maturity and, finally, the intimately gratifying, sensual and aesthetic preciousness of being afraid. It is incorrect to see in this story a kind of subjection to fear and terror, of the subject's disabling 'passionate attachment' to his own subordination to fear:[4] through affect – by successfully linking ideas and cues to emotions and physical sensations – the boy performs recreational terror, and so fear can take its correct place in building character. The boy's reaction to the fish in his bed is itself childish and playful, but in being taught how to 'shudder' he learns how to master his performance of fear, pain rethought as its aesthetic assumption.

The Gothic setting of the story also demonstrates how the nineteenth-century craze for the Gothic returned to medieval forms and images – the haunted castle being the most obvious metonym – helping us to step back from the modern understanding of fear and terror to begin a more meaningful analysis of the medieval resonance of persecution. Enlightenment thought perceives fear to be inimical to civilization and knowledge (liberty, reason, law, order); psychoanalysis views fear as a kind of anxiety which reflects some anomie or repressed experience. Michel Foucault's influential theory of punishment and pain suggests that torture, ordeal and punishment are forced upon the individual's body by institutions, to effect a deperson-alizing conformity, in which pain destroys the individual.[5] Likewise, René Girard's theory of the relationship between terror and the sacred, whilst rightly stressing the importance of communal celebrations of past violence, supposes that the audience identifies with the per-petrator, not the victim, of such sacred violence.[6] Elaine Scarry has influentially argued that pain effects the 'unmaking' of subjectivity, but, as Talal Asad argues against Scarry, 'thinking about pain' is not, in religious culture, 'necessarily a private, thought-destroying event'.[7]

Medieval culture (like the nineteenth-century sublime and Gothic) valorized fear and pain. Consider the Platonic emphasis on 'holy terror' (*theos phobos*), a kind of awesome effect religious objects can have on us, or Augustine's declaration that 'he who is in pain is alive', or the beautiful ode by Judah Halevi (d. *c.* 1141) on what it is to tremble 'with holy fear':

> Can a body
> be a room
> to hold a heart
> attached to eagle's wings,
> when a man
> detests his life, only wants
> to roll his cheeks
> in the earth's
> best soil;
> trembles with holy fear,
> always weeping . . .[8]

Jewish and Christian selfhood starts with fear – with Adam declaring 'I was afraid' (Genesis 3:10) – and the first biblical stories give fear a key role in the acquisition of individual, social and divine knowledge (the words 'fear' and 'afraid' feature some thirty times in the book of Genesis alone); similarly, we might think of the much-repeated medi-eval liturgical motto taken from the Office of the Dead, 'the terror of death upsets me' ('*Timor mortis conturbat me*'), or that 'the fear of the Lord is the beginning of wisdom' (Psalm 110:1), or the famous opening line of St Anselm's first meditation: 'I am afraid of my life' ('*Terret me vita mea*').[9] In the words of Richard of St Victor (d. 1173), 'Great fear must be followed by pain': 'a prayer which comes out of a contrite and humiliated heart is more likely to be heard; humiliated by fear, broken by repentance.'[10] For Tertullian (150–222 CE), a founding father of Latin Christianity, Christians are 'a race of men ever ready for death'.[11] To act piously from fear is, according to the Talmud, almost as good as acting from love.[12] Edmund Burke's description of the 'delightful horror', rousing us to 'the strongest emotion which the mind is capable of feeling', strongly recalls medieval ideas of edifying fear.[13] This is one of Søren Kierkegaard's points in his discussion of the story of Abraham and Isaac; 'only one who knows anguish finds rest', and fear and terror help us to make our moral and ethical choices and so become moral citizens.[14]

Enlightenment thought holds 'conduct' to be separate from and valued more than 'feeling'; but in the Middle Ages as in the Gothic fear and related extreme feelings were actively cultivated as part of a serious and sustained set of ideas about what it was to be an intellectual subject, to be *moved* ardently, properly and constructively, interlinking behaviour, emotion and morality. Edmund Burke's *Philosophical Enquiry into the Origin of our Ideas of the Sublime and the Beautiful* (1757) makes very clear that an emotionally and aesthetically valuable kind of fear should not become an actual violence because, as with a phobia, by making a thing feared we make it precious and intimate and yet removed from ourselves. Horror is only 'delightful', to use Burke's term, if it builds, rather than destroys, one's character; likewise, Augustine and others proposed that fear and terror should be welcomed into one's intellectual development but should also be mastered and controlled, to be turned to a constructive empathy and rhetorical force.[15] Medieval clerical thinkers returned time and again to gaining the right kind of religious experience of imaginative persecution, arguing for the importance of humble fear in causing the soul to repent.[16] Such recreational pious persecution is quite different to the socially destructive and personally catastrophic 'sweet violence' of the tragic.[17]

If we wish to uncover how medieval people thought, we must take seriously how they felt; for the very idea of knowing, reading, viewing or retaining something was considered an engagement of the physical senses and the emotions. This book explores the various imaginative ways in which persecution and pain were welcomed into the everyday worlds and cultural lives of medieval people; I explore how medieval people placed their most precious symbols and themselves in positions of persecution, subject to violence. I trace the relationship between feeling and persecution, from *cognition* to *actualization*: that is, from the intellectual processes associated with pain, terror, fear, to the performances and rituals in which these feelings were engendered and made material. My working definition of what it is to 'feel persecuted' follows Aristotle's definition of fear as 'a painful or troubled feeling caused by the impression of an imminent evil that causes destruction or pain'.[18] This study considers culture, and cultural production, in terms of meaning, feeling, aesthetics, emotion and affect – which might apply to Jews and Christians equally. What follows is a discontinuous account of emotions, styles, fears and cultures, with material drawn from medieval English literary and visual sources, France, Germany, Italy, Spain and the Low Countries; I do not assume a homogenous 'Christian' or 'Jewish' experience of the Middle Ages. This study puts interdisciplinarity into practice, necessarily leading the scholar into unfamiliar and daunting places, aiming to explore the experience of medieval people whose lives and culture did not always know or respect disciplinary boundaries.

In contemporary culture, the 'power of nightmares' and paranoid fantasies animate our media with rolling news, loudly warning of imminent violence and chaos. We have our own characters and narratives – terrorist cells, apocalyptic global warming, AIDS, SARS, MRSA, swine flu – which teach us, in part, about Islam, weather-patterns and epidemics. But they also teach us about ourselves, about how we remember. We willingly subject ourselves to narratives of *terror*, religious fear and valorized images of suffering, of identity under attack; just such precious, even pleasurable, work was done by the medieval material considered in what follows.[19]

Ne Timueris: Devotional Violence

In the lovely pages of the early fourteenth-century Luttrell Psalter, one of the most richly illustrated books made in medieval England, is the injunction *ne timueris*: don't be afraid.[20] Directly beneath these words is a vivid scene of torture (illus. 1). Two Jews, crudely profiled with misshapen faces, whip Christ, who is bound, nearly naked, to a column. This seems to be a paradigmatic example of medieval 'anti-Semitism': vulgar and pervasive, flagrantly untruthful and unfairly violent. Such artefacts from late medieval England offer a unique opportunity to think about the aesthetic rather than politico-social construction of Judaism, as England had no Jewish community between 1290 and *c.* 1650. Jews were comprehensively expelled from England in 1290

1 Flagellation of Christ. Luttrell Psalter, England, *c.* 1350. BL Add. MS 42130, f. 92v.

by Edward I (*r.* 1272–1307): the English monarchy and aristocracy had become impossibly indebted to the Jews, and the expulsion of the Jews was a symbolic assertion of the king's control of his realm.[21] The English context of 1290 to *c.* 1650, in which there was no visible or organized Jewish community, allows us to retreat from an emphasis on actual victimhood and consider instead its cultural resonances. Late medieval England provides us with a context in which the Christian image of Judaism *must* be doing something else other than reflecting eyewitness encounters with Jews, Judaism and Jewish space. How might Sir Geoffrey Luttrell have read this violence? And what pleasure or instruction might he have gained from looking at an image which revels in its own bloodiness?

The image shows the Flagellation of Christ, demonstrating Christ's humanity and his degradation. The biblical authority for the details of the scene is scant.[22] Nonetheless, such scenes of Jews engaged in torturing Christ's body, a 'sensibility that combines pain and penitence [which] crested in late-medieval Europe', were very widespread.[23] The Vulgate Bible says only that the Jews 'gave him blows' (John 19:3), '[they] began to spit on him, and to cover his face, and to buffet him, and to say unto him: Prophesy: and the servants struck him with the palms of their hands' (Mark 14:65) and that they 'mocked' him (Luke 23:11). The column and flails were later, but persistent, inventions. The scene is based on Pseudo-Bonaventure's phenomenally widely read *Meditationes Vitae Christi* (*Meditations on the Life of Christ*), translated into English by Nicholas Love (d. *c.* 1424) as the *Mirror of the Blessed Life of Christ*:

oure lord was despoilete, bonden to a pilere, & harde & sore
scourgete, & so stant he nakede before hem alle, *that fairest yonge
manne of alle children that ever were born* taking paciently of thoo
foulest wrecches, the hardest & most bitter strokes of scourges,
& so is that moste innocent, fairest & clennest flesh, floure of alle
mankynde, alle to rente & full of wondes . . . [24]

A fixed point of purity in a moving sea of cruelty, the superlative
beauty and innocence of Christ is emphasized, contrasted with the
Jews' foulness. The Luttrell Psalter image gathers together the most
familiar cues through which Jews were represented in medieval
Christian culture, placing a moment of violence in a luxurious and
pious setting. A Jewish text, David's psalm, becomes the setting for a
celebration of the degradation of the Jewish image through the abjection of Christ.

The Jews are quickly recognizable: most obviously, their disfigured faces, with bulbous noses and exaggerated features; their profile
positioning, contrasting with Christ's gaze out into the viewer's world;
their active physicality as opposed to Christ's passivity; the lower
nakedness of the left-hand Jew versus the modesty of Christ; the
harsh line of their bodies and their bright parti-coloured clothing,
juxtaposed with Christ's soft lines, his skin which blends with the skin
of the parchment manuscript. The flagellating Jews direct the viewer-
reader's gaze to the centre of the page and to Christ's body, while the
flails (each with three ropes, to suggest the Trinity) and the Jews' red
clothes (suggestive of the blood of martyrdom) point towards the
lesson of the Passion: that Christ suffered for mankind, that his suffering was needed. For the medieval reader-viewer, the ugly violence
of the Jews holds beauty within it, of Christ's sacrifice and mankind's
redemption. The image would have stimulated the viewer's pathos –
an emotional, affective, penitential reaction. It is also a neat summary
of the medieval understanding of a (Jewish) cruelty (*crudelitas*),
which is opposed to (Christian) clemency (*clementiæ*): as Thomas
Aquinas (1225–1275) wrote, citing Seneca, 'those are called cruel who
exceed due measure in punishing', 'cruelty implies excess in exacting
punishment' and cruelty is a 'lack of mercy which withholds benefi-
cence'; the Jews in this image perform such a cruelty and, in doing so,
allow Christ to demonstrate mildness, sweetness of temper and tem-
perance. The cruel, according to Aquinas, are 'those who punish
another, not because of some fault he has committed, but because of

the pleasure they take in his being hurt'. Aquinas concludes that cruelty is a *deliberate* kind of 'human wickedness' (as opposed to 'sheer beastliness') and that 'savagery is directly opposed to the gift of piety'.[25]

The image is adjacent to the text of Psalm 48, raising further issues of meaning. This book is full of *imagines verborum*, marginal illustrations which reveal hidden textual meanings and draw out unexpected or memorable images from the text.[26] Likewise, over several pages, the Luttrell Psalter illustrates and explicates all of Psalm 48 with images of Jews attacking Christ: the Betrayal of Christ by Judas (f. 91r), Christ before Herod (f. 91v), the Mocking of Christ (f. 92r), and the Scourging of Christ (f. 92v). This is then a cycle of Passion images to accompany Psalm 48: as a word-play image, the illustrator *used* the image of Christ's suffering body to make tangible and memorable the spirit of Psalm 48, an invective against 'the folly of worldlings, who live on in sin, without thinking of death or hell'.[27] The psalm is not on first sight about violence, but inveighs against those who love money and worldly things: 'They that trust in their own strength, and glory in the multitude of their riches, / No brother can redeem, nor shall man redeem' (Psalm 48:7–8), 'they are laid in hell like sheep, death shall feed upon them./ And the just shall have dominion over them in the morning; and their help shall decay in hell from their glory' (Psalm 48: 15–16, the text adjacent to the Flagellation image). So these images work to associate Jews with matters of flesh (the imposition of violence) as opposed to spirit (the transcendence of this violence), and the sinfulness of worldliness given all Christ suffered for mankind. Likewise, St Augustine powerfully glosses Psalm 48:16 with the words

> Do you really want to have eyes only for present things, and no more? He who rose from the dead gave us promises about the future, but he did not promise us peace on this earth or rest in this life.[28]

The *Glossa Ordinaria*, the popular explanatory commentary on the medieval bible, repeated these lines of Augustine's, and glossed the lines '*Ne timueris*' with the admonition '*Ne timeantur potentes*': do not be afraid of the powerful.[29]

So in the rendering of Psalm 48 in the Luttrell Psalter, Jews are understood as physically powerful, Christ and Christians as spiritually strong but physically weak. The image offers a neat example of how

Jewish violent agency was created, represented and re-energized, only fifty years after the Jews' expulsion from England. Michael Camille has argued, regarding this and similar images in the Luttrell Psalter, that 'the Luttrells were learning to hate . . . not a real but an imaginary people', but he also suggests that the Luttrell family might have had an 'ancestral grudge' against the Jews because Geoffrey Luttrell's grandfather had been indebted to the Jews of London.[30] However, such Jewish violence against Christian bodies must, in this kind of context, be understood as an aesthetic experience which *enriched* the medieval reading experience through vivid and engaging images which interact with the text, a 'heightened and intensified experience of reading, through the discovery and appreciation of all the riches both apparent and concealed in the words.'[31] Moreover, as pictorial representations of the spirit of the psalm, the gaudy and insistently embodied Jews of the Luttrell Psalter distract our eyes, 'present things' calling out for our attention. Following Augustine's interpretation, medieval readers were to retrain their eyes, to see in the text and image something other than what it at first seems to represent. In a pious reading which sees the scene of violence as edifying, it makes good sense: to quote Augustine's explication of Psalm 48 again,

> Someone lives a bad life, yet he or she lives on, flourishes, strikes fear into others, and is widely honoured. Someone else leads a good life, but is criticised, reviled and slandered, but he or she toils on. It seems like darkness. But hidden in the root are vigour, fertility, and riches promised . . . The wicked will rue it inwardly . . . and repent of their taunts, but their repentance will be too late, and sterile.[32]

The Jews in the image from the Luttrell Psalter remake the text of the psalm through violence. They stand for wickedness, temporary power, agency, activity, contrast; but, most potently, they teach the reader, through their attention-grabbing and instructive violence, how to discern the correct, spiritual message encoded within the psalm.

Increasingly, and throughout medieval Europe, the Crucifixion became described as a specifically 'Jewish' crime, an interpretation informed by such images of Jewish violence against Christ's body. On the paradoxically luxurious page of the Luttrell Psalter, the image tells the viewer that when one is worldly, one inflicts violence on Christ just as the Jews did. The juxtaposition of the Jews as wicked rich men and Christ in the glory of persecution helped the Luttrell family think about their place in heaven, for the image demonstrates that the cruel, crude Jewish bullies on the page are the bad men whom the psalmist had in mind. Such a reading does not alter the fact that, in the Luttrell Psalter, we are gazing on a scene of horrible and shameful violence.

Medieval readers like Sir Geoffrey Luttrell would have turned this image of horrific agency into one of beauty; it is a 'mind-genre' and an ostensive image (an intellectual cue), not a surface aesthetics. Both image and text are concerned with *transforming* fear, from a negative violence against weakness into a positive and valorized pose of weakness. So the viewer gazed on Christ's *passio* – his affliction, his suffering – but also, in the terms of medieval thought, experiencing a perceptual *passio* through *disciplina* (both physical and mental training): as Nicholas Love's *Mirror* explains, through 'devoute imaginacion' the tortured Christ is at once 'a piteuouse siht & a joyful siht' – piteous 'for that harde passion that he suffrede for oure savacion', joyful 'for the matire & the effect that we have therbye of oure redempcion'; after 'long exercise of sorouful compassion' can this be felt, 'not onely in soule but also in the body'.[33] Medieval conceptions of emotion were focused on the two main affective attitudes of love and hate, *passio* being the word used for strong or overpowering emotions, such as hatred and fear, and to describe that which must be endured; but *passio* also described the imprinting of something on one's mind, on the receptive intellect. Aquinas described this imprinting in terms of *passio*, a physical ordeal: minds retain a kind of physical impression or wound in the *parte sensitiva* of things seen and remembered. Such a perceptual *passio,* and related rhetorical figures of *contentio* (antithesis), *contrarium* (contrasting contraries) and *oppositio* (negation), are representative of the ways readers and viewers experienced and mediated imaginary persecution.[34]

Like fans of contemporary horror films, medieval viewers would have found their way into understanding a scene of violence through other ways of reading: metaphorical, allegorical, typological. To invoke contemporary horror films is not a flippant device with which to suggest the relevance of my medieval sources. The 'instructive' Jew of the Luttrell Psalter, whose violence helps the Christian reader to read memorably and affectively, is similar to the tropes of the horror genre described in the many scholarly studies in film, media and literary theory which have explored what recreational horror does for its audiences.[35] The similarities between medieval and contemporary horrors include an abiding concern with power and control, a focus on extremes of emotion and graphic moments of physical violence, a fascination with distorted, strange or impossible bodies, a concern with how human morality is formed and malformed, and, always, a repetitious conflict between good and evil. And, like contemporary horror films, an image such as that from the Luttrell Psalter is highly aware of its own constructedness, and textuality: not only in that the marginal illustration is in dialogue with the text, but also that, as a luxurious devotional book, *design* is paramount. This kind of image demands to be read, actively and intelligently.

Susan Sontag has acutely described how 'for two thousand years, among Christians and Jews, it has been spiritually fashionable to be in pain'.[36] Both contemporary horror and medieval images of Jewish violence cause their audiences to gasp in revulsion, stimulating (and simulating) anger, disgust, fear, a whole world of intense but studied emotion and physical reaction. As with other texts and images from the Middle Ages, those which have been described as 'anti-Semitic' are invested in their own 'rhetoricity' and violent aesthetics, their capacity to be read and to move their audience, to bring the feeling of persecution into their audiences' intellectual worlds, turning the infliction of pain into its assumption.

Feeling, In Theory

By emphasizing the subjective nature of their religious experience and the humanity of Christ, medieval people demand that we acknowledge their feelings. In terms of the later Middle Ages, this is often understood via 'affective piety', spectacular performances of religious empathy, sensation and suffering; 'affective piety' has come to cover those expressions of desire, usually focused on mystical union with Christ's body, 'at times profoundly erotic, at other times deeply spiritual', in which personal emotion and the expression of physical feeling seem to confront doctrine, ritual and religious order.[37] Accounts of 'affective piety' have tended to focus on how medieval religion *used* the body in the quest for practical and personal religious experience, and have foregrounded the individual's desire to touch, to know, to feel, their religion.[38] The medieval body offered an agency in which sensations such as pain, violence against one's self, terror, eroticism, enclosure and fear were actively welcomed into one's life;

the vocabulary of wounding and bleeding was consistently described through the diction of sweetness and pleasure.[39] The integrity of the human body was queried, repeatedly returning to the fantasy of the inviolate, coherent body through describing its rupture; bodies were 'lived in the knowledge of their vulnerability'.[40]

'Feeling', like 'the body', is a historically specific and socially constructed category; the languages people use to articulate their feelings derive from their cultural and social norms and the kinds of feelings that are valorized change with time and context.[41] Religious 'feeling' is manifested in specific vocabularies and visual forms – in the case of late medieval Christianity, for instance, of love, longing, heat, thirst and wounding, with specific religious and mystical valence. Such registers query the distinction between mind and body; and this is why 'affect' can be a particularly valuable term. 'Affect' refers to the connection of the mind with the physiological, of emotions with ideas, of feeling with intellect.[42] Using the terms of affectivity allows us to consider both the community's role in creating the individual (i.e. social constructionism) whilst, at the same time, valuing the individual's experience of feeling and emotion.[43] Affectivity also allows us to think beyond problematic and anachronistic terms of literacy/illiteracy, to consider instead the sensory and emotional engagement that texts and images made possible. 'Affective piety' is therefore not just an 'aesthetic' description but can be seen as similar to the 'constructive sentimentalism' recently proposed by the philosopher Jesse Prinz, according to whom moral education derives from emotional disposition: one feels, say, disgust (the emotion), and thus confirms a moral position of intolerance.[44] Thus mystical texts exhorted the reader/listener to experience 'felinges & stiringes' through visions of Christ's Passion 'with the innere eye of thi soule', to watch bloodthirsty scenes of Christ's suffering.[45]

Medieval people did not see books and pictures as something separate from themselves – either from their minds or bodies – but as recreational objects which could touch, impress, hurt or wound the reader or viewer. This has been called 'affective literacy' and 'vision as touch';[46] Michael Camille has described, regarding the ideas about 'intercommunication' set out in the *Policraticus* of John of Salisbury (*c.* 1120–80), how 'when reading a text, the [medieval] subject moved his mouth, arms and hands, interacting with the discourse he was performing.'[47] Camille extends this kind of performative 'reading' to the viewing of sculpture, and, by implication, to all legible practices which called for the audience's engagement. Similarly, in Middle English, verbs for the arousal of emotions very frequently connect the experience of emotion with physical action: 'achaufen' (to kindle an emotion), 'amoven', 'arisen', 'blasen' (to be fervently emotional, literally 'to blaze'), 'boilen' (to boil with emotion), 'bresten' (to burst with emotion), 'dilaten' (to stretch or broaden one's emotional response), 'farsen' (to stuff or cram oneself with emotion), 'flaumen' (to be ablaze with emotion), 'hungren' (to crave emotionally), and so on.[48] There is an inherent element of somatic affectivity within our word 'emotion', from the Latin 'e + movere', to transport, to move out;[49] 'felen' – to feel – connotes both tactile sensation (a sensory experience) and sympathetic or emotional reaction.

Later medieval objects – books, altarpieces, rosaries, chaplets, diagrams, jewellery, amulets – were not remote from the viewer but a stimulus to affective responses, touching the viewer, as one might be touched in love or violence; like Christ's body and blood in the Eucharistic wafer, devotional objects could be so close that they could move into the viewer, reader or user. Medieval reading could be 'performative', as medieval people 'enlivened the silent page with the imagination of noisy scenes, enriched individual prayer through association with liturgical celebration, and made the individual's quiet encounter with the static book itself a species of sacred performance';[50] likewise, viewing images could be 'a total experience of communication involving sight, sound, action and physical expression'.[51] Medieval English people described 'quicke bookis' – living books – the word made flesh.[52] In some ways medieval practices of reading and seeing are close to modern cinema – sharing an inherent correspondence of the reading-viewing process to perception and emotion – a medium, like film, which 'not only puts movement in the image, it also puts movement in the mind'.[53] In sum, the languages of both emotion and reading are suffused with the diction of physical engagement; the physiological reaction to reading or viewing is mirrored in the medieval rhetoric of feeling 'excited' and 'aroused'. 'Reader-response' theories recall medieval ways of interacting not only with books but all forms inscribed with meaning:

> the literary work has two poles, which we might call the artistic and the aesthetic: the artistic pole is the author's text and the aesthetic is the realization accomplished by the reader. In view of this polarity, it is clear that the work itself cannot be identical

with the text or with the concretization, but must be situated somewhere between the two . . . As the reader passes through the various perspectives offered by the text and relates the different views and patterns to one another he sets the work in motion, and so sets himself in motion, too.[54]

This is not to suggest a pure theory of reader-response (in which the reader alone puts *meaning* into a text): rather, meaning may have been directed by medieval authors, scribes and artists, but an aesthetic and affective reaction or response is accomplished by the reader or viewer.

John of Genoa (Johannes Balbus; d. 1298), a Dominican aesthetic theorist, wrote in his *Catholicon* that sentimental and violent images should be used 'so that the mystery of the incarnation and the examples of the Saints may be *more active in our memory* through being daily presented to our eyes' and '*to excite* feelings [*affectum*] of devotion, these being aroused more effectively by things seen than by things heard'.[55] Affective memory could not be achieved simply by bedazzling 'beauty': it required formal and emotionally engaged mnemotechnic (the practice of aiding the memory), which mirrors the physiological terms of emotion in its language of 'active' memory; as Jill Bennett writes on 'empathic vision':

> In the medieval view where all memory-images were believed to have an emotional component acquired in the process of their formation (because they are comprised of images that produced a state of affection in the beholder when they appeared), it is impossible to conceive of images (that is, memory-images and, by extension, the art images used to stimulate memory) as operating simply through processes of cognition – or of recognition. Viewing, on this account, is not restricted to retinal impression and interpretations; the engagement of the senses implies a transformative process through which the properties of images are transferred to the viewer. In effect, one becomes the image through an encounter with it.[56]

Medieval texts and images were not separate from their audiences, but things with which one came into emotional and physical contact. Indeed, the act of seeing was described as 'transmissive', a reception of light akin to the reception of grace, with the corporeal arts of seeing and reading having the capacity to afflict, strike and remake the person, as images were 'carried' physically via the eye into the soul.[57] This was an 'emotional' art of memory, a deeply personal 'engagement of the senses', making 'each memory as much as possible into a personal occasion by imprinting personal associations like desire and fear'.[58] Medieval visual culture might not only be interpreted iconographically – relating to textual, theological or cultural significance – but also as 'cues or heuristic devices which access memory, and which are . . . emotionally tagged'.[59] Thus the Middle English terms for the making of memory describe remembering as if one is a book or a surface on which to be marked: 'emprenten' (to impress something in one's memory), 'exteinten' (to blot something from one's memory), 'fichen in mind' (to *fix* something in one's mind), 'meven to minde' (to move something into one's imagination).[60] So medieval people understood the capacity of images and texts to comfort and antagonize – 'to edify and horrify . . . to thematize the *Angst* of penitential experience';[61] this goes hand in hand with the understanding of affective literacy and affective vision, in which one's body and mind moved with, and sometimes merged with, a text or image being looked on, or which might cause one to cry, shriek or faint. Such ideas are of crucial importance in understanding what it was, in the Middle Ages, to welcome an experience of Christian-Jewish conflict into one's life.

This brief discussion of feeling and affectivity is important for what follows in as much as such affective images, texts, prayers, rituals and meditations – like that already discussed from the Luttrell Psalter – were often constructed around fear, pain and similar charged emotional states, such as disgust, eroticism, morbidity. Fear – Aristotle's 'painful or troubled feeling caused by the impression of an imminent evil that causes destruction or pain' – was, from ancient times into the Middle Ages, a branch of rhetoric (and, as such, a key to knowledge and based around an adversarial relationship against which it is pleading or persuading). Aristotelian fear is a consequence of a 'state of mind' which can be mastered, manipulated and, especially, used to great effect on one's audience. 'Fear makes men deliberate, whereas no one deliberates about things that are hopeless', writes Aristotle.[62] Aristotle suggests that 'it is often preferable that the audience should feel afraid' and it is therefore

> necessary to make them think they are likely to suffer, by reminding them that others greater than they have suffered, and showing that their equals are suffering or have suffered, and that

at the hand of those from whom they did not expect it, in such a manner and at times when they did not think it likely.[63]

Fear was part of an ongoing examination and redefinition of myriad emotions and species of fear – such as *kataplexis* (terror), *ekplexis* (consternation), *agonia* (anxiety), *aidos* (shyness), *oknos* (shrinking), *aiskhune* (shame) – and was ubiquitous in rhetorical manuals, repeatedly held to produce stirring, pleasurable and satisfying effects.[64] To imagine pain, to think of terror, to place oneself at Christ's Passion, in exile, or in another moment of persecution and violence, and to feel afraid was edifying *because* it was disturbing. The art of being shocked into feeling afraid, or at least to manipulate one's audience into an aesthetic of fear, was bequeathed by Aristotle to the medieval world, as was a notion that through practised fear one apprehends, and is able to aspire to, confidence, success and strength. Like fear, pity also figures in Aristotle's *Rhetoric*; Aristotle claims that 'all that men fear in regard to themselves excites their pity when others are the victims', contrasting pity (an aesthetic reaction) with shock (a visceral reaction).[65] Thus pity is a kind of fear in which one experiences another's suffering as if it were one's own, in a transference which is similar to the empathy with which medieval people often used books and images; pity is a kind of self-involving empathy, based on an image of persecution.

Persecution in Theory and Practice

Religious history has recently been seen in general as 'a discursive domain in which the notion of agency is richly played out;'[66] in medieval European culture, this is reflected in the self-inflicted austerities – isolation, fasting, discomfort, penitence, rhetoric of abnegation – which became more valued, and more frequent, than the actual penetration of the flesh.[67] Fear was, as Mary Carruthers says, 'the first step in the way of meditation' and, in this spirit, Mitchell Merback has elegantly documented how images of the Crucifixion, the cornerstone of Christian contemplation, depicted not just grace and salvation but also torture and capital punishment, a 'vulgar and disgraceful' penal episode designed for 'aesthetic shock'.[68] Likewise, the primary mode in the Christian representation of Jews was one of moral allegory and contrast, suffused with images of disgust, violence, bloodiness and torture, as we have seen in the example from the Luttrell Psalter.[69] It is essential here to restate that there is a clear difference between 'actual' power (which medieval Christians almost universally had over Jews) and that which is imagined (in which medieval Christians valorized weakness and martyrdom and represented themselves as under attack from Jews, and others). That is to say, a rhetoric and aesthetics of fear not only does not necessarily connect with an experience of disempowerment, but actually reverses this power-dynamic. Paranoia has been described as a technology of the self which 'seems to require being imitated to be understood, and it, in turn, seems to understand only by imitation'; paranoia works by 'blotting out any sense of the possibility of alternative ways of understanding'.[70] To adopt the pose of a victim, or to identify with a martyr was, paradoxically, one of the most empowering kinds of subjectivity available in medieval culture.[71] As described in the 'Last Beatitude' (Matthew 5:10), 'Blessed are they that suffer persecution for justice' sake: for theirs is the kingdom of heaven,' describing persecution as the way to Perfection.[72] Likewise, St Paul writes (2 Corinthians 12:10), 'I please myself in my infirmities, in reproaches, in necessities, in persecutions, in distresses, for Christ. For when I am weak, then am I powerful.'

St Augustine argues that 'the things which disturb the mind', which he defines (quoting Virgil) as 'desire and fear, gladness and sorrow', should be well-experienced 'in a manner consistent with the Holy Scriptures and wholesome doctrine'.[73] The alternative, *impassibilitas*, is evil: *apatheia*, an 'insensitivity', a life without the fear or knowledge of pain, which must surely be judged 'the worst of all vices'. To be without pain would lead, Augustine says quoting Cicero, to 'savagery of mind, and stupor of body'; similarly, the rationalist Roger Bacon (d. 1294) wrote that 'he who is always fortunate and passes his life without vexation of mind is ignorant of the other side of nature'.[74] Pain is experienced as an 'emotional and spiritual' state and, as in the Grimm brothers' story, 'pain', fear and terror are absolutely not proofs of death, but rather 'a sign of life', a physical *and* an emotional life, for such feelings can only be present in a living creature; separate from the late medieval emphasis on *imitatio Christi*, the rejection of the body by Neoplatonism, and the performance of suffering as the penalty for sin, Augustine makes clear that one needs to *feel* religious terror:

> if *apatheia* is a condition such that there is no fear to terrify and
> no pain to torment, then it is a condition to be avoided in this
> life if we wish to live rightly, that is, according to God.[75]

Augustine later cites 2 Timothy 3:12 ('Whoever will live piously in Christ shall suffer persecution') to suggest that 'the Catholic faith may indeed be strengthened by the dissensions of heretics'. Throughout, Augustine argues that the 'will' and the 'passions' must be united, not at odds with each other, making clear that to *feel* persecuted is a key component of a 'good' religious subjectivity. Pain and fear were generally viewed 'as a function of the soul' with no separation between Christ's physical suffering at Calvary and his mental anguish.[76]

To strike a pose of weakness and to play the role of martyr is to play the 'philopassionist' card, that is, to describe oneself as loving and welcoming pain, to welcome the persecution of the body and mind.[77] It would be easy to see such fantasies as a consequence of a kind of sado-masochism (to use an anachronistic term), but they can also be seen in terms of a well-developed Christian culture of *clementia et mansuetudine* (clemency and gentleness) which actively sought out the image of cruelty in order to confirm its own mildness. At the same time, such fantasies of abjection disrespect and disavow the human body. Neoplatonism, in particular, held the human body in low esteem, as being amongst the most inferior kinds of matter. The Neoplatonic soul – eternal, universal and superior – not only existed separate from the body but bliss in one's soul was more easily achieved through the repudiation and denigration of the body. As Talal Asad argues, such a submission to, or evocation of, edifying pain is in itself a kind of agency.[78] Thus medieval people often welcomed pain, violence, terror and disgust into their own worlds, via the Jewish image, because to experience these things was, in one way or another, edifying.

Therefore the images of violence and the kinds of pain examined here are those ardent, emotional, aesthetic and intellectual ideas which imagined persecution in order to animate religious minds and produce a religious response. Such conceptions of edifying fear are not limited to the famously vivid Christianity of the later Middle Ages: for instance, the thirteenth-century *Nizzahon Vetus*, one of the most vituperative anti-Christian Jewish works of medieval Europe, opens not with an assertion of power but of weakness:

> My help comes from the Lord, Creator of heaven and earth. Blessed is he who gives power to the weak and increases strength to them that have no might.[79]

The author of the *Nizzahon Vetus* quotes the Psalms (121:2) and Isaiah (40:29) not simply to reflect his marginalized status as a Jew living in medieval Europe; the citations of scripture put him in authorizing positions of victimhood. These lines can be compared with the description given by Bernard of Clairvaux (1090–1153) of the transformation of humiliation into humility, of need into strength:

> [The righteous should] rejoice, as is fitting, that it is not so much persecution which is increased as reward, and let them rejoice that they bear many things for Christ, so that with him a more abundant reward may wait for them . . .[80]

Medieval Christian representations of Jews and Judaism appear to oscillate around these opposite poles of pain and terror: at one, Jews were the historical and actual victims of Christian rulers, soldiers, crusaders and neighbours, suffering bloody tortures at their hands. At the other, Jews are represented torturing Christ, Christians, Christian symbols and, through child-murder, well-poisoning and the like, are represented as continual persecutors and terrorizers of Christians, *stimuli* of Christian *pathos*.

Such a focus on the rhetoric of Christian–Jewish conflict has emerged in some remarkable and brilliant recent scholarship. Jews adopted and adapted Christian languages of the hatred of Jews and applied it to Christians; likewise, having been labelled as 'dogs' by Christian polemicists, medieval Jews said it was Christians, not Jews, who 'bark'.[81] In controversies surrounding the purity of blood, Jews and Christians heaped invective upon each other, in the Middle Ages and beyond.[82] The 'memory' of slaughter and expulsion inspired martyrologists in Germany and France, whilst medieval Jewish and Christian discussions of conversion probed and complicated the very notion of religious identity.[83] Christian narratives of persecution by Jews did not translate simply or seamlessly into the Christian persecution of Jews. According to St Augustine's famous definition, a monster is so called from the verb 'to demonstrate' (*monstrare*), 'because monsters are signs by which something is demonstrated':[84] that is, the 'something' made monstrous is 'something else', an exemplary sign.

So what *utility* is there in an image of Jews persecuting Christians and to fostering fear if it is not to blame those of whom one has made oneself afraid? Such images allowed one to make an aesthetic and rhetorical feeling of persecution, concordant with the religious ideal of gentle victimhood *and* with the intellectual ideal of being physically engaged with one's reading through personal associations like pain and fear. But it is crucial to mention the role of real persecution here too, for the ardent, solipsistic fantasy of being persecuted could give rise to other kinds of persecution.

During the outbreak of the Black Death across Europe in 1348–50 Jews were accused (sometimes along with Christians) of being involved in sowing the disease by poisoning local wells. This allegation accompanied many other reactions and interpretations (for instance, blaming astrological factors for the illness) and 'scientific' or scholarly reactions did not blame the Jews, whilst Pope Clement IV issued a bull which formally denied the allegation.[85] On a general level, the allegations surrounding the Black Death reflect increasing stigmatization of Jewish communities, itself partly a consequence of increased pressure (particularly from the mendicant orders of friars) for Jews and Christians to live apart. In specific places, mainly in central and northern Europe, Jews were attacked due to the raising of this allegation: at Strasbourg, according to the Worms *Sefer Minhagim*, the Jews put themselves to death in an act of martyrdom to save themselves from their Christian persecutors. It is hard to identify how far the aesthetic of Jewish persecution that Christians had developed in their religious and emotional lives 'crossed over' into actual persecution, because fantasy *can*, but does not usually, become reality.

Imitatio Christi (imitation of Christ) and *devotio moderna* (the later medieval spirituality of humble discipline) developed this emphasis on the edifying religious experience of 'excited feelings', of fear, pain, hope and love. In the words of the Cistercian monk William of St Thierry (d. *c.* 1148), *amor*, love of God, is a 'vehement will' based around the repeated meditative contemplation of the Passion.[86] It is not an overstatement to say that such devotional habits called for, even depended on, an *aesthetic* fantasy of Jewry. Religious technologies of perceiving, feeling, immersion, sensation, not only required the worshipper to imagine their own sinfulness and to imitate Christ's Passion, but required the idea of a persecuting agent. Mystical theological writing repeatedly voices the need to feel threatened in order to feel comforted; moreover, the mortification of the self through Christ was the path to spiritual riches, and graphic descriptions of the assault on Christ accompany entreaties to Christ to 'wounde my thoughte', to 'buffete the soule and wounde with-inne', to transfer, through symbolic violence, the ordeal Christ suffered at Calvary into the worshipper's heart and to inflict a wound of love, like a Jew, on Christ.[87] This kind of welcomed pain is not frightening or alienating, as it might appear to a modern reader, but offered a useful and welcome kind of empathy; this is 'exemplified in the penitential pantomimes and "defiling practices" of mystics and ecstatics like Catherine of Siena' which 'actively geared itself to the pursuit of pain as a positive force in spiritual, and thus human, affairs'.[88] Indeed Catherine of Siena (d. 1380) developed an entire theology based around the difference between 'holy fear', 'the perverse fear and love that killed Christ', and 'slavish fear' (the fear of personal suffering); as Catherine exclaims, 'I beg you in mercy to punish me!'[89] This paradox – of merciful punishment, of longed-for pain – animates most mystical writing but the subject in question in this book is those ways in which medieval people made present, made immediate, violence between Christians and Jews through media – through books, images, churches, maps and theme parks.

Through such imagery medieval people placed themselves personally within a cosmic cycle of Christian redemption, which celebrated the 'indescribable beauty' of Christ's suffering at Calvary. St Anselm (d. 1109) wrote that the greater we emphasize Christ's sufferings at Calvary, his 'fatigue, hunger, thirst, beatings, and crucifixion and death between thieves',

> the greater is the love and generosity that he has shown toward us . . . For it was fitting that just as death entered the human race through the disobedience of a human being, so too life should be restored by the obedience of a human being . . . [which] demonstrate[s] the indescribable beauty that belongs to our redemption.[90]

This 'indescribable beauty' was based around those things which Aristotle described as being fearful: a 'painful or troubled feeling', 'the impression of an imminent evil', the anticipation of destruction or pain. This reached its extreme and most sensational form in the *humiliati*, the ascetics of later medieval Europe who combined the rhetoric of mysticism with apocalypticism, messianism, auto-abnegation including flagellation, and violently anti-Jewish invective, in which Jews were 'wicked children' and 'most faithful followers of antichrist'.[91] But such ascetics were only extreme currents within a dominant culture of edifying poses of meekness and victimhood. An anonymous Bohemian Augustinian commentator, writing around the year 1400, considered an image of the crucified Christ thus:

He is shown to us crucified, wounded, beaten and crowned with thorns, and similarly the saints. And the vision causes the heart to tremble, the soul is wounded, the mind is touched, the spirit feels compassion and repeats in it the whole Passion of Christ and of the saints.[92]

This example neatly encapsulates the movement from recognition (seeing and 'reading' the image of the crucified Christ) through affective response (the trembling heart) to edifying compunction (the wounded soul, the touched mind, compassion properly felt), leading to the endless repetition of Christ's Passion. Contemplating the holy was emphatically not the same as looking at or reading about something holy; proper contemplation intended to move, or transport, the viewer or reader, and it is within this expressive and immersive mnemotechnic, and its attendant valorized fear and empathy, that the Jewish stereotype is located within medieval Christian culture. Thus the emphasis in my enquiry is on how medieval people *experienced* this kind of mediated pain, not just what such pain might mean to us today. All the artefacts considered here are concerned with making 'a literalized space for the imagination's deployment';[93] conflict, violence and pain, solipsistic feelings of persecution, built subjective expression and held within them the image of beauty.

CHAPTER 2

The Violence of Memory: Seven Kinds of 'Jewish' Torture

He asked himself what demon drove Mischa continually to uncover
and to torture this strange region of sensibility – and as he did so
he reflected yet again how strangely close to each other in this man
lay the springs of cruelty and of pity.
—Iris Murdoch, *The Flight from the Enchanter*

I: The Rhetoric of Persecutory Violence

A 'spiritual regimen' written for a fifteenth-century English gentleman instructed its reader, at mealtimes, to use five breadcrumbs to make the Sign of the Cross on the dining-table, as a reminder of Christ's Passion.[1] The torments of the Passion were, according to the regimen, to be remembered everywhere. There is nothing frightening or bloody about five breadcrumbs; they were, however, an ardent symbol fashioned from something tiny, domestic and familiar. The breadcrumbs focused the mind, trained the memory and brought Christ's Passion into everyday life.

Memory does not equate to loss, but rather makes lost or absent things present or felt again. The rhetorician Cicero tells us that it was when a ceiling collapsed at a dinner-party that the art of memory was invented: the seating plan, the identities of the terrified faces, the mangled bodies of the victims, were violently imprinted on the memory of the survivor, Simonides.[2] Classical rhetoric bequeathed to the Middle Ages a set of principles for making an experience feel persuasively effectively grievous, and making an existing emotion feel the more intense; such principles inform medieval representations of the imperilled self (or Christ) and imaginary Jewish persecutor.

This nexus of intellect and pain appears frequently. The twelfth-century story of the 'death by stylus' of Eriugena, the scholar stabbed to death by his pupils and their pens, aptly reflects 'the violence of intellectual tranmission'.[3] Martyr-saint cults, like that of St Catherine of Alexandria, showed how 'knowledge and faith were frequently acquired and disseminated through violence, both intra- and inter-culturally'.[4] In one medieval manuscript of Gregory the Great's *Moralia in Job* 'violent and monstrous imagery' parallels the 'trials' undergone by the spiritual reader, 'to whom [these violent images] act as spurs to greater achievement'.[5] Beginning with St Augustine's memory of being whipped as he studied, Mary Carruthers has described how medieval memory-images often depended on working in 'an active, even violent, manner' and how books and bodies were described in a relationship of affliction, of incising patterns on soft fleshy surfaces;[6] *punctus* (piercing) and *compunctus* (compunction) provided a singularly potent, and painful, vocabulary for the acquisition of knowledge. 'Inventional violence' – the torture of interpretative discovery and composition – was a creative, and beautiful, force.[7] There was an 'enduring affiliation between music, representation and bodily violence', not least in practices of pedagogy and specifically in the world of Jewish violence and Christian martyrdom described in Chaucer's 'Prioress's Tale'.[8] In the 'scientific' field of optics, 'violence to the self' was described within the act of seeing something.[9] We might remember that in the later Middle Ages torture and ordeal were equated with revelation, conversion and the discovery of truth.[10] The 'threat of violence' structured, and continues to structure, lived subjectivity, with punishment 'beautified' into a 'locus of pleasure'.[11] So the idea or memory of violence, the imaginative trope of violence, is invoked, as opposed to its actual imposition.[12]

Three pertinent examples of rhetorical violence provide powerful frames through which to understand medieval fantasies of edifying violence between Christians and Jews; in their established modes of persuasive design, these examples help us to think about how cultural artefacts might *move* their audiences. These examples are taken from key texts which would have been known to someone like Sir Geoffrey Luttrell and indeed to most medieval Christian schoolboys in the Latin West, as these texts were part of the *trivium* (of logic, rhetoric and dialectic) which formed the basis of the medieval curriculum: Quintilian's *Institutio oratoria*, the pseudo-Ciceronian *Ad Herennium libri IV* and Prudentius' *Psychomachia*. These texts were the foundation for some of the most influential medieval treatises on rhetoric, from the Isidore of Seville's seventh-century *Etymologies* to Stephen Hawes's *Pastime of Pleasure* (1506), and each connects terror with rhetorical utility, joining fear, violence and juxtaposition to eloquent expression. Such texts, ultimately based in the world of ancient legal pleading, focus on violence, tyranny, sex, conflict, piracy, an 'imaginary world' far from the concerns of courts of law.[13]

Quintilian's *Orator's Education* is a training programme of effective speech, including a guide on how best to appeal to emotion: 'the life and soul of oratory, we may say, is in the emotions'.[14] The text was well known throughout the Middle Ages, although in fragmentary form.[15] Quintilian suggests that emotion (*adfectus*) 'is most involved where there is personal danger' and that the arousing of tears is the 'most effective' of all emotions.[16] Quintilian's 'emotion' is not 'feeling' as we might understand in modern English: the Latin word, *adfectus*, translates the Greek *pathos*, in which 'the passions' are 'vehement', emotions are 'violent . . . powerful agents of disturbance'.[17] For Quintilian, love is *pathos*, 'concerned with anger, hatred, fear, envy and pity', whereas affection is *ethos* (*mores*, ethics); love as *pathos* disturbs where *ethos* calms.[18] This emotion is to be used for persuasion, 'in arousing emotion which is not there or in making an existing emotion more intense'.[19] Quintilian surmises

> The person who will show the greatest power in the expression of emotions will be the person who has properly formed what the Greeks call phantasiai (let us call them 'visions'), by which the images of absent things are presented to the mind in such a way that we seem actually to see them with our eyes and have them physically present to us.[20]

This is not just a kind of imagination but a specifically empathic kind of thought based around one's identification with suffering; to evoke pity, says Quintilian, 'let us believe that the ills of which we are to complain have happened to us, and persuade our hearts of this.'[21] His terms are not far from those of later medieval meditative spirituality, which exhorted the reader or listener to 'make present' in one's mind, 'with the innere eye', the trials of Christ.[22] Quintilian gives what seems to be almost a description, *avant la lettre*, of how medieval people responded to images of Christ's tormented body on the Cross or to the martyred corpses of the saints:

> Suppose I am complaining that someone has been murdered. Am I not to have before my eyes all the circumstances which one can believe to have happened during the event? Will not the assassin burst out on a sudden, and the victim tremble, cry for help, and either plead for mercy or try to escape? Shall I not see one man striking the blow and the other man falling? Will not

the blood, the pallor, the groans, the last gasp of the dying be imprinted on my mind?[23]

Quintilian describes suffering-for-empathy, a celebration of an image of pain through which to build one's 'mind' through vivid 'imprinting'. From such visions, says Quintilian, we get emotions and *enargeia* (*illustratio* or *evidentia*): 'a quality which makes us seem not so much to be talking about something as exhibiting it'.[24]

The utility of violence and ugliness was also recognized in one of the most widespread treatises on rhetoric, the pseudo-Ciceronian *Ad Herennium* (the basis of Ciceronian rhetoric in the Middle Ages). Here, the author describes how important it is that images 'adhere' (*haerere*) in the mind, as on a wax tablet, in a physical and material kind of contact. To do so, 'we establish likenesses as striking as possible':

> if we set up images that are not many or vague, but doing something; if we assign to them exceptional beauty or singular ugliness; if we dress some of them with crowns or purple cloaks, for example, so that the likeness may be more distinct to us; or if we somehow disfigure them, as by introducing one stained with blood or soiled with mud or smeared with red paint, so that its form is more striking, or by assigning certain comic effects to our images, for that, too will ensure our remembering them more readily.[25]

To the modern reader, the *Ad Herennium* seems to be describing how to make a particularly *bad* image: one without delicacy, complexity, ambiguity, subtlety – in other words, something outside good (post-medieval) artistic expression. But this, suggests the author of *Ad Herennium*, is precisely the most *active* image – engaged in activity, extreme, stained, smeared and disfigured (*deformabimus*) – because *figurae* are not produced for delicacy but for instruction and memorial retention. Such a position was repeated by many in the Middle Ages: the best kind of educative and memorable image was 'gross and sensible' (in the sense of being felt).[26] To see how the handbook of rhetoric was used in religious writing we might compare the passage from *Ad Herennium* with Bernard of Clairvaux's twelfth-century description of the soul's understanding of its own evils:

> My brothers, which of us, if he suddenly noticed that the clothing which covers him was spattered all over with filth and the

foulest mud, would not be violently disgusted and quickly take it off and cast it from him indignantly? But the soul which finds itself contaminated in this way cannot cast itself away as a man can cast away his clothes. Which of us is so patient and so brave that if he were to see his own flesh suddenly shining white with leprosy (as we read happened to Moses' sister Mary), he could stand calmly and thank his Creator [Numbers 12:10]? But what is that flesh but the corruptible garment in which we are clothed?

And how should we think of this leprosy of the body in all the elect but as a rod of fatherly correction [Proverbs 29:15] and a purgation of the heart?[27]

Bernard combines activity (spattering mud, casting off one's clothes) with disfiguration (dirt and leprosy), making a biblically resonant inner world of 'singular ugliness' and disgust with which to describe the soul. Bernard's prose may not be modelled on the *Ad Herennium*, although it might well be; but Bernard's description of the besmirched Christian soul is absolutely aligned with the kinds of guidance in *Ad Herennium* about how to make an active image through rhetorical violence.[28] Moreover, it can be clearly seen how the kinds of active image described in the *Ad Herennium* and by Quintilian were easily amenable to allegory, medieval Christendom's dominant mode of interpretation.

Medieval schoolboys would also have been familiar with Prudentius' *Psychomachia*, an enormously influential Late Latin poem of visualized battles between virtues and vices;[29] the poem describes the struggle between good and evil in the individual and the struggle between the Church and paganism/heresy. The *Psychomachia* imagines learning – moral learning and the development of a moral self – as a conflict between extremes; moreover, it repeatedly finds an edifying role for conflict, terror and shock. So Discord (surnamed Heresy) is 'torn asunder and parceled out to unclean creatures', her body thrown to dogs and 'thrust into foul, stinking sewers'; Soberness smashes the lips of Indulgence with a rock,

the teeth within are loosened, the gullet cut, and the mangled tongue fills it with bloody fragments; Her gorge rises at the strange meal; gulping down the pulped bone she spews up again the lumps she swallowed.[30]

The *Psychomachia*, scenes from which are frequently reflected in Romanesque and Gothic art and architecture as well as in medieval thought, offers little in the way of narrative; rather, violent *tableaux* culminate in the highly ordered building of an apocalyptic temple/ Temple (largely quoting the Apocalypse). The gory bloodiness of the *Psychomachia* is what makes for a memorable moral lesson in a very similar way to the scenes of contrast between Christians and Jews which became so widespread in the later Middle Ages.

Other writers on memory and rhetoric – notably the Italian grammarian Boncompagno da Signa (d. after 1240) and the English-man Thomas Bradwardine (d. 1349) – developed mnemotechnical theories out of the fearful image of violence, replete with conflict, spilt blood, rent limbs, 'foulness', harlotry and grotesquery; da Signa affirms 'that offensive acts and unexpected events cling more fervently to the memory'.[31] As Jody Enders writes, 'the memory image was persuasive and dramatic because it was violent', and this book responds to Enders's challenge that medievalists should 'resituate the memory image within the violent and performative rhetorical contexts for which it was intended, all the while recalling how its virtual violence might be translated into speech.'[32] This has nothing to do with the stereotype of the 'barbarous' and violent Middle Ages, and everything to do with personal, pious, moral and intellectual education.

II: Maternity and Murder: The Virgin and the Massacre

Comfortable fantasies and Passional images of scourging, slapping, being spat on, mocked and victimized were recreated and mediated almost everywhere in medieval culture, to interrupt, to punctuate, one's life with what Jacobus de Voragine (d. 1298) called the 'bitter pains' and 'scornful mockery' of Christ's Passion.[33] The Middle English translation of Thomas a Kempis' *Imitation of Christ* called this 'cotidiane mortifyinge', everyday debasement and mortification, the crucifix 'ever redy'.[34] One meditated on the Passion in baseness and atonement in as much as Christ suffered for mankind, purchasing mankind's redemption with His blood; yet such suffering was also valorized for, as the German mystic Eckhart (*c.* 1260–1327) explained, 'whatever we suffer in this world and in this life will have an end'.[35] The medieval Christian was both 'like a Jew', in that Christ had suffered for mankind, and subject to 'Jewish' violence, in that *imitatio* depended on empathy with Christ's ordeal. Eckhart argued that it is death that gives being: 'The martyrs are dead and have lost their *life* but have received *being*' – after suffering, after martyrdom, comes a pure, noble and higher kind of being.[36] Likewise, Bernard of Clairvaux (*c*. 1090–1153) stated in his preface to his commentary on Psalm 91, with a striking directness:

> you are killed all the day long by many fasts, by labours oft, by vigils above measure, besides those things that are within, sorrow for sin and multifold temptation. You are being killed; but it is for the sake of Him who died for you. If you abound in tribulation for Him, you will abound in consolation through Him . . . For with Him you will find that great tribulation itself becomes a certain consolation.[37]

As Georges Duby commented, 'the imitation of Christ [became] above all the imitation of his agony' (although Duby saw this primarily as a sentiment of 'the people' rather than 'monks and university professors').[38] It is in this spirit that Christ's body was repeatedly ravaged by violence and became subject to new kinds of pain and suffering and such images were welcomed into one's own life, in an empathic imitation of Christ.

An ivory figure, now pristine and untouchable in a museum display cabinet, shows a beautiful young woman sitting on a throne and holding her baby, gazing at him (see illus. 2). She smiles, lovingly. The baby touches his mother's jewelled breast, meeting his mother's gaze, and returns the smile. This woman is the Virgin Mary in a conventional pose as Queen of Heaven, with the infant Christ. She appears to be serene and composed but, as she holds her baby, she tramples with her left foot on a malformed and diabolical beast, half-cow, half-dragon.

Behind the Virgin a parallel scene is taking place, also involving an enthroned monarch, mothers and children. One mother crouches, desperately grabbing her baby's arm; but the baby is hoisted aloft by its ankle, held by a bearded man with a sharp profile, who brings a long, sharp knife down towards the prone baby. Another mother wrings her hands in grief as her infant is held and stabbed in the back by another man. A king, enthroned, looks on. The king is Herod the Great, the client-king of Judea, and babies are being murdered in the mass infanticide, the Massacre of the Innocents, ordered by Herod

2 Enthroned Virgin with Child trampling the Beast, with Massacre of the Innocents on reverse. Ivory, Paris, early fourteenth century. Toronto, Art Gallery of Ontario, Thomson Collection 14.

(Matthew 2), following the announcement by the Magi that the King of the Jews had been born in Bethlehem.

This is the drama depicted on an early fourteenth-century Parisian ivory figure (now Toronto, Art Gallery of Ontario, Thomson Collection 14).[39] I use the term 'drama' because this is, emphatically, a dramatic object, a figure (in the sense of being an embodied form), not a statue (literally, a standing, or static, thing). The viewer must engage, somatically, with it: we must either move around the figure, or turn the figure in our hands, in order properly to feel its meaning. This remarkable and fascinating artefact is unique, and thus unrepresentative, but, in seamlessly joining together a scene of gentle tenderness with what its cataloguers call a 'painful scene of massacre', the figure articulates a world of feeling and interpretation which brings together pleasure and pain, linking Jewish child-murder with Christ's Passion, and through a mode of engagement with the viewer which is *active* and violent.

To understand how the Toronto figure works we must look at the terse gospel account of Herod's killing of the children of Bethlehem:

> Then Herod perceiving that he was deluded by the wise men, was exceeding angry; and sending killed all the men children that were in Bethlehem, and in all the borders thereof, from two years old and under, according to the time he had diligently inquired of the wise men. / Then was fulfilled that which was spoken by Jeremias the prophet, saying: / A voice in Rama was heard, lamentation and great mourning; Rachel bewailing her children, and would not be comforted, because they are not. (Matthew 2:16–18)

From the account given in Matthew, the Massacre of the Innocents was understood through prophecy, as a fulfilment of the Old Law (the description of Rachel's 'lamentation ... mourning, and weeping' for her children in Jeremiah 31:15). On this basis, the brief tyrant-legend of the Massacre of the Innocents became an important commemorative feast in the medieval Church, in which the Massacre of the Innocents was understood as a foreshadowing, a prefiguration, of the killing of Christ by the Jews, in which children bear 'witness to God not by speaking but by dying'.[40] The Massacre was celebrated as Holy Innocents' Day (28 December), in England called Childermas;[41] relics purportedly of the slain children were held in Padua,

Lisbon, Milan and Salisbury.[42] In England, at Childermas adult authority was reasserted as boy-bishop festivities, in which boys appeared to usurp the authority of deacons through violent or coarse sermons, came to a close.[43]

The Toronto figure encapsulates the figural understanding not only of the life and death of Christ but of the relationship between Jewish and Christian Law. The Innocents, according to the common medieval understanding of the story, died for Christ.[44] Born in Bethlehem, Christ and his blood had long been sought by the Jews: his death prefigured in the Massacre, the shedding of his blood at the Passion prefigured in his Circumcision, the Virgin's love of her infant son cognate with her bringing him into the world to die. The beast at the Virgin's feet in the Toronto figure is the devil, and is often represented as being trampled by the Virgin, fulfilling Genesis 3:15 ('I will put enmities between thee and the woman, and thy seed and her seed: she shall crush thy head, and thou shall lie in wait for her heel') and Apocalypse [Revelation] 12:4 ('and the dragon stood before the woman who was ready to be delivered; that, when she should be delivered, he might devour her son'). The Toronto Virgin's passive, decorous victory over the satanic dragon speaks of the paradoxical power of her weakness: in offering her infant son's martyrdom for mankind, she secures victory over evil.

Thus the Toronto figure is replete with devotional meaning, contrasting Old and New laws through the imagery of childhood, maternity, violence and rule. But the figure demands too that we consider how it was used. The figure requires its user to *move* between childbirth and child-murder to foster a tactile and intimate aesthetic shock: the movement from prefiguration (Massacre) to incarnation (Christ-Child) to Mary as Queen of Heaven, and the parallel mental movement, are mirrored in the viewer's somatic movement around or with the figure, the body once again being led into a perceptual *passio*, the sculpture's 'enlivened space' engaging the user too in a contrast of textual-liturgical memories.[45] The Toronto figure makes a jarring but highly meaningful contrast between tenderness and violence, with a kinaesthetic personal experience, moving one's muscles as one moves one's eyes around the figure and one's mind (or one's 'mind's eye') through the violent life and death of Christ.

The gathering of imagery in the Toronto figure is identical to the writing of Jewish violence and Christian retribution in Chaucer's 'Prioress's Tale' from *The Canterbury Tales* (late fourteenth century), one of the Christian *ur*-texts of Jewish infanticide. The tale, told by a Prioress, describes the murder of a Christian boy by the Jews of an Asian city and his miraculous posthumous singing. The tale ironically forces the reader to connect the Prioress and her Christian protagonists and the Jews her tale traduces. The Christian boy's mother is described as a 'newe Rachel' (vii:627), using Rachel to evoke maternal Marian grief for lost children and Holy Mother Church.[46] The Prioress's affective, eloquent narration of the tale is introduced by a prologue heavily indebted to the liturgy of Childermas, and the repeated patterning of Jewish child-murder is suggested in the Prioress's description of the Jews as the 'cursed folk of Herodes al newe' (vii:574) who have in their heart 'the serpent' Satan (vii:557).[47]

Like the Toronto figure, the 'Prioress's Tale' has a capacity to *move* its audience: by evoking the pathos of child-murder, Chaucer's Prioress launches a rhetorical tour de force, a fervent exclamation ('O mooder Mayde, O mayde Mooder free!', vii:467) of Marian piety. The narrative's moving power is paralleled in the reaction of the Christian townspeople in the Prioress's story to the miracle of the little boy: the abbot starts to cry, 'salte teeris trikled down as rein' (vii:674), and passes out, ecstatically, lying on the ground; his somatic reaction to the boy's miracle is then copied by the abbot's convent, who 'lay on the pavement/ Wepynge' (vii:677–8); the boy's *passio* stimulates an imitative reaction by the convent. Thus the movement between Jew and Christian, violence and pity, facilitates and demands a physical, emotional and somatic movement. This violence responds to the other violence in the tale which is that done to the little boy by his schoolteacher, who threatens him with violence if he fails to learn his song 'by roote'; this 'inventional violence', a violence at the point of a text's composition and delivery, is 'positive, creational, and generative of aesthetic beauty', even as it narrates pain, fear and persecution.[48]

III: Morbid Lullabies

The Toronto figure shows how medieval people welcomed the violent aesthetic of the Passion into their everyday lives, submitting their most cherished symbols to 'Jewish violence', re-inflicting loving wounds on Christlike bodies and inflicting vengeance on the devil. Such artefacts placed torture next to comfort, using the rhetoric of violent shock, whilst making the Passion central to daily lived experience. Likewise, late medieval mock-lullaby lyrics are based around an aesthetic of shock, contrast and empathy. Like the Toronto figure, these lullabies are concerned with brutality towards children. Such 'spiritual lullabies', which appear in English from the mid-fourteenth century, employ to great effect a poetics of jarring violence in which the tone and comforting conceits of the lullaby are adapted with the infant Christ foretelling his horrific trials; in some lyrics he comforts his mother, in others she comforts him. Far from being a song of comfort, these morbid lullabies cause distress whilst showing the wisdom and divinity of the Christ-Child. Thus the expected convention of the hushed child is reversed, in the idiom of late medieval popular prayer, to give a startling and forceful image of the child's body tortured by Jews.

The best known of such poems is the *Coventry Carol*, with the refrain 'Lully, lulla, thou little tiny child';[49] this poem was part of the Coventry pageant of the town's Shearmen and Tailors and was sung by female characters as part of the prefigurative dramatization of the Massacre of the Innocents.[50] The 'little tiny child' addressed is the Christ-Child. The poem evokes 'Herod, the king,/ In his raging', in a violent contrast to the 'pore child' hushed by the lullaby. Another such anonymous lullaby, 'Lullay, lullay, my lityl child', from mid-fifteenth-century England, is narrated by the crying Christ-Child in the manger, 'laid . . . in a wispe of hay', asking how might he 'fall apon a slep?' ('fall asleep?');[51] he resigns himself to wait, to 'suffre the paines that I may', thus forming the startling image of the new-born infant anticipating his crucifixion. The child then addresses his mother:

Seys thou noghte, thou fair *may*,	*Do you not see, maiden*
And *heris thou noghte* also	*do you not hear*
How Kinge Herod, that *keyn* knight,	*stalwart*
And of his peres mo	*and his many fellows*
That be abowte night and day	
My body for to *slo*?	*slay*

Both the mother-child intimacy and the physical torment to come are made much more forceful by the very inappropriateness of writing torture within a lullaby. Moreover, Mary's lullaby refrain, 'Lullay,

lullay, my lityl chyld', is rendered impotent within the foretold inevitability of Christ's martyrdom. The child cries because of the 'dred' of the 'paines' to come, but resigns himself to suffering on the Cross, his hands bound. Each stanza of the lyric closes with the promise that he will 'Suffre the paines that I may,/ It is my Fader will'; the refrain of the lyric is the 'lullaby', spoken by Mary to her infant:

> Lullay, lullay, my lityl child,
> Slepe and be now still.
> If thou be a litill child
> Yitt may thou have thi will.

This poem graphically asks its audience to imagine and communicate with the body of the tortured infant, to connect the bleeding man on the Cross with the newborn infant in the manger, making intimate St Bernard of Clairvaux's statement that 'This baby is God himself, reconciling the world to himself.'[52]

A somewhat earlier example, with the refrain 'Lullay, lullay, litel child, why wepest thu so sore?', appears in the commonplace book of the Norfolk Franciscan John Grimestone (*fl.* 1372).[53] The narrator lulls the little child, 'that were so sterne and wild/Now . . . become meke and mild,/ To saven that was forlore' ('to save that which was lost'). From this starting point the identity of the little child as Christ becomes increasingly clear, as the narrator reflects ruefully on the 'appel' that mankind chose against his Father's will; for this reason, the infant – 'thu litel thing . . . thu litel king' – is destined to 'suffren peines mo[re],/ In heved, in feet, in hondes two': that is, in the form of the Five Wounds of Christ. The lyric, which becomes a bleak asseveration rather than a lullaby, closes thus:

That peine us make of *senne* free,	*sin*
That peine us bringe, Jhesu, to thee,	
That peine us helpe *ay* to flee	*in return*
The wikkede *fendes lore.*	*fiend's teaching*

The poem answers its refrain 'why wepest thu so sore?' with the repeated 'peine' to which the little child must be subjected. In all these poems the narrator-meditator, the 'comforting' voice of the lullaby, causes grim violence to the Christ-Child, suffering in each poem on behalf of mankind.

As Marina Warner says, 'lullaby and elegy' become linked in a kind of duet, 'obsessively spell[ing] out . . . dangers', dipping 'infants prophylactically in the imaginary future of ordeals and perils'. But Warner, in describing these lullabies' 'weak domestic magic', suggests that such lyrics might have been sung by medieval mothers to their children, as if she imagines them to have been composed in a mother-child scene for the purpose of hushing a child to sleep.[54] It is much more likely, given the clerical 'literary' manuscripts in which these poems are found and their accomplished construction as well as their thoroughgoing violence, that such lullabies were an adult perform-ance of emotional empathy with the Christ-Child, staging and per-forming a precious, intimate compunction with Christ's suffering. In doing so, such lullabies make the 'bogeyman' about which Warner eloquently writes central to the idea of growing up, being secure and *feeling* persecuted in a spiritually edifying way.

The idea of a specifically Christian childhood imperilled by 'Jew-ish' violence is also closely linked to the rite of circumcision, at once the bloody marker of Jewish difference but also the valorized com-memoration of Christ's humanity, 'the imposition of a new and saving name' and 'the shedding of his blood'.[55] Whilst surgical circumcision for medical reasons was sometimes practised by medieval Christians, the rite was more frequently invoked as an aesthetic cue to call to mind the Jews' first shedding of Christ's blood and what Leo Stein-berg calls Christ's 'volitional act', the 'voluntary gift of his blood'.[56] Allegations of the Jewish mutilation of Christian boys' genitals were suffused with the imagery of circumcision.[57] Christ's Circumcision increasingly came to call to mind pain and tears as emphasized by Pseudo-Bonaventure: Nicholas Love's English translation graphically describes the 'paine in his swete tendire body', how Jesus' 'tendre flesh was kut'.[58] The Feast of the Circumcision was celebrated on 1 January, New Year's Day, so, in a very practical and familiar sense, the Chris-tian year started with Circumcision.

Later medieval culture repeatedly returned to the image of cir-cumcision as a precious and memorable moment of edifying violence not as a violent slur on Jewish masculinity.[59] John Lydgate's *Lyf of Our Lady* (c. 1415) provides the most detailed medieval English treatment of the Circumcision of Christ. Lydgate's treatment starts with an evocative description of the 'colde Januarie,/ With fresty berde', the time of the Feast of the Circumcision, a day 'so high and gloriouse' (IV:1, IV:21).[60] His description of the Circumcision is based on

Pseudo-Bonaventure's *Meditationes* and foregrounds the rite's affective painful pleasure:

And withe a knife made full sharpe of stone,	
His mother loking with a pitous eye,	
The childe was *corve* ther-with all, anon,	*cut*
That all aboute the rede bloode *gan gon*	*began to flow*
Withoute a boode, as saithe Bonaventure,	*Without delay*
That for the paine he did endure,	
And for sharpnes of the *sodden smerte*,	*sudden pain*
The childe *gan* wepe that pité was to *here*.	*began, hear*
Wherfore his mother, of verrey tendre herte,	
Oute *brast on teres* and might her-self	*Burst into tears,*
not *stere*,	*restrain*
That all *bydewede* were her *eyne* clere,	*moistened, eyes*
Whan she sawe him that she lovede soo,	
So yonge, so faire, weping so for *woo*.	*woe*
But he *a-noon* in all his passion,	*forthwith*
For all that he was so yong of age,	
In manere he had pité and compassion,	
To see his modir so wepe in hir rage;	
And put his hande unto *hir visage*,	*her face*
On mouthe and *eyne, passingly benyngne*	*eyes, of great*
	gentleness
And as he *couthe* goodly made a signe	*was able*
Withoutyn speche, to *stint* her weping,	*stop*
That came to her of motherly pité. (IV:29–51)	

Lydgate emphasizes weeping and pity, but also eloquently shows the intersubjective transmission of affect between Christ and the Virgin: the child weeps when his foreskin is cut, causing his mother to cry, fostering the child's compassionate response. The diction – of red blood flowing, 'the sodden smerte' and the Virgin's grief – is highly imitative of Passion scenes; the infant's gesture – reaching for his mother's face – was a well-known gesture of Christ's love for the human soul and the quasi-erotic Sponsa-Sponsus (Bride and Bridegroom) imagery in which Mary is the Church to her son who is the Word of God.[61] The moment of violence in Lydgate's poem is also a moment of love, and it is in this bloody and transformative moment of pain that the infant, human Jesus shows his wisdom, pity, compassion and divinity.

IV: A Child is Being Beaten: The Tring Tiles

Such aestheticized recreations of the struggle between flesh and spirit, sin and goodness, torture and its transcendence, are common to medieval Christianity and effective rhetoric, both valuing aesthetic suffering. Johan Huizinga called this 'that perpetual oscillation between despair and distracted joy, between cruelty and pious tenderness' characteristic of the Middle Ages.[62]

In this vein, the Tring Tiles, an early fourteenth-century English frieze of clay tiles executed in sgraffito, narrate a set of humorous, ferocious and miraculous stories about the boyhood of Jesus, replete with a kind of inventional violence, a founding myth full of painful knowledge.[63] The tiles tell their stories in narrative pairs; on the left of each pair, the young Jesus is wronged or victimized; on the right, through miraculous transformation or vengeance, Jesus corrects the situation. The tiles include the tale of a little boy whose father would not let him play with Jesus; miraculously, Jesus draws his playmate out through the keyhole. In another set, Jesus turns the village children, who have been hidden from him by their parents in an oven, into pigs. Another pair of tiles shows the young Christ being bullied, his Jewish playmate destroying little pools Jesus has made beside the river Jordan; in the answering tile, Mary instructs Jesus, having killed the bully, to restore the bully to life, the bully being sent on his way with a kick from Jesus. In most of the miracles Jesus is overseen by Mary or Joseph. The tiles were probably used as mural decoration in a parish church in or around Tring (Hertfordshire).[64]

One pair of tiles (illus. 3) includes a dramatic scene of violence, at once both everyday and shocking: on the left-hand tile, a seated schoolmaster slaps the young Jesus (centre) across the face, as Mary looks on. On the right-hand tile, Jesus (still at the centre) is watched by two adult teachers and two cripples, to whom he lectures.

This story is derived from the Latin *Gospel of Pseudo-Matthew*, a set of early medieval stories about the childhood of Jesus;[65] here, the boy's teacher, Levi, reproaches Joseph for thinking more of his son than of the elders, neatly voicing the conflict between the 'old' (past) and 'new' (present) Laws of Judaism and Christianity. The young

3 The infant Jesus is beaten by Levi the schoolmaster; Jesus lectures his teachers. Tring Tiles, English, clay, early fourteenth century. British Museum.

Jesus overhears, and ominously warns his teacher: 'I know when you were born and how long you have to live'. A quarrel develops, in which Levi beats Jesus on the head with a rod of storax (the branch of 'honour and grace' with odour of 'the purest balm' mentioned in Ecclesiasticus 24:21–3, so suggestive of the sweetness of the violence inflicted on Jesus). Jesus responds to Levi: 'Why do you hit me? Know of a truth that he who is smitten teaches the smiter more than he is taught of him.'[66]

In the *Gospel of Pseudo-Matthew* Jesus merely confounds Levi and miraculously cures infirm people around him from blindness and lameness. In later versions, the young Jesus strikes the schoolmaster dead then miraculously revives him, though this is not suggested in the tile.

The Tring Tiles are closely related to an early fourteenth-century illustrated manuscript of the Anglo-Norman *Enfaunces de Jesu Crist* or *Evangile de l'enfance*, which contains poetic versions of most of the stories included in the tiles together with similar illustrations.[67] The *Enfaunces* starts with the Annunciation (f. 1r) and the Massacre of the Innocents (f. 4r), and then narrates Jesus' miraculous childhood. It provides the same story as the tile from Tring: Levi strikes Jesus for refusing to answer a question; Jesus responds by demanding that Levi explicate the Hebrew alphabet, which Levi is unable to do; Jesus the prodigy does this instead (f. 18r; see illus. 4).[68] In the Anglo-Norman text, Jesus then turns to lecture the heretics and criminal hypocrites ('*herites*' and '*felons ypocrites*') around him who are lame and dumbstruck, apparently the grim-faced characters on the right-hand tile from Tring. Through the little Jesus' great help and sweetness ('*grant socur*' and '*douçur*') he makes the lame able to walk, and the mute able to speak, signs of healings ('*signes del saner*') which terrify the Jewish masters. Versions of the story were reasonably well known, and are found in a few other sources from medieval Europe, and there are several similar artefacts which manifest the new, affective stories of 'popular culture' vernacular in luxurious, innovative formats (such as picture books, clothing, tile sequences and drama).[69]

This story makes the narrative of the supercession of Levite law by Christian wisdom approachable, miniature, pithy. It is also a more intimate version of the well-known legend of Christ among the Doctors in the Temple (Luke 2:41–51), with the added element of Levi's violence. The story is also remarkably similar to those narratives which became very popular in the later Middle Ages, featuring Jewish violence against Christlike children, notably the 'Jewish Boy of Bourges' put in an oven by his father, preachers' *exempla* in which the Christ-Child appears weeping or as bleeding flesh, and the young victims of Jews in Christian ritual-murder cults.[70] In all cases an imperilled innocent is victimized by a 'Jewish' figure; the victims' willing assumption of violence answers the Jews' prerogative to inflict this violence. In the richly decorated manuscript of the Anglo-Norman *Enfaunces* Jesus has his hair pulled at school, answered by

4 The young Jesus is beaten by his teacher. From *Evangile de l'enfance*, MS. Selden Supra 38, fol. 18r, early fourteenth century.

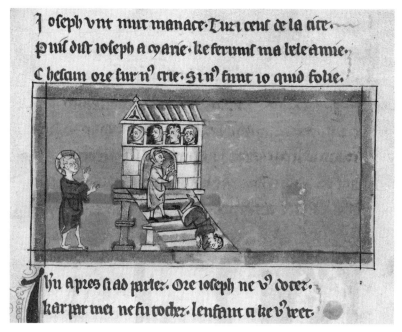

5 Jesus' friend is kicked down the stairs by a school bully. From *Evangile de l'enfance*, Library, MS. Selden Supra 38, fol. 20r.

the sudden death of the assailant (f. 10v); Jesus is bullied by a Jewish boy who jumps on his back (f. 11r), again answered by his being slapped by Jesus and killed; a childhood friend of Jesus is pushed down a flight of stairs by a Jewish bully (f. 20r; see illus. 5); a Jew breaks Jesus' pitcher, but Jesus manages to take the water home to Mary in the folds of his gown (f. 21v); yet a further story in the Anglo-Norman *Enfaunces* describes Jesus being slapped by another teacher.[71] The tortures go on and on, inflicted on the infant Jesus by his peers and by adults, and inflicted by Jesus in revenge. As well as being highly generic, such stories displace the very real violence not between Christians and Jews but of medieval pedagogy, in which learning a lesson was directly related to a master's infliction of violence upon the pupil.[72]

The villains of the Tring Tiles are Jewish: temporally, they are characters from Jesus' childhood in Judea; literally, the cognate 'Infancy Gospels' and Anglo-Norman *exempla* insistently name these characters as Jews ('*lé Gius*'); and, iconographically, the hooked, sharp noses, manual gestures of resistance and violence, pointed headgear juxtaposed with Jesus – always depicted in three-quarter view with a halo – point to their Judaism. In effect, the tiles fill in Jesus' Passional biography, between the childhood prefigurations of the Massacre of the Innocents and the Circumcision and the violence inflicted at the Crucifixion.

The slap in Jesus' face is a moment of brutality and also a moment of memorable drama, calling to mind the ubiquitous 'Jewish' slapping hands we find throughout medieval culture in scenes of Christ's Passion. This tile makes evident the abiding relationships in medieval culture between pedagogy and violence, devotion and suffering, as well as showing how fresh and *further* abuses against Christ's body were developed, here heightened by depicting violence against the child. At the same time, the Tring Tiles memorably depict Christ's own capacity for mischief and vengeance, the so-called 'Malevolent Acts' of Christ, to afflict or strike down those who doubt him, figuring a religious history made up by violence and retribution. Moreover, the Tring Tiles introduce a violent contrast between Christian and Jewish bodies. The mode of viewing the Tring Tiles is similar to modern day strip-art: this is not anachronistic, as the tile sequence, no doubt explicated in sermons as well as repeatedly viewed by congregants, is an intermedial narrative poised between seeing, reading, and re-telling/hearing. As tiles which would have been displayed on a wall (or, possibly, a floor), a somatic reaction is invited, as the eye and the body move with the narrative; in each case from left to right, from injustice to resolution, from violence to miracle, again akin to the perceptual *passio*.

The suggestion of Sigmund Freud's 1919 essay in the title of this section, 'A Child is Being Beaten', refers to that 'pleasurable quality' of fantasy which has its starting point in violence and punishment, the theoretical basis of the connection between pleasure and suffering. Whilst Freud's suggestion that the onlooker to the scene of violence experiences a sexual stimulus which leads to masturbation has become the best-known aspect of 'A Child is Being Beaten', the essay also suggests the edifying potential and vicarious nature of violence. 'The fantasy of [being beaten] is connected with feelings of pleasure', writes Freud, but 'the real experience of [watching] beating scenes was felt to be unbearable'.[73] Freud notes that 'the beaten child is never the fantasising child', but that the fantasizing child uses the beating fantasy to organize their relationships with those they love.[74] The winsome Christ-Child we find so frequently in medieval images, sermons and poetry was not only the recipient of love, but of a proleptic violence which foreshadows the Passion; the wounded child, the victimized child, the child being beaten, was also the incarnate God sacrificed by the Jews on behalf of mankind, the living bread, and an attention-grabbing assertion of violent embodiment.

V: Jewish Child Murder and the Domestic *Passio* of William of Norwich

To understand religion on one's own terms, to make it as much as possible a part of one's intimate experience, was to make something memorable and emotionally resonant: in other words, like the Toronto figure and the Tring Tiles, to domesticate and to familiarize the Bible, around an affecting polarity of violence and victimhood, persecution and mercy. Christ's Passion was considered omnipresent and beyond time: 'ever redy', in the words of Thomas à Kempis, whilst medieval mnemotechnic held that each memory made the thing remembered present again. These two considerations can significantly help us understand that most 'medieval' of allegations against Jewry, sacramental child killing, usually called 'ritual-murder' or 'blood libel'. As well as being highly charged and locally specific cults, often connected with micro-politics, devotional fashions and anti-Jewish persecutions, we can see such stories as personalized and emotional reconstructions of Christ's Passion.

The *ur*-text of William of Norwich's life, Thomas of Monmouth's *Life and Miracles of St William of Norwich*, sheds a great deal of extra light on how such stories were understood in the Middle Ages. Thomas's *Life and Miracles* concerns the events of 1144, when William, a skinner's apprentice in Norwich, disappeared. His death was subsequently blamed on the city's Jews (who allegedly concealed the boy's death in concert with corrupt local Christians). William's body and the shrines in which it was placed came to be the source of many miracles and the sainted boy can be said to be the first such example of a church-sponsored cult of a child slain by Jews. Thomas's text, written around 1172, some three decades after the events it describes, aims to establish William's sanctity and the Jews' culpability.[75] But, in addition to the practical aim of launching William as a saint, it is an erudite, wordy, imaginative piece of Latin prose, written for Thomas's bishop, William Turbe (d. 1174). It is not, and never was, a 'legal' or 'factual' indictment of the Jews, but rather a treatise on divinity and martyrdom as understood by a medieval monk.

6 The Martyrdom of St William of Norwich, Loddon (Norfolk).
Fifteenth-century painted screen.

Such accounts of these Christian boys' martyrdoms at Jewish hands
are designed to be imitative: imitative of each other and of Christ's
Passion. The English accounts all developed in highly literate and
cosmopolitan Benedictine monasteries (the main accounts coming
from Norwich, Bury St Edmunds, Gloucester, Winchester, Canterbury and Lincoln) between 1150 and 1255, and the earliest Continental

reports of ritual murder probably came, likewise, from books circulating between monastic houses. Later, in at least one fifteenth-century book of hours, the prayers to and images of Robert of Bury St Edmunds, an East Anglian boy-saint, appears in place of the Nativity, Robert's death removed from medieval Bury and placed at the moment of the birth of Christianity, the point when Judaism becomes Old to the Christian New.[76] On the mutilated fifteenth-century rood screen at Holy Trinity, Loddon (Norfolk), the *passio* of William of Norwich appears within a scheme of images on the life of the infant Christ (illus. 6). The Loddon panel shows William strung up and spread-eagled, in a parody of the Crucifixion, and genitally wounded, to suggest the Circumcision; in other images of the boy, his attribute is the Three Nails of his Passion, a miniature version of the Five Nails through which Christ suffered. At Loddon William of Norwich's death is both Christlike and saintly. This would have been important to lay people's engagement with these boys' cults, seeing the Jewish murder of Christian boys as a reference to the biblical past rather than the local present; indeed, in the *Life and Miracles of St William*, William's death is repeatedly described as a mockery of Christ's Passion.[77] The imagined bloodstained corpse of a boy like William could stretch time, connecting the murderous Jews of medieval Norwich with the biblical violence of the Crucifixion.

Thomas's *Life* is written in seven books, which do not give a continuous, linear account of William's life, but a brief account of William's infancy and martyrdom (which occurs in the first book), followed by miracles, visions, the punishment of the Jews, an imaginary 'rhetorical' version of a Christian-Jewish disputation in the presence of King Stephen, the various reburials of William's corpse, further miracles, the death of William's mother, finishing with yet further miracles. Following a long preface, the very first incident in book I is a strange dream which Elviva, William's mother, had:

> It appeared to her as she slept that she was standing in a road with her father Wlward, a priest, a man very famous in his time. And lo! as she bent her eyes upon the ground, there at her feet she beheld a fish which is [commonly] known as a luce [*qui vulgo lucius dicitur*]. The fish had twelve fins on each side, and they were red and as it were dabbled with blood. And she spake to her father and said, 'Father, I see a fish, but I greatly marvel how it should have come here or how it can live in so dry a

spot.' To whom her father made answer, 'Take it up, my daughter. Take it up and put it in thy bosom' [*in sinu*, in the bosom
or lap]. Which when she had done, the fish seemed to move in
her bosom and by degrees to grow so fast that now she could
no longer hold it. So it glided out, and escaping by her sleeve
and suddenly taking to itself wings, it flew away, and, passing
through the clouds, betook itself to heaven, which opening to
receive it.[78]

The story of little William begins in a visionary mode, of mysteries,
similitude, signs and portends, setting the scene for a text which deals
in rhetoric as evidence and emotions as facts. The dream is described, by Thomas, as a '*sompnium presagio*', a dream of forewarn-
ing or presage, and in it can be seen the entire story of William and
his martyrdom. The fish represents William the martyr, speckled red
with the blood of martyrdom. The twelve fins call to mind a range
of valorized duodecimal ideas: the twelve sides of the Temple and
the twelve gates of the New Jerusalem, the twelve tribes of Israel, the
twelve Disciples, and the combination of the sacred and the secular
(3×4), all of which represent aspects of William's life and death.[79]
The fish leaps inside Elviva's bosom or lap like the Holy Spirit leaps
in Mary's womb (Luke 1:41). Elviva's father's injunction ('Take it up,
my daughter. Take it up . . ', translating '*Tolle filia, tolle illum*') alludes
directly to the famous biblical line '*tolle tolle crucifige eum*' (John
19:15), 'Take him up, take him up and crucify him', shouted by the
Jews at Christ's trial (and included in the Easter liturgy), thereby
prefiguring William's martyrdom at the hands of the Jews. William
the martyr is, in his earthly life, a 'fish out of water', not meant for
Norwich but ready for Heaven; the martyr will, one day, transform
and ascend at Easter (and, indeed, William was martyred in Easter
week). In keeping with medieval dream theory, which returned
repeatedly to exploring the liminal 'middleness' of visionary dreams,
Elviva's dream gives her an elevated knowledge, a kind of divine
revelation, mediated through mundane imagery, 'poised between
opposed categories of transcendent and immanent, divine and
demonic'.[80]

In no way does Thomas even pretend this is a witnessed report
of a historical fact, but rather that it is a rich memory-event – retrospective and prophetic, allusive and ripe for interpretation: the *luce*
is at once a likeness of previous figures, a likeness of William and

a figure of what will befall him.[81] Recollection of the murder of William is not of an event, but of a set of discourses and cues, to the death of Christ and to saintly martyrdom, and this is the purpose served by the *luce*. In the *luce* are gathered together the key facets of William's life and martyrdom, as a kind of icon: the word *luce* figures the candles and lights (Latin *lux*) that becomes William's motif (he is born on the feast of Candlemas, signifying 'that he would greatly love candles and the brightness of them').[82] Speckled with blood and out of water, the *luce* figures William's martyrdom. With an English term, *luce*, rather than a Latin one, William's image is familiar, non-elite, vernacular, domestic. Thomas of Monmouth uses this technique – an English word within florid Latin – at two key points: the *luce*, and the *teazle* ('*quod vulgo teseillun dicitur*') with which the Jews torture William.[83] Moving out of Latin into English, local things (a pike and a thistle), like familiar people ('Gillilda, wife to Thurgar of Mildenhall', 'Hervey the baker') appear suddenly and emphatically in the Latin prose. They provide key coordinates around which the reader can apprehend and remember William's story, as Passional martyrdom erupts in twelfth-century Norwich.

Likewise, we might consider the account of Liviva (a minor character 'borrowed' from the local cult of St Edmund).[84] Liviva had a dream that, the Saturday before Palm Sunday, she was attacked by Jews in the High Street of Norwich's Market Place:

> And as they held me they broke my right leg with a club and they tore it away from the rest of my body, and running off with all speed it seemed that they were carrying it away with them. O only too true forewarning of my vision![85]

Liviva passes out in pallor, and then recovers consciousness, but never stops lamenting for the rest of her days. This is a characteristically vivid piece of writing, combining the strikingly grotesque trope of the detached limb within the intimate, levelling and public space of Norwich's High Street; Liviva is literally 'ripped off' by the Jews at the Market. The torn limb calls to mind a range of similar images, not least the Massacre of the Innocents and the Wounds of Christ, but also the manicule, the pointing fingers of manuscript marginalia which called the reader to attention, and the raised hands and kicking legs we see throughout the medieval culture of gesture. In its narrative context, Liviva's 'too true' dream is understood as proof of the Jews' guilt, as the affective dreamscape of her assault by Jews in the market is 'read' and 'felt' as potent conjectures (then as evidence) of the extraordinary way in which William would be murdered.

It may seem strange, given that the entire project of William of Norwich's cult is based on the idea of Jews murdering Christians, but Jews occupy only a few pages of Thomas's long text, and we gain little sense of Jewish life in medieval Norwich from it as a source. What such stories of the Jewish murder of Christian boys do is make intimate the story of Christ's Passion by using a combination of sensational and extreme images within the everyday, local and familiar. These stories thus made present – and thereby made medieval people the conscious and active agents in – Christ's Passion. The emphasis in these boys' stories is on the wonderful and miraculous, vivid scenes of emotion and cruelty, and, especially, key imitative moments of torture. Thomas says the Jews wanted to mock the Passion of Christ, but the sense and meaning of the entire project is based on rereading William's death as a heightened, clarified, remembered version of Christ's Passion. It might be said that the 'memory-work' a text like this performs is not to remember the Jewish murder of a Christian child, but to remember Christ's Passion as intimate and 'cotidiane'.

VI: Violence as Rhetorical Conjecture

Thomas's *Life of St William* also includes a fascinating account of a disputation between the Jews and Christians of Norwich. Thomas does not give an account of the Jews' trial for causing William's death; the trial scene concerns the retributive murder of Eleazar the Jew, in whose house William was murdered and who concealed the boy's body in woodland. The Jews present their complaint for Eleazar's murder before King Stephen, accusing a local knight of murdering Eleazar to rid himself of debts; Thomas writes an 'imaginary' account of their suit. At length and with elegance the Jews set out an orderly case against a Christian knight, Simon de Nodariis (Novers), summarizing, with some wit:

> *Atque, ut rem manifestius exequar, debitor miles aut soluere uoluit et potuit, aut uoluit nec potuit, aut noluit et potuit, siue, quod restat, nec uoluit nec potuit.*

And to make the matter plainer, this knightly debtor either would pay and could; or he would and could not; or he would not and could; or lastly, he neither would nor could.[86]

The Jews speak nicely, but they are, Thomas implies, bearing false witness before an illegitimate court. The king sides with the Jews against the knight; the bishop acts in the knight's defence, saying that the knight was with Eleazar when they were attacked by brigands, and argues that they, Christians, should not have to defend themselves against Jews who have recently, 'as report says', killed a Christian boy. The king adjourns the case and the Jews meet in London and assemble a bribe: this is offered to the bishop and refused. When the court reconvenes, the king further defers the case of the trial 'to another season', and the matter seems to be dropped. For Thomas of Monmouth, this is further evidence of 'that most crafty and avaricious race, the Jews' and, in their attempts to bribe the bishop, evidence of their guilt of the murder of William.

Thomas makes clear that this account is not an eyewitness report but rather a 'rhetorical version': the terms Thomas uses are '*disceptationem supposui*' (a supposed or theoretical discussion), '*coniecturalis*' (conjectural or speculative) and '*declamationis*' (suggestive of public, rhetorical contest).[87] Thomas's account is a wonderfully lively piece of writing and there can be little doubt that it was written as an exercise in rhetoric and writing rather than 'fact' as we might now understand it. Thomas summarizes that 'testimony of revelations' and 'manifold arguments' serve as 'proofs' that William was slain by the Jews:[88] 'revelation' and 'argument' are in themselves proof. The trial is a long and formal discussion of the propriety of credit and debit in terms of Jewish-Christian relations, and little considers the case of William's death. However, the trial account is framed by two vivid moments of physical grotesquery: beforehand, the description of the death of Eleazar and, afterwards, the description of the death of the Christian Sheriff John de Cheyney who had protected the Jews. Eleazar suffers a swift and horrible death which itself is an explicit repetition of the death suffered by little William: Eleazar 'was enticed out of his own house, was killed by the hands of Christians in a wood, and exactly in the same way [as William] was left in the open air and exposed to be torn to pieces by dogs and birds'.[89] Sheriff John, meanwhile, starts to suffer from a flux of blood from his backside, his body gradually weakening;[90]

he eventually dies due to the constant bleeding. As has often been noted, the sheriff's death recalls that of Judas, who 'being hanged, burst asunder in the midst: and all his bowels gushed out' (Acts 1:18). Even though the Vulgate mentions Judas's viscera where Thomas of Monmouth describes John's blood, the legal trial framed by two violent spectacles is an effective method: the elegant and serpentine rhetoric of the trial is answered in its contrast, the bloody and gruesome punishment by God. Thus Thomas vividly shows how the guilt of the sheriff and the Jews is not determined by legal justice, but by affective retribution which calls to mind earlier violence against William and Christ.

Affectio – broadly translated as emotion – and repetition are the guiding principles of Thomas's story. Things felt, things remembered and repeated, things believed and things perceived are much more important in the way Christians define themselves against Jews than who did certain things or when these things were done. When Thomas of Monmouth is writing about the 'proof' of the Jews' guilt, he does not have a forensic idea of Jewish guilt, but an interpretative and emotional one.

We might approach medieval Christian stories like those of Jewish child-murder not as 'known' recollections of actual events – of proof, bodies, evidence, crimes – but as stimuli to emotional engagement and as stories which gather up various local elements and religious images – of sainthood, martyrdom, the Christ-Child – to be rearranged personally, ardently and locally. In the fervent memory of Christ's Passion, in the drama of martyrdom and redemption, and, most potently, in the dizzying extremes of Christian good – unsullied, virginal, native, innocent – and Jewish evil – international, depraved, bloodthirsty, emphatically embodied – these stories are designed to shock, to stimulate empathy and compunction, with their vivid and highly coloured scenes of violence and emotion.

Thomas's *Life and Miracles* never achieved a great readership, although the story he told has often been repeated in one form or another. Such stories rely on the image of child murder, but they seem also to promise retributive violence towards Jews. Do such stories necessarily hold within their fantasies of Jewish violence against Christians a promise of Christian violence to Jews? More often than not, the stories were retrospective and solipsistic, looking back to the Bible and into the devotional world of medieval Christianity. At Norwich, the consequences of the allegations against the Jews do not seem to have been grave; but, famously, as at Lincoln in 1255 and Trent in 1475, Jewish communities were attacked as a consequence of such stories.[91] It is impossible to assess how far the sensuous world of blood, grief and rage imagined in these stories encouraged and endorsed the behaviour of those who attacked the Jews, but we can be confident that the precedent of Christ's Passion with which such stories resounded worked for medieval Christians in framing and stimulating the generic, familiar violence in which they were engaged.

VII: Swearing Oaths Like a Jew

An unusual wall painting from the church of St Lawrence at Broughton (Buckinghamshire) warns against curses, oaths and slander (illus. 7); it dates from the fifteenth century and is one of several such depictions in late medieval England of the injunction against swearing *per membra*, making oaths on the limbs and wounds of Christ's body.[92]

At the centre is the *pietà*, the Virgin holding the dead, mutilated body of Christ. Nine young men direct various acts of violence and desecration against them. In the lower right corner one holds Christ's foot and in the upper left corner another holds a hand; these limbs have been ripped from Christ's body as the result of having sworn an oath on it ('By Christ's wounds' or similar). Likewise, the man to the right of the Virgin holds the sacred heart, and the man in the lower left corner holds bones (like Shakespeare's Hotspur swears, 'Heart!' on Christ's heart and 'Christ's bones!').[93] The image goes beyond scripture in suggesting that Christ's body was torn apart (akin to the medieval punishment of being quartered after hanging, or broken on a wheel), although it is consonant with late medieval devotions to the Five Wounds and the Bleeding Heart of Christ, in which wounded limbs and organs are represented by themselves.[94]

The two figures at the lower centre of the picture are engaged in some kind of gaming: the board between them seems to be for tables or merels, chequers, dice or 'hazard' game. Much of what we know about such games of chance – the precursors of modern dice and counter games – is from injunctions and invective against them; the usual adjectives which accompany such games are 'cursed' or 'unlawful' and, in the Broughton painting, the playing of these games has become a serious kind of blasphemy. In the Towneley play of the Crucifixion, the games played in the tavern become representative of hell and are mixed with a range of 'Jewish' ills, such as usury and backbiting: Tutivillus, the devil, addresses the evil-doers at the Day of Judgment thus:

Welcom, my *lefes!*	*dears*
Fals iurars and usurars,	*Those who swear false witness*
To *simony that clevis,*	*those who cleave to simony*
To *tell*;	*to count them one by one*
Hasardars and *dysars,*	*dicers*
Fals dedys forgars,	*forgers of false deeds*
Slanderars, *bakbytars* –	*backbiters*
All unto hell![95]	

Hell has become a provincial tavern. Likewise, in the Broughton image the Passion goes on anew, 'ever redy', repeated, redone, in the everyday curses and games of late medieval English people. The young men are, in part, represented as Jews. They are standing with the rent limbs of Christ, a pose which would have called to mind a continuum of the Jewish tearing of Christian limbs, from the Massacre of the Innocents to the allegation of ritual-murder. The Bible would have shown medieval Christians that one of the things Jews do *as Jews* is play dice: the casting of lots for Jesus' coat (Matthew 27:35). All the men wear distinctive hats and odd-coloured hose, parti-coloured outfits being symbolic of the Jews at the Passion.[96] The image parallels Chaucer's description of the 'yonge folk' – three young men – in 'The Pardoner's Tale' who were given to 'riot, hasard, stywes, and tavernes' and, in particular, to swearing oaths that were

so grete and so *dampnable*	*damnable*
That it is grisly *for to heere hem swere.*	*to hear them swear*
Oure blissed lordes body they *totere* –	*tore apart*
Hem thoughte that Jewes rente	
him *noght ynough* –	*not enough*
And *ech of hem* at otheres	
sinne *lough* (VI:472–6)[97]	*each of them, laughed*

The Pardoner's young rioters are then both like Jews and *worse than* Jews as they tear Christ's body apart. Another fourteenth-century warning against swearers, in John Bromyard's widely read *Summa praedicantium*, invokes the Jews as the 'original' blasphemers, but

7 'Warning to Swearers', swearing men ripping limbs from the dead Christ, Broughton (Buckinghamshire). Wall painting, *c.* 1470.

explicitly says that Christians who swear are even worse and go even further than the Jews in their physical attack on Christ:

> The Jews did not know Christ to be God; they blasphemed against Him and mocked Him when a mortal man, but the Christians, knowing Him to be God, do this to Him when He is reigning in glory. The Jews gave Christ's body unmaimed, but the Christians cut it up in pieces, limb by limb, with the devil's sword, i.e. their tongue.[98]

Moreover, the Broughton image intersects with many *exempla* stories used in sermons of the swearer's vision of a bloodied, wounded child (the Bloody Child *exemplum*).

A version of this story appeared in the *Festial* by John Mirk of *c.* 1382, one of the most widespread sermon texts in later medieval

England. According to Mirk's story, a great man was sent by the Emperor to be a justice over a group of people; prior to this great man's arrival, the people could swear no oath but 'yey' and 'nay'; after the justice's arrival, the people started to swear on all kinds of things. The justice and his men

> wer so wont for-to swere by Godys passion, and armes, and sides, and blody wo[u]ndys, that all the pepull toke at hom[e] so in use, that all the pepull swere as horribull as thay did.[99]

Swearing is then a kind of mass-blasphemy, and akin to a conversion by an alien evangelist, here in the form of the justice. One day, the justice was sitting in his court, 'in sight of all men', when 'the fairist woman that ever that seghen', dressed in green, appears; she is carrying a 'faire child in hur lappe'. The child is 'blody and all tomarturd', that is, bloodily martyred. The woman asks the justice what should happen to those who have thus abused her child; the justice answers that such people should be put to death. The woman answers thus:

> 'Thou and thy men with your horribull othes han dismembryd my sonne Ihesu Cryst, that I am modir to, and soo ye have ta[u]ght all this lond. Wherefor thou schalt have thyn owne dome'. Then anon, in sight of all the pepull, the erth opened and the justice fell do[w]n into hell.

Unsurprisingly, Mirk's little story ends by telling us that the people amended their blasphemous ways. The narrator then turns to the audience, moralizing and threatening, to instruct the listener to do as Christian men should: to cease one's oaths and to revere properly Christ's Passion and his wounds.

The story as given in the *Festial* returns us to the shocking and memorable image of the Christ-Child subjected to violence. The instructive, educative role of this wounded childish body is very clear here: it is Mary who shows the 'tomarturd' body of her little son, a domestic and maternal take on the late medieval tradition of the *ostensio vulnerum*, the extravagant ostensive act of the suffering Christ showing his wounds: an act of viewing which is also an act of violent touching. In another version of the story, a wounded Christ-as-youth appears to a monk who wishes to return to secular life; the bloodied Christ says 'You are crucifying me again', and so the monk remains cloistered.[100] The point the story makes most forcefully is that in one's everyday transgressions one is, like a 'Jew', repeating the tortures of the Passion of Christ; through inflicting these wounds one discerned right from wrong and one confirmed one's faith.

The onus is placed on the reader/viewer to produce meaning by putting themselves 'inside' the artefact, as the reader/viewer was not only imaginatively present at the Passion but involved in it. A common visual scheme, the warning against breaking the Sabbath in the form of the 'Sunday Christ', similarly brings the Passion into the mundane world of the medieval worshipper.[101] In these images the implements by which medieval people made their livings represent the Instruments of the Passion, vividly staging an intimate violence to Christ's body in which the medieval worshiper became 'like a Jew' for breaking the Sabbath.

From the starting point of violent rhetoric, we have seen not only the intimacy of graphic violence but also the highly serviceable and familiar nature of the 'Jew' who inflicts this violence. In the image of attacking a body was a constellation of practices about sacred violence, suffering infancy, and compelling, moving reading, viewing and remembering. The Toronto figure evoked violence to represent the Virgin and Child's passive triumph over evil, whereas the warnings against swearers align the late medieval Christian with the Jews, wounding Christ anew. The Christ-Child was not only a powerful reminder of maternal tenderness and infantile stainlessness (the image with which we are familiar from Madonna and Child portraits), but was also very often imagined as bloodied, tortured, the victim of his audience, performing his gore. Another glimpse at the Luttrell Psalter (f. 169r) corroborates this: here, next to Psalm 93:6 – 'They have slain the widow and the stranger: and they have murdered the fatherless' – shows three scenes of violence (illus. 8), including an unkempt man hacking two children's bodies apart. The image shows the atrocities afflicted on the English by the Scots, a fourteenth-century conflict in which the book's donor, Geoffrey Luttrell, had taken part;[102] but this image also evokes the Innocents and the imagery of the wounded Christ-Child, as the Scots become like Jews in their ferocious violence, as fourteenth-century persecution shades into its biblical analogues. This image, of a child's torn body in the midst of a luxurious manuscript, eloquently reflects the decorative violence through which medieval people sought to feel the poignant shock of Christ's Passion. As in the Eucharistic sacrament, in which Christ's

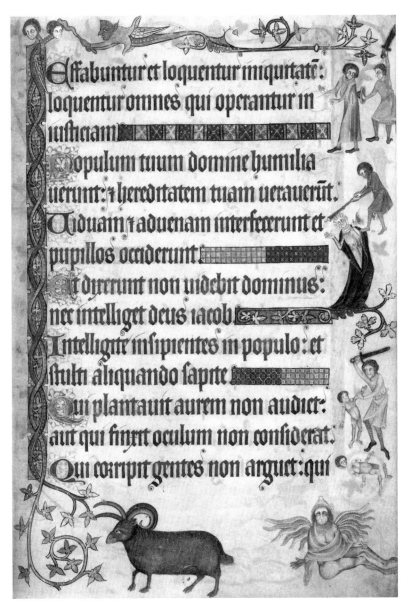

Effabuntur et loquentur iniquitate: loquentur omnes qui operantur iniusticiam

Populum tuum domine humiliauerunt: z hereditatem tuam uexauerunt.

Uiduam z aduenam interfecerunt et pupillos occiderunt.

Et dixerunt non uidebit dominus: nec intelliget deus iacob

Intelligite insipientes in populo: et stulti aliquando sapite

Qui plantauit aurem non audiet: aut qui finxit oculum non considerat.

Qui corripit gentes non arguet: qui

8 Scottish atrocities against the English, reminiscent of the Massacre of the Innocents. Luttrell Psalter, England, *c.* 1350. BL Add. MS 42130, f. 169r.

bloodied body appeared anew, Jewish violence on Christ's body was used to stimulate an intense, but familiar, memory. To return to this scene of special pain was treasured because it was instructive and intimate, and the place where devotional and emotional subjectivity started.

CHAPTER 3

The Jewish Profile and the History of Ugliness

The art of caricature . . . [is] thus based . . . on the contrast between
cruelty on one side and credulity on the other.
—Vladimir Nabokov, *Laughter in the Dark*

Ugly Violence: Profile, Position and Violent Counterpoint

Medieval visual images and textual descriptions of Jews are best
understood as affective memory-images, designed to bring the edifying and pleasurable experience of fear, violence and contrast into
the medieval reader/viewer's aesthetic world. However, many such
images immediately appear 'racist' to the modern reader. Post-
medieval 'racial' vocabularies, particularly that of the Nazis, caricatured and vitiated the image of the Jewish face and body, seeking
to conjoin degenerate physicality and degenerate morality, around
the idea that there is something of a 'Jewish look', that one can 'look
Jewish'.[1]

   'Race science' and its modern analogues are indebted to medieval
modes of representation; however, medieval representations cannot
be said to have either the same meanings or the same aesthetic register as these modern versions. Medieval thought and law held that the
tainted Jewish or heretic soul was manifested in the Jews' perceived
ugliness.[2] Likewise, Giotto's images of Judas use physiognomy to indi-
cate wickedness, such as the rounded forehead of a stupid person and
the 'slanting nose' which reveals a 'crooked soul'.[3] Medievalists are
primed in 'reading' types of gesture, expression and pose as expressions of both inner character and interpersonal engagement. Too
often, however, we recognize an image as a type, or as a stereotype,
without considering the ways in which we have recognized it as such:
are Jews really depicted in profile simply because medieval artists saw
them as 'racially' 'different', subhuman or physically 'fallen'? Moshe
Barasch takes Jewish 'racial' difference for granted when he writes that

medieval artists 'preferred to depict [Jews] in profile, a view that makes the racial characteristics stand out more clearly'.[4]

Modern racist imagery emerged from the conjunction of physiognomics (facial features read as evidence of character) with fantasies of racial purity, as proposed by Wilhelm Marr (1819–1904) and others.[5] Physiognomy was codified by the Swiss theologian Johann Caspar Lavater (1741–1801), his work grounded in art-historical methods, his 'evidence' taken from European portraiture rather than socio-anthropological observation; Lavater's analytical images may remind the modern reader of racial science but were used as portraitists' models and exemplars.[6] Early portraiture and the associated medieval art of caricature had, long before Lavater, employed modified, exaggerated or stylized physical features to suggest moral character, to form a memorable image and to dramatize a kind of formal violence.

Indeed, physiognomic manuals circulated in the Middle Ages, the most widespread being the anonymous *De physiognomia libellus* and *Physiognomia Latina,* Michael Scot's *Liber phisionomie* (*c.* 1230), Pietro d'Abano's *Compilatio physionomiae* (*c.* 1295), the pseudo-Aristotelian *Physiognomonica* and *Secreta secretorum*, and sections of Albertus Magnus' *De animalibus.*[7] Most of this physiognomic theory came to Christianity via Arabic and Hebrew versions of Aristotelian traditions; its wisdom was very similar to that which would later be given by Lavater. The fifteenth-century English translation of the *Secreta secretorum* by John Lydgate (?1370–1441) and Benedict Burgh (d. *c.* 1483) includes a section on 'the Crafft of physionomie', 'the excellent science, celestial and divine'.[8] Lydgate and Burgh describe how 'loking in facys' [*faces*] allows one to judge 'proporcioun' and thereby understand 'disposicioun'. Lydgate and Burgh advise kings to learn physiognomy: their fundamental advice is to avoid men who are 'feble of Colour', those who have deformed faces, those who have red, white or black spots around the eyes. A long hook-nose is the sign of a 'liere', 'as Oold philisoffres clerly doth devise'; he who moves his hands when talking 'is a disceyvour'; one must 'nevir deme mannys disposicioun' from one attribute or member alone: one should be sure to 'Behoold al signes'.[9]

Even though physiognomy only spread through Latin Europe from the twelfth century, from the early Middle Ages visual culture of the human face and body position (also known as 'view') had specific valence, with Jews, as well as other 'outgroups', very often represented in profile view or position.[10] 'Position' refers to the mode in which

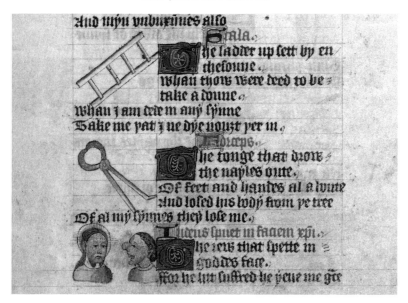

9 Instruments of the Passion: the ladders, the tongs, the Jew spitting in Christ's face. From Verses on the *Arma Christi*, San Marino, CA, Huntington Library MS HM 142, f. 8v, England, mid-fifteenth century.

we view the subject (such as 'frontal', or 'three-quarter', or 'dorsal', or 'profile'). For instance, in an Eastern or Byzantine Christian icon, particularly one of Christ in Majesty (Pantocrator) or of a saint, the position is usually frontal; this allows for an uninterrupted, undistracted meditation on the subject and evokes the inscrutability and ineffability of divinity.[11]

Medieval culture had well-established and well-defined registers of beauty and ugliness, grace and immorality.[12] Judas is almost always uniquely depicted in profile, at the Betrayal or receiving the sop at the Last Supper, as profile represents an active, forceful and jarring presence;[13] at his suicide, Judas is usually depicted in frontal position, an exemplary, hanging sign. From such fixed modes of representation we cannot posit a fixed 'racial science' in the Middle Ages; rather, there were distinctive and established modes of portraiture and caricature which, being tied to religious morality and affiliation, would later be used to inform or corroborate racial science.[14] Very early English images of Jews other than Judas tend to show them in profile – for instance, the famous 1233 tallage-roll graffiti of 'Mosse-Mokke' and 'Avegaye', Jewish financiers of Norwich.[15] The Jewish profile *viewed in profile* was certainly a well-known, indeed ubiquitous, convention in Byzantine art and was firmly established in England by the twelfth century and remained, apparently, fixed and stable throughout the Middle Ages. A clear example is provided by a fifteenth-century *Arma Christi* image-text scheme (illus. 9). The green-faced Jew gazes and spits on the side of Christ's face, inviting a clear comparison and contrast in representational registers of Jewish crime and Christian grace. Christ does not meet the Jew's eye, but rather looks outward into the reader's world.[16] 'Position' – not perspectival or mimetic realism – is the governing principle of such representations.

These are images of an idea of a Jew, rather than images of Jews. We cannot analyse or counter this kind of stereotype with evidence, logic or argument because, as Hannah Arendt suggested, apparatuses of dominance and subjection 'construct their own realities and thereby resist empirical proof'.[17] Instead, we might think of this kind of stereotype as emotionally involving and expressive, best understood in terms of affect or feeling rather than intellect (through which ideas might be proven, known and reasoned, rather than asserted or felt). Such medieval devotional images might be considered as affective devices, not as failed or rudimentary attempts at mimesis, perspectival naturalism or 'art'.[18] Hans Belting describes the 'era of images', in which images communicated with the viewer through emotion, touch and presence, preceding modern cultures of naturalism and connoisseurship (Belting's 'era of art').[19] In brief, medieval theories of optical vision and *perspectiva naturalis* were configured around the potential of the eye and the image to interpenetrate physically, intellectually and emotionally, be it through optical 'extramission' (according to which the eye gave out rays which hit the image) or 'intramission' (according to which the image penetrates the eye).[20] 'Decoration', design and devices, grotesques and drolleries, served memorial and intellectual engagement; Frances Yates proposed a way of understanding medieval visual culture in terms of 'corporeal similitudes' and 'spiritualised human images' as set out in Scholastic treatises on memory, whilst Mary Carruthers's work shows how memory, often described as a kind of impression or wound made in the viewer's mind, was at the very basis of the medieval concept of representation.[21] Images, devotional poetry and religious drama sought to concentrate the viewer's attention, to involve the viewer, actively and affectively, in the recital and performance of salvation, and to put before the mind – or the mind's eye – matters of the spirit.

Jews do not have uniform or consistent 'racial characteristics' and medieval people did not have a modern 'racial' theory of humanity.[22] Profile positioning was used to evoke and suggest particular doctrinal *and* emotional responses. The Jewish profile's prevalence suggests that the medieval Christian world equated Christianity with beauty, Judaism with ugliness, but this is necessarily part of a sophisticated process of reading, interpretation, feeling and moral comparison. In his discussion of 'honesty', Thomas Aquinas described in the *Summa theologiae* (*c.* 1266–73) how beauty, whilst sensuous in origin, has three prerequisites: 'perfection', 'appropriate proportion', and 'clarity'; whilst he admitted that not all beautiful things are virtuous, Aquinas concludes that 'beauty of body consists in shapely limbs and features having a proper show of colour. So also beauty of spirit consists in conversation and actions that are well-formed and suffused with intelligence.'[23]

There was little discussion in the Middle Ages of 'ugliness'; rather 'not-beauty', those things without appropriate proportion, were considered aesthetically disruptive.[24] 'Ugliness' (deriving from the Old Norse *ugglig*, something to be feared) is, after all, often merely a way of describing something incongruous or strange. No stereotype makes sense by itself: to understand the stereotype not only must we have encountered it before, but we must be able to judge it, separate it, distinguish it, from other 'normal' and 'positive' depictions around it.[25] St Augustine raised this issue in his treatise *De ordine* (*On Order*), where he suggested that if poets took ugly things out of their works their poetry would become vexatious, 'a rough sentence within a polished text makes the flight of fancy and the more ornate passage stand out': without coarseness, 'beautiful passages' are 'obscured by their own brilliance'.[26] Augustine makes clear that ugly things are needed for both moral and aesthetic order.

Such ugliness, based on an exaggerated body, is often described as 'grotesque'. Not unlike the term 'anti-Semitism', the 'grotesque' is frequently invoked in terms of medieval culture as if we all understand what it means. Moreover, like 'anti-Semitism', 'grotesque' is a postmedieval term (from the French, a fanciful style of sixteenth-century decoration, from the Italian *grottesca*, referring to the decoration of the ancient grottoes under Rome) and this is true for much of the vocabulary we now have to describe such images: 'uncanny', 'bizarre', 'misproportioned', 'disjointed', 'blemished', 'weird' (in the sense of the unusual; in the Middle Ages it referred to fate), are all post-medieval terms. Grotesquery is characterized by incongruity, distortion, and would have been called, in medieval English, 'outlandish' (literally 'foreignness', but generally used in the Middle Ages for Saracens, invading enemies and new-fangled strangeness) or 'crooked', 'foul', 'ugly', 'gross', 'strange' or 'misshapen', all adjectives indicating malformation, imperfection, bent-ness, foreignness or deformity rather than some inherent, timeless quality of grotesquery. Christ, on the other hand, represented the equally intangible archetype of beauty, 'the clannest ['purest'] complexione that ever was or miht be' as Nicholas Love described it;[27] the beautiful suffer pain, and the ugly cause it. Similarly, beautiful images are godly images, whereas Jews attack such images, as in a fifteenth-century collection of Marian miracles which includes two stories about Jews who insult and efface holy pictures.[28]

The Jewish Profile and Violent Agency in the Salvin Hours

The Salvin Hours is a lavish and beautiful medieval manuscript. It is characterized by its decorative scheme which insistently and grotesquely depicts Jews in violent, ugly stereotypes. The pairing of 'lavish' with 'ugly', 'beautiful' with 'violent', may seem strange to modern readers, but the Salvin Hours demonstrates how these terms are far from incompatible; indeed, they might be said to combine and inhere in the religious aesthetics of this early Gothic devotional book, based around a visual rhetoric of contrast and violence, conflict and dissonance.

The Salvin Hours is an English manuscript book of hours dating from around 1270, illustrated by two artists.[29] The book was probably made in Oxford.[30] It is a spectacularly elaborate production and would, assuredly, have been a *de luxe* commission, possibly for semi-public devotions (given its large size and splendid decoration). The book's anti-Jewish decorative scheme has been noted before, commented on in several studies, although little consideration has been given to the ways in which Jewish and Christian subject positions have precise and pervasive meanings in the illustrations.[31] As a book of hours, the Salvin Hours is about Passional memory, whether remembering Christ or the saints. It seeks to make the Passion the defining mode of devotional affect and response, and Passional imagery in the book bridges the life of Christ, the lives of the saints, and the *memoria passionis* of the medieval worshipper.

10 Christ before Caiaphas, Salvin Hours. England (?Oxford), *c.* 1270. BL Add. MS 48985, f. 29r.

In almost all of the images by Artist 1 (who illustrated the book's first twenty-nine folios) profile positioning is deployed for 'negative' (that is, non-Christian) characters to dramatic effect. The decorative scheme of the book opens with a Tree of Jesse image (f. 1v). Here, the Jews of pre-Incarnation scripture (David, Solomon and so on) are shown either in three-quarter or frontal view. Indeed, Artist 1 is careful in this image to avoid profile positioning; the subjects interact with each other or gaze upwards to the holy central figures, giving the image its sense of progression, order, purpose and focus. Conversely, on the facing illustration of the Betrayal (f. 2r), now badly rubbed, Judas is depicted sharply in profile, kissing the gently drawn three-quarter positioned Christ. Artist 1 thus employs position to mark the Jews of the Tree of Jesse image as Hebrews (or pre-Incarnation figurations of the Law) rather than as Jews who, in rejecting Christ, assured their ongoing abjection.

A useful and clear case-study is provided in Artist 1's image of Christ before Caiaphas (f. 29r; see illus. 10), although most of the book's images feature similar profile positioning. In this image, the Jews' profiles, marked by their forcefully beaked noses, militate against the soft folds of the robes and the rich and elegant detail of the frame. In the Caiaphas image, three Jews (two of them in profile) apprehend Christ, seeking narratively and visually to contain or arrest him.[32] Caiaphas is depicted in profile too, likewise bearing the sharply beaked nose. In this way, Caiaphas represents a distortion in profile of images of Christ enthroned in Majesty (always depicted in frontal mode).

The two profile Jews – the two 'false witnesses' of Matthew's gospel (Matthew 26:3–5) – encroach on the space allotted within the initial, demarcated by Caiaphas' scroll, indicating their violent movement towards Caiaphas. The book – the New Law – Christ clutches is compositionally (or mathematically) at the centre of the initial, but the Jews compete for the eye's attention, with their darkened skin (which counterpoints not only Christ's whiteness but the gold illumination of the background) and harshly drawn profiles. The riot of hands surrounding the book halts Christ's progress just as the Jews prevent the viewer's clear contemplation of Christ's body. Christ steps on the Jews' feet; this may appear to the modern viewer as a bungled attempt at perspective, but it may also foreground Christ through His supercession of the Jewish body. This supercessionism is further articulated through the parallel between the rear (non-profile) Hebrew and Christ; this non-profile Jew, his face visually echoed in Christ's, pushes Christ forward, establishing both Christ's Hebrew destiny (his link to the Jews, his fulfilment of typology) and his supercession (as marked by the profile Jew between the Hebrew and Christ). Likewise, Caiaphas' left foot is placed behind the frame whereas Christ appears to be stepping out of the frame and, throughout the image, the Jews interact with each other, creating a sense of the audience's exclusion.

Such opening images set up a contradistinction between Christian and post-incarnation Jewish bodies, based not so much on appearance but on modes of depiction. In fact, style and position act as meaning. Such images serve to separate Christian from Jew, fulfilling the Augustinian position that the Jews' ongoing but abject survival testifies to their punishment for the rejection of Christ and their dispossession from Christian reward.[33] Whilst this kind of profile positioning does allow for an exaggeration of the nose and signifies a threatening stance, it is also crucial in the way the image is put together to be read. Images such as that of Christ before Caiaphas are essentially playing with perspective, as manipulations of view and subject-position in a way which is complementary to narrative. Medieval images were not necessarily constructed to present a narrative or representational whole but were rather often concerned with presenting a disrupted version of a complete narrative;[34] similarly, a discontinuous narrative which demands to be 'read' rather than 'seen' has repeatedly been described as a feature of pre-modern images, depending on the 'intellectual movement of the viewer', in Dagobert Frey's terms.[35] The Jews in the Caiaphas image might be seen as disruptive, as they are anti-immersive and obtrusively drawn. Position is used to mark a range of moral contrasts and contrapuntal relationships – the Jew in profile is the abject Jew, the Jew in three-quarter view is the typological Hebrew Jew from whom Christ is descended, and Christ in three-quarter view is the figure of Christianity and its harmonious beauty.

The Jews' profile positioning in the Salvin Hours returns us to those devices of ugliness and shock described in medieval mnemotechnic. The Jews gain their meaning from being crude, visually disagreeable and represented in a contrary register to Christ; Boncampagno da Signa included in his treatise on memory numerous characteristics – 'ugliness of figure', 'curve of the nose', 'deformity', 'mutilation', 'variety of clothing', 'passion', 'fear' – which are the hallmarks of the medieval Jewish stereotype.[36] This Jewish profile intensely articulates mnemonic functions of exaggeration, grotesquery, abbreviation, synecdoche, hyperbole, contrast, antithesis and making strange, ostentatiously excluded from conventions of *pulchrum* (aesthetic beauty, beautiful in itself) and *aequalitas* (the Augustinian term for 'evenness', connected with the perfect nature of God), but is more, rather than less, expressive for doing so.[37] Thus the Jews prevent a fully focused, uninterrupted gaze on Christ and they interrupt the harmony and delicacy of the book. In this way, the reader-viewer undergoes their own Passion within their *memoria passionis*, oscillating between grace and ugliness, beauty and pain, good and evil, Christian and Jew. So the violent and aggressive interactions imagined between Jewish and Christian characters are mirrored in a 'decorative violence': the incongruous Jews prevent aesthetic unity or harmony and in doing so articulate profoundly their role as obstacles to Christian progression. They act to stimulate Christian ire, both as violent agents and as crude, but attention-grabbing, forms. Thus the Jews become objects of the viewer's antipathy not simply because they are 'ugly' and 'Jewish' but because they create a tension in modes of looking (or 'scopic regimes') invited and required by the images.[38] That the Jews obstruct 'correct' reading complements their status as 'hermeneutically handicapped'

11 Martyrdom of St Laurence, Salvin Hours. England (?Oxford), *c.* 1270. BL Add. MS. 48985, f. 88v.

(to use Rita Copeland's felicitous phrase): the Jew in the Christian book both reads with difficulty and makes reading difficult.[39]

Subsequent images in the Salvin Hours are not concerned with the Gospels, but the profile grotesque remains central to the book's decorative scheme. Artist I having set up the visual modes of Christian and Jewish difference, Artist II depicts the persecutors of the saints if not as 'Jews' then in the 'Jewish' visual register. The stunted, busy persecutors of St Andrew (f. 54r), the fierce sword-wielding decapitator of St Paul (f. 66v), the four cheerful and industrious flayers of St Bartholomew (f. 80v), one of the gurning roasters of St Laurence (f. 88v; illus. 11), the agile Danish archers taking aim at St Edmund (f. 95v) and many more, are painted in the same way: profile positioning, beaked or elaborately snubbed noses, features defined in heavy black line, boldly coloured vestments. The crucial exception is the armour-clad English soldiers who cut down Thomas Becket (f. 99r; illus. 12); the abject profile was, it seems, not appropriate for Englishmen, no matter how malign. In short, apart from in this one case, those responsible for post-biblical martyrdoms are depicted 'as Jews' in profile. Again, these characters are unable to be consonant with Christian representation but it is from this dispossession that they derive their expressive potency.

The use of profile for these characters does not show that the thirteenth-century illuminators thought of them as Jewish. Rather it shows the ongoing Christological validity of persecution, connecting the life (and *passio*) of Christ with that of the saints. At each point, devotional representation is figured as a kind of visual competition between the worlds of 'good' art versus bad, soft lines versus harsh, pastel versus bold shades, and profile versus other positions. Most importantly, these images show the theological coherence and importance of the vitiated Jewish image; such a stereotype is not in any simple way a marker of social hatred but rather an ardent yet highly schematic articulation of moral counterpoint. The Salvin Hours is a useful example because it brings together a range of Christianity's adversaries in one mode of depiction. Throughout the book, the contrast between (Jewish) grotesquery and (Christian) elegance produces a scopic conflict akin to the perceptual '*passio*'.[40] The conflict between Jewish and Christian depictions serves to 'move' the viewer, 'wounded' in vision, in an imitation of Christ's suffering. That is to say that style *is* meaning in the Salvin Hours, style does not follow or supplement meaning. The Jewish profile acts – in style and in content – to bring conflict into the reader or viewer's own religious, textual and visual experience.

12 Martyrdom of St Thomas Becket, Salvin Hours. England (?Oxford), *c.* 1270. BL Add. MS 48985, f. 99r. The erasure of St Thomas's face is likely post-medieval.

Rhetoric and *compunctio cordis*: 'The Angell Saide to Thee'

Just as a visual rhetoric of a Christian representation of Jews could serve moral, mnemonic and aesthetic purposes, a text could 'move' its audience, and stir *compunctio cordis*, a heartfelt compunction and a kind of wounding, through a similar kind of violent contrast. As in visual images, the Jews of medieval literature are often conspicuous in their blunt yet excessive physicality and their predictable simplicity; they are obvious in their harshness yet make reading difficult. The following Middle English lyric, addressed to the Virgin Mary at the foot of the Cross, is illustrative:

> The angell saide to thee that the fruit of
>   thi body sulde be blyssyde;
> Ande now, in the *dome* of the Jewys,   court
>   Crist es a-cursede.
> At his burth thu harde angels singinge;
> Ande now thow seys his frendis wepinge.
> At his burthe kingis and schiperdis did   5
>   him *omage* and wirschippe;   homage
> And now al maner of men don him *despite*   disgrace and
>   *and schendschyppe.*   humiliation
> At his burth thou *wantyd* womanes wo;   were without
> Bot, as thow wel *fellys*, now it is noght so.   feel
> Some time thou hadest cause
>   for to singe 'Alullay.'
> Bot now thi songh is all of '*wylaway*'.   alas   10
>
> *Somtym* thou fed him with thi sweet milk   once
>   to his *esse*;   comfort
> Ande now the Jewys feding hime wyt bitter
>   gall to his *disesse.*   discomfort
> Som time thou founde him in the
>   midil off the doctors in the temple;
> And now thou findyst hime hanginge
>   in the midil of the Jewes on the krosse.

The lyric is found in two sermon manuscripts, associated in both with Good Friday, itself a moment of heightened anti-Jewish *animus* and expression in Christian liturgy.[41] One of the poem's editors suggests that it is part of an Easter drama, and the poem's vivid *tableaux* have a highly visual impact. More plausibly, the lyric requests that its reader imagines themselves *at* the foot of the Cross, a 'making present' like the *enargeia* or *illustratio* as prescribed in rhetorical handbooks and mystical writing.

The lyric, with its distinctive narrative juxtapositions, is constructed around alternating lines contrasting the Nativity (the repeated 'At his burthe', 'Somtym') and the Crucifixion ('And now'); this contrast is cleverly made through present-tense (referring to death) and perfective (referring to life) diction. The lyric gathers together a range of conventional Marian *topoi* – the Christ-Child as fruit, the angelic chorus at the Nativity, the Virgin's painless birth, maternal lactation – interrupted by and contrasted with a graphic and sensational account of Christ's distress and a sustained and uninflected adversarial stance towards the Jews. Whilst the poem is sensational and affective, and metrically irregular, it is also tightly constructed and rhetorically sophisticated and succinctly dramatizes Christ's life-cycle through a Marian lens. It is noteworthy that the lyric opens with the Annunciation, the temporal intersection which, as Daniel Arasse has argued, became the paradoxical moment at which Christian ideas of perspective developed.[42] The Annunciation is also an ideal point of suspense – between old and new, Jew and Christian, pain and redemption.[43]

This lyric is, in effect, an extended *contentio* rhetorical *topos*, gaining its power through the juxtaposition and connection of 'blyssyde' (1) and 'a-cursede' (2), 'alullay' (9) and 'wylaway' (10), 'esse' (11) and 'disesse' (12), Christian and Jew; in other words, meaning is made through antitheses which cause the reader to oscillate between extreme emotions. *Contentio* is not just a contrast or antithesis as it is now understood, but rather evokes a struggle; *contentio* is the term used by Cicero in his description of public rhetoric precisely to evoke its antagonistic – indeed contentious – nature, and was described in 1560 by the English rhetorician Thomas Wilson (1523/4–1581) as 'when our talke standeth by contrary wordes or sentences together'.[44] Sometimes called *antithesis, antitheton* or *contrapositum* and closely linked to the modern idea of antithesis, this rhetorical device juxtaposes contraries of both words and ideas, arriving at the truth through discrediting its contrary or opposite;[45] the *Ad Herennium* states that 'through antithesis contraries will meet';[46] Isidore of Seville said that 'among the ornaments of speech [antitheses] remain the most lovely', a point he illustrated with examples such as 'Good is set against evil, and life against death' (Ecclesiasticus 33:15) and 'wealth struggles against poverty, right thinking against depravity, sanity against madness – in sum, good hope against desperation in every circumstance' (here quoting Cicero).[47] The 'discourse of opposites' was used for both clerical and 'unlettered' readers;[48] in European thought of the later Middle Ages, juxtaposition was not simply a rhetorical device, but can be seen as 'indicative of a mode of thinking in which perception was aided by the creation of opposing categories.'[49]

In this way the poem has an accomplished narrative structure, for it progresses by looking back with fondness at the Nativity but is repeatedly halted, arrested, with the jarring counterpoint of the Passional 'now' (14) from which the poem speaks. The lyric sets up two sets of mental images, Nativity and Passion, and makes each more powerful, and indeed more memorable, by aligning them. So here too the reader or listener experiences in each couplet a kind of *passio* – from security and life to martyrdom and death – in an adversarial version of the Passion attuned to precisely the same poetics as the images of the Jew in profile. Again, the Jew is conspicuous and invasive. This devotional *passio*, in which the reader is buffeted between Christian and Jew, is absolutely parallel to the *passio* of the eyes: 'something one underwent or endured . . . a state in which the line between pain and pleasure is indistinct.'[50] The overlong final line, awkwardly excessive, leaves the reader irresolutely considering the immediate and intrusive 'now' of Christ's torture on the Cross and, by locating the reader amongst the Jews, effectively revives the Jews as stimuli to a religious feeling based around discomfort and fright. Such an artefact functions, affectively, through engendering an emotional response in its audience, rather than depicting emotion per se. The Jews of the lyric play a very similar role as the profile visual representation: to be halting and shocking and *difficult*, an *imago agens*, an active image. Indeed, the lyric moves not through moral progress and judgement but through visualized scenes similar to the *loci* (places) and *tableaux* set out in mnemotechnical treatises.[51] As Augustine's pupil Licentius cries out as he considers the necessity of evil in defining good, 'the clashing of contraries, which we love so much in rhetoric, gives body to the overall beauty of the universe'.[52]

The lyric is an expressive Jewish–Christian clashing of contraries. Whilst we might read nowadays striving for immediacy and immersion, wanting a narrative in which we lose ourselves, here is an adversarial encounter between Jewish and Christian *rhetorical modes* which disrupts the reader and militates against progressive narrative. It thereby stirs the reader/listener's *compunctio cordis*, literally 'compunction of the heart', a jarring pain and awareness of sin which is the emotional trigger to prayer.

Stephaton: Another Witness at the Passion

The Salvin Hours features an image of the Crucifixion (f. 40r; illus. 13), by Artist II, which offers a further example of violent counterpoint; the vulnerable body of Christ is at the centre of the image, the delicacy of his skin and facial expression suggesting humanity and composure. The crucifix is set within the initial as in a 'T and O' design reminiscent of *mappae mundi*, signifying the universally encompassing scope of the Passion.[53] However, the borders of the image and the borders of Christ's body are disturbed, and the image shows the artist working with two distinct styles of positioning. Christ is speared on his right side by the Roman solider Longinus who wears a pointed Jew's cap but is painted in the same style as Christ, with subtly expressive facial detail, elegant flowing drapery, and in three-quarter view. Longinus gestures to his eye, a reference to the legend that he regained his sight when Christ's blood spurted into his eye.[54] Thus in 'acknowledging' Christ he is freed from the kinds of depiction applied to the others characters in the initial. On Christ's left, 'Stephaton', the sponge-bearer, is clearly 'Jewish' here, not because of his actual or imputed religion but because of his *visual* affiliation – in crude, harsh profile – with the three further Jewish torturers.[55]

The 'Jewish' sponge-bearer gave Christ a vinegar-soaked sponge at the Crucifixion when Christ cried out with thirst (Matthew 27:48; Mark 15:36; John 19:29); he is not named in the Bible.[56] Like so many of the stories considered here of Christians and Jews in an emblematic moment of conflict, Stephaton and Longinus became standard iconographic and devotional images in the Middle Ages, even though their biblical authority is fleeting. One early medieval thinker, Pascasius Radbertus (d. *c.* 859), identified the vinegar and gall offered by the Jews to Christ as emblems of faithlessness, vinegar denoting the 'corruption of vices' and 'soured' post-lapsarian human nature.[57] Stephaton's sponge figured the Jews, 'puffed up [with] the vinegar of sin and corruption, and drawing all the dregs of shameful things into

13 Crucifixion, Salvin Hours. England (?Oxford), *c.* 1270. BL Add. MS
48985, f. 40r.

themselves'.[58] In Stephaton and Longinus are encoded a whole world
of fear and feeling, contrast and response.

In the Salvin Hours image Longinus and Stephaton distract us
from the Crucifixion at the centre and force the viewer's meditative
gaze away from Christ's body. Stephaton's disruption of the frame
provides a kind of perspective against the image's ground;[59] Christ's
tormentors move with impetus towards the central figure's vulnerable body, twisted in torment on the cross. Only Christ gazes out from
the image; the other characters gaze inwards, busily absorbed in their
tortures. The conjunction of bold profile view and physical movement in this image catches the eye; the Jews' transgression of the
frame's boundaries, which again recalls the *mappa mundi* in which
Jews and others cluster around the edge of the world, helps create
rival visual jurisdictions, between edge and centre, as the centripetal
gaze on Christ's body and the green cross is offset by the centrifugal
detail provided by the Jewish tormentors.

Dysmas, the Good Thief at Christ's side during the Crucifixion
and the first recipient of Christ's salvific blood, became a popular
subject in late medieval art because, 'for suffering patiently and obe-
diently, for his literal realization of the ideal of *imitatio Christi*, he is

rewarded with the crown of martyrdom';[60] what's more, his counterpart, Gestas the Bad Thief, dies damned and in pain and in doing so foreshadows eternal torments, 'antithetical models for a culture tuned to pain's instrumentality in the pursuit of redemption'.[61] The 'invention' of the similar figure of Stephaton, marginal but ubiquitous in Passion scenes, reveals how Christ's Passion was increasingly constructed around affective contrasts (or 'spectacles of alterity' as Michael Camille aptly calls them), moving between opposite moral and representational modes, and was thereby attractive and useful to medieval people.[62] The medieval interest in Stephaton is cognate with the preoccupation with Christ's wounds and the litany of abuses heaped on Christ's body by the Jews.[63] Stephaton reinforced the sense of adversarial blood and victimhood so important to the Passion, and reinvigorated the Jewish component of it. In English writing, Stephaton is identified not by name but as a Jew (for example, the *Metrical Life of Christ* says that 'A Jewe out went,/ And in his hond a sponge hent/ And filled hit with roten wyn').[64] Whereas Longinus is blinded and then regains his sight, Stephaton lingers, violently assertive, and thus the pairing reveals the forward (salvational) and backward (sacrificial) nature of Christ's blood.

Judas's Hair

The convention of depicting Jews in a halting, disruptive profile can be traced back to the depiction and description of Judas, who was considered both a representative and paradigmatically treacherous, violent Jew. Judas has already been mentioned in terms of his profile physiognomy, as his features interrupt the Last Supper, and as a parallel to the eviscerated sheriff in the miracles of William of Norwich. Judas became defined by three arresting moments: first, the giving of the sop at the Last Supper (John 13:21–7), the moment at which Judas's special treachery is identified and at which 'Satan entered into him'; secondly, the 'Judas kiss', through which Judas revealed Christ to the Temple authorities (Matthew 26:48; Luke 22); and, thirdly, Judas's suicide, by hanging from a tree (Matthew 27:5), as his bowels rupture and explode (Acts 1:18). These three moments – all of which emphasize intense embodiment through theatrical gesture and an 'excessively corporeal' and therefore 'Jewish' Judas[65] – are powerful images of physical violence and decorative or aesthetic violence at the heart of Christian devotion. We might truly say that Judas is the most *active* of Christian *imagines agentes* (active, or lively, images, as described in *Ad Herennium*) – emphatically bodily, horrifically inappropriate, resolutely different, violently obscene, of the utmost importance in sealing Christ's fate and, crucially, arresting: not in the modern sense of an arraignment, but in terms of commandeering our attention, arresting the narrative. This jarring decorative activity has been noted by Susan Gubar in her recent 'biography' of Judas; within her first few pages Gubar describes the 'mystic incongruities', 'incongruous reinventions' and 'incongruous portraits' of Judas.[66] Gubar contends that 'Judas in his most notorious persona has to be approached as the principal figure through whom Christians have understood Jews and Jewry', and indeed since Jerome (d. 420) the Jews are said to have taken their name from Judas, not Judah. Gubar's repeated use of the term 'incongruous' suggests the capacity of Judas to grab attention, to shock his audience and to assert himself as a memorable, active, disgraceful and aesthetically violent character. This 'frenzy of the visible', to use a modern term from the scholarship of photography and pornography, masters difference through effecting its own power, constructs its own system of knowledge, suggests 'hard core', visceral answers to intellectual questions, whilst placing truth and its contradiction side by side.[67]

The biblical account of Judas is famously incomplete, but the synoptic gospels show Judas as actively responsible for the betrayal of Jesus, a necessary evil in as much as the betrayal led to the Crucifixion and thereby to Redemption. The Satanic aspect of Judas's character is most forcefully foregrounded in the gospels of Luke, in which Judas is defined as a 'traitor' (Luke 6:16), and John, in which Jesus intuits that, amongst the apostles, 'one of you is a devil' (John 6:71). Judas does not feature as an important agent in the Pauline epistles, which focus largely on the punishment of Judas, and the contradictions in the biblical accounts are many.[68]

An innovative treatment of the story of Judas survives from late thirteenth-century England, in the *Judas* ballad ('Hit wes upon a Scere Thorsday'), a short dramatic poem.[69] Here, Jesus commands Judas to go to Jerusalem 'oure mete for to bugge' ('to buy our food'), and gives him thirty pieces of silver to do so, a mockery of redemption described in the terms used to represent the meat of Christ's Eucharistic body. At Jerusalem, Judas meets his 'soster, the swikele wimon' ('sister, the treacherous woman'); she tells him that he deserves to be stoned for following Jesus, 'the false prophete'. Judas and his 'sister' then go up on a rock and he falls asleep in her lap; when he wakes, the 'platen of selver from him weren itake' ('the pieces of silver were taken from him'). At the poem's climax, Judas is so angry and upset by this,

He drou hymselve bi the top,	He tore his hair until
that al it lavede a blode	it was bathed in blood;
The Jewes out of Jurselem	The Jews from Jerusalem
awenden he were wode	thought he was mad.

Then Pilate – 'the riche Jeu' – appears, and offers to give Judas money in return for Jesus. Judas refuses at first, but agrees when Pilate offers the thirty pieces of silver. The apostles gather for supper, Jesus enters and declares that he knows that 'Ic am ibought ant isold today for oure mete' – 'I have been bought and sold today for our food'. The little poem closes with Judas's treachery revealed by Jesus, and Peter swearing his loyalty.

The poem, often called the earliest English ballad, is comprised of several dramatic speeches without biblical authority: first, Christ's sending of Judas to Jerusalem to buy provisions for the Passover *seder* meal; secondly, Judas's 'soster' who, Delilah-like, causes him to fall asleep in her lap and thereby lose the money; third, Judas's perverse plan to reclaim the money, by selling Jesus to Pilate (here become Jewish);[70] Jesus perceives Judas's treachery and, as in the biblical account, allows Judas to identify himself as the traitor at the Last Supper. The poem closes with a succinct contrast between Judas and Peter, one a faithless apostle, the other a faithful one. The poem exemplifies the move, common in late medieval religious media, towards a violent adversarial relationship between Christ and the Jews, here marked by Pilate's presentation as 'the riche Jeu', rather than Roman governor (Luke 3:1). The poem presents a series of memorable moments of characters in contact and conflict, progressing through pairs of characters acting upon each other: Christ's command to Judas, Judas's betrayal by his sister, Pilate's deal with Judas, Christ's identification of Judas, Judas's contrast with Peter. Moving through these contrasts suggests a range of juxtapositions constituted by moral-emotional *tableaux*: Judas with his head in his sister's lap, Judas at the Passover table with Christ, the proleptic promise of the arrival of Pilate's men.

How far the poem exculpates Judas (by fabricating the heretical sister) or confirms his treacherous nature (his perverse wish to sell

Jesus to procure the food) has been much debated by critics.[71] The poem succinctly encompasses, through Judas, the human, quotidian process leading up to the Crucifixion, God's sacrifice for mankind understood through personal conflict. It is carefully modulated in its series of dramatic dialogues, its characters' potent gestures, its structure of questions followed by answers, and its subtle movement from Maundy Thursday ('Scere Thorsday') to the Crucifixion, marked by the cock that crowed (Matthew 26; Mark 14:30; Luke 22; John 13:38). The emphasis on Judas more broadly reflects the importance placed on personalized witnessing of the events of the Passion, as laid out by Pseudo-Bonaventure and other later medieval mystical writers.

The Middle English *Judas* ballad tells us that Judas 'drou hymselve bi the top, that al it lavede a blode/ The Jewes out of Jurselem awenden he were wode': Judas pulls at his own hair, drawing his own blood, until the Jews of Jerusalem believe him to have gone mad. Judas's violence against himself is in itself an eloquent sign of the workings of a guilty conscience, but the image it produces – of Judas's bloodied hair – feeds into one of the most common, and misunderstood, medieval images of Judas: the red-haired traitor.

The imputed redness of Judas's hair has been commented on frequently, largely because of the reference in Shakespeare's *As You Like It* to 'hair. . . of the dissembling colour', 'something browner than Judas's' (III:4:6–7).[72] This red hair finds its expression in numerous – but not all – medieval visual depictions of Judas. A striking example occurs in a stained-glass window by the glazier James Nicholson (*fl.* 1518–40) at King's College, Cambridge: Judas at the Last Supper, with red hair and a red beard, sharply profiled, hook-nosed, leans forward to receive the sop, entirely active and physical. Judas's red hair has been seen in relation to a range of other vilified peoples as 'part of an ancient and worldwide aversion to red hair, the origins of which are unknown but have been variously guessed at'; implausible 'folkloric' suggestions have been put forward, concerning the red hair of foxes, the Italians' dislike for red-haired Germans, the English hatred of red-haired Danes, and so on.[73] Other critics have argued that this red hair has a mimetic relationship to the frequency of red hair amongst European Jews. To be 'Judas-born' is, in English folklore, to be born with red hair; a 'Judasbart' – a 'Judas beard' – was, in late medieval and early modern German, a red beard; a red beard in old Danish was a 'Judasskæg'.[74] Judas's complexion was also proverbially red or freckled, and his red hair was shared with

Cain.[75] Likewise, various red flowers and berries, often poisonous or foul-smelling, have been given names connecting them with Judas, suggesting both the tree from which Judas hanged himself and the red blood of his, and Christ's, martyrdom.[76] Such idioms point to the enduring domestic labelling of things incongruous with the epithet of Judas, but many of them also specifically explicate incongruous redness with the blood and violence with which Judas was consistently connected. From the very first biblical accounts of his death, in Matthew and Acts, Judas was bloodstained by 'blood money' and his death in the 'field of blood' (Aceldama, *ager sanguinis*).[77]

Judas's red hair is a bloody marker, not an 'ethnic' fact. The making of a physically distinctive Judas is cognate with the 'marking' of Jews with the Jewish badge following the Fourth Lateran Council of 1215; but in Christian physiognomic theory red hair was also perfectly suited to Judas as it indicated 'folynesse,/ lak of providence and discrecioun, Of freting wretthe ['biting wrathfulness'] with Oute Occasyoun.'[78] As a performed 'sign', the red hair of Judas has more in common with other Christian symbols of spilt blood and violent martyrdom.

The 'red stain' suggestive of martyrdom was well established in medieval European culture, connoting a victim's spilt blood; for Judas, this red mark suggests his role in Christ's Passion. St Edmund was depicted on the Wilton Diptych, a fourteenth-century royal altarpiece, wearing red socks, recalling Hugh of St Victor's description of the Church as a dove with red feet, 'for the Church moves through the world with her feet immersed in the blood of the Martyrs'.[79] The robin redbreast, used as an icon of the boy-saint Robert of Bury who was said to have been ritually murdered by Jews, had its breast dyed red with Christ's blood after picking a thorn from Christ's crown at Calvary.[80] The red ruby figured the blood of the martyrs, 'who, as they shed their blood, send up ardent prayers for their persecutors'.[81] Thomas Aquinas's attribute is a ruby on his breast, and the ruby was used by Chaucer in 'The Prioress's Tale' to describe the Jews' infant victim ('of martirdom the ruby bright'). The English poet John Lydgate addressed St Edmund as the 'richest' ruby, 'rubefied with blood / In thy passion'.[82] As Lydgate described St George's martyrdom, 'In his blode, as eny rose rede, He was baptised', turning the stain of bloody violence into a valorized image of baptism.[83]

14 The Death of Judas. From an ivory diptych, France, early fourteenth century. Victoria and Albert Museum.

The 'ugly' red hair of Judas is linked to the other affective moment of violence through which he was frequently represented: the rupturing of his bowels at his suicide. Examples are legion, and the scene is particularly common in late medieval French and English ivories, where Judas's viscera issue from him prettily, like a bloody rosebud (illus. 14). Judas represented the heinous sin of suicide;[84] he was also the countertype of Christ, hanging from a tree, blood issuing downwards opposed to ascendant spirit.[85]

An image from the celebrated *Très Riches Heures*, the book of hours made for Jean, duke of Berry (d. 1416), speaks eloquently of Judas. This manuscript is famous for its illustrated calendar, in which peasants neatly labour against a backdrop of towering châteaux and brilliant lapis lazuli skies. In contrast to these beautiful images, the book also finds a place for shocking images of violence and horror: Christ as the Man of Sorrows, an open wound in his side dripping rich carmine (f. 75r); the Horseman of Death who makes his way towards a city's walls as legions of skeletal zombies wield scythes at terrified, fleeing soldiers (f. 90v); a crowned, naked and recumbent Lucifer, torturing souls in hell as he is himself tortured (f. 108r); and Judas hanging, his eyes and mouth opened in surprise and terror, his bowels flowing out from between his open legs, from the tree on which he has hanged himself (f. 147v; illus. 15).

Judas appears in a part of the manuscript which was laid out by the Limbourg brothers, but finished and mostly illustrated by Jean Colombe in the 1480s.[86] The image of Judas complements the 'violent imprecatory' Psalm 108:2 cited immediately below the image:

Deus laudem meam ne tacueris
quia os peccatoris et os dolosi
super me apertum est

O God, be not thou silent
in thy praise: for the mouth
of the wicked and the
mouth of the deceitful man
is opened against me

The psalm closes with an appeal to Christ to protect the worshipper from persecution (Psalm 108:29–31):

[29] *induantur qui detrahunt*
mihi pudore et operiantur sicut
deploide confusione sua [30]
confitebor Domino nimis in
ore meo et in medio multorum
laudabo eum [31] *quia adstetit*
a dextris pauperis ut salvam
faceret a persesquentibus
animam meam.

[29] Let them that detract
me be clothed with shame:
and let them be covered
with their confusion as
with a double cloak. [30]
I will give great thanks to
the Lord with my mouth:
and in the midst of many
I will praise him. [31]
Because he hath stood at
the right hand of the poor,
to save my soul from
persecutors.

In the medieval Vulgate bible, this psalm was understood explicitly as referring to Judas, with the following explanatory headnote:

David in the person of Christ, prayeth against his persecutors; more especially the traitor Judas: foretelling and approving his just punishment for his obstinacy in sin and final impenitence.[87]

In the image from the *Très Riches Heures*, Judas's blue cloak lies beneath him, referring to the psalm ('covered with . . . confusion as with a double cloak'). The blue cloak is also a fallen, disgraceful counter-version of the Virgin's blue mantle (depicted throughout the manuscript) whilst the red tunic worn by the hanging Judas again suggests the red of martyrdom, calling to mind the role Judas plays in Christ's death.[88]

So, read with the psalm, this image of Judas is designed to stage the vengeance of the righteous against 'persecutors', showing Judas, the arch-detractor, 'covered with . . . confusion' and 'clothed with shame'. The image of the hanged man, bowels rent and mouth agape, thus makes iconographical sense; but we also need to consider what the image does in terms of our movement through the book. Judas turns to face his audience only in death, not unlike a freeze-frame in contemporary film. The freeze-frame appears to its audience to stop an image in motion, by appearing to stop the medium itself: the frame is frozen and thereby the narrative freezes. But the freeze-frame is not an error, but rather an effect: it works artificially to make static a thing that is in movement. The only movement in the image is the viscera falling from between the dead man's legs; unlike almost all of the other pictures included in the manuscript, this image is haltingly static: nobody is doing anything, there is no narrative and little movement, the body hangs. This kind of image is, literally, arresting: it asserts body, shock, and a malformed ugliness, an aesthetic jolt as potent as the pull of the noose around the anti-hero's neck. Contemporary theories of traumatic memory suggest that traumatic events cannot be organized on a narrative level and so appear as violent, radical and intrusive breaks, repeating the moment of trauma and disturbing their narrative context:[89] likewise, the hanged Judas is a frozen moment of intense violence.

As the text of the psalm makes clear, the reader/worshipper is invited to bring conflict into his or her experience in this psalm, at once remembering one's detractors, swearing vengeance against them and gazing on an antithesis of Christ's redemption. Just as Christ's Eucharistic body and blood disturbs time by being 'ever redy', instantly accessible, Judas's eerie hanging is between heaven and earth, a point of suspension: he is going nowhere, and, likewise, our progress through the book is arrested. The continuous movement of the reader through the book of hours – literally, the hours of one's life marked as progression through Christian time – hangs still, in an aberrant disruption to liturgical time and personal time, as Passional violence asserts itself in the midst of opulence.

15 Death of Judas with fallen cloak and flux of blood, from *Très Riches Heures du Duc de Berry*. France, Jean Colombe, 1480s. Chantilly, Musée Condé MS 65, f. 147v.

CHAPTER 4

The Jew's Hand and the Virgin's Bier: Tangible Interruption

After I had cut off my hands
and grown new ones
something my former hands had longed for
came and asked to be rocked.
—Denise Levertov, *Intrusion*

Touch

Medieval thought imagined seeing and reading as a kind of physical interpenetration; likewise, we often use vocabularies of touching and attaching to describe retaining a lesson – information we have *grasped*, a memory we *held* or to which we *cling*, a point or insult that *stuck*, arguments that *applied*, *hanging* on each and every word, attention-*grabbing*, a notion within our *grasp*, information *dragged* out of someone, an idea to which we have become *attached*, a fantasy by which we are *seized*, an *idée fixe*. This chapter explores the medieval image of Jephonius the Jew who appears at the Dormition or Funeral of the Virgin with amputated or withered arms and literalizes this relationship between attachment, touch and exemplary information; he does so in a way which is thoroughly indebted to an aesthetic of 'Jewish' violence and interruption.

This Jew had reached for the Virgin's bier as the apostles bore her to her burial. His hands stuck to the bier and were, according to different sources, either cut off or remained stuck; they were only restored when the Jew converted to Christianity. A lavish fourteenth-century English Gothic book of hours, the Taymouth Hours, possibly made for the English or Scottish royal families, provides a potent and representative example (illus. 16).[1] The Jew, in a red gown, hangs from (and boldly constrasts with) the Virgin's blue bier. He grabs violently at the blue fabric, and the active violence of his gesture is indicated in his bared legs and twisted body. Potently, his misshapen, crudely drawn profile face looks against the direction of the funeral cortège, contrasting with the serene, purposeful faces of the apostles moving with the bier from left to right. The Jew sticks to the bier, also obstructing

16 The Jew disturbs the Virgin's Funeral, Taymouth Hours, fourteenth century. BL Yates Thompson MS 13, f. 133v.

the reader's progress through the book. The image of the Jew's twisted body realizes the narrative of the text directly above, Psalm 101:3: 'Turn not away thy face from me: in the day when I am in trouble, incline thy ear to me. In what day soever I shall call upon thee, hear me speedily.' An Anglo-Norman gloss, in red, around the image, inveighs against the cruelty, deafness and blindness of the Jews ('*li jeus*'), further extrapolating Jewish perfidy from the psalm.

In a world in which gesture, in particular manual gestures and formal public gestures, were pre-eminent modes of communication, the Jew's stuck or amputated hand was a potent symbol indeed.[2] Biblically, a good hand equals 'strength and power, and no one can resist thee' (2 Paralipomenon [Chronicles] 20:6), a hand that gives, cures or defeats;

> And if thy right hand scandalize thee, cut it off, and cast it from thee: for it is expedient for thee that one of thy members should perish, rather than that thy whole body be cast into hell (Matthew 5:30).

A withered hand, a disembodied hand, a hand cut off, is the hand of desecration, the hand of the thief, the murderer and the Jew; but this hand also grabs attention, ripe for miraculous healing.

Jephonius' ripped-off hand is, first, a grotesque. Secondly, it is an abbreviation, a part, without proportion, which functions independently of the whole from which it originates. Thirdly, it is interruptive

– the hand sticks, it adheres, arrests progress, a bodily disarticulation which is also a moral dislodgment. According to medieval anatomy, God gave hands to man (instead of paws, as animals have) and therewith gave him reason and discretion;[3] accounts of medieval people losing their reason describe them gesticulating wildly, signifying randomly and incorrectly with their hands, transgressing the highly ordered *expositio* of medieval *gestus*.[4] The active hand and the hand removed from the body, uncanny limbs at once active and static, human and mechanical, fascinated medieval people much as they do people today.[5] Representative of a kind of stubborn, total embodiment, such hands figure in the Middle Ages as that which both arrests and proves Christianity: slapping, tugging, sticking to things, gesturing, pointing, *grabbing* attention, shocking, miraculous: profane yet funny, gory and ridiculous but often instructive and the bearer of moral and aesthetic information, the hand being a 'didactic and mnemonic device', a 'system of mnemonic places' which literally points things out for memorial retention.[6]

The Jew's hand is precisely representative of medieval ideas about memory and memorable images:

> Because the memory retains distinctly only what is extraordinary, wonderful, and intensely charged with emotion, the images should be of extremes – of ugliness or beauty, ridicule or nobility, of laughter or weeping, of worthiness or salaciousness. Bloody figures, or monstrosities, or figures brilliantly but abnormally colored should be used, and they should be engaged in activity of a sort that is extremely vigorous.[7]

Vigour, violence, extremes of piety and its desecration, the contrast of lament and grotesquery, are central to the idea of the Jew's stuck hand; thus, in Thomas Bradwardine's memory-theory, 'limbs or some means of attaching . . . other images' should be joined 'in an active, even violent, manner' to produce the best kind of memory-image.[8]

The Origins of Jephonius

The story of the Virgin's Dormition and Assumption to Heaven, and the accompanying popular story of Jephonius the Jew, fills a substantial void in Scripture about what happened to Christ's mother after the Crucifixion. The Vulgate biblical account utterly lacks information on Mary, and gave only unspecific, implicit, veiled clues: the reference to 'A woman clothed with the sun' (Apocalypse [Revelation] 12:1) and allusions from the Canticles were produced as a kind of 'evidence' of the Assumption of the Virgin: that is, that, at the end of her earthly life, Mary ascended to heaven both body and soul (hence the lack of physical relics of the Virgin's body on earth).[9] Early Christians, certainly until the sixth century, were agreed that they knew little about what happened to the Virgin at the end of her life and it was only with the circulation of apocryphal texts and traditions – including a fifth-century 'tomb of Mary' at Kidron in Jerusalem – that the life and death of Mary was expanded. From the fourth century, an established narrative emerges that Mary underwent a 'dormition', a 'repose' or a physical death, which was followed by her assumption to heaven, both body and soul, in a kind of Resurrection, and thus occurred the Coronation of the Virgin as she became Queen of Heaven. Byzantine traditions state that the Virgin died at the age of 80, Western traditions at 60.[10] The *Transitus Mariae* of Pseudo-Melito of Sardis, the prototype and template of all subsequent Latin and English versions of the story, describes the death, funeral and assumption of the Virgin;[11] similar accounts, one attributed to Joseph of Arimathea, others from Coptic and Syriac sources, all held that there was indubitably a funeral and tomb of the Virgin (which, according to some accounts, was found empty three days after her entombment), that a Jew or group of Jews attacked the bier, and that Mary's death was accompanied by miracles.[12] Eastern ideas and beliefs about the death of the Virgin, including Pseudo-Melito's account, were communicated to the West by Gregory of Tours (d. 593/4) in his influential *De gloria martyrum* (*The Glory of the Martyrs*); the feast of the Virgin's Assumption (in the West) or the Dormition (as celebrated in the East) was an important festival in medieval Christianity, held on August 15, preceded, like Easter, by processions and fasting. From earliest times, the events of the Virgin's death were imitative of Christ's Passion, entombment and Resurrection;[13] indeed, in the East, the feast of the Dormition was sometimes called a 'Summer pascha', with imagery of lament, suffering and empathy. These traditions surrounding the Virgin's death emerged from theological concerns about the integrity of the Virgin's body, the extent of the Virgin's divinity or sanctity, and a desire to humanize whilst deifying the Mother of God.

The hostility of the Jews to Mary is not incidental or peripheral, but central to accounts of the Virgin's death and Assumption from the sixth century onwards.[14] This is unsurprising given that Mary's death was modelled on that of her son. Most stories involved a certain Jerusalemite Jew – often named Jephonius but elsewhere Athonius, Reuben, Yophana, Sophonius, Belzeray, Fergus – who attacks the Virgin's body or her funeral bier as it is being transported to her tomb. According to the most common versions of the story, the apostles' funeral singing arouses the Jews into anger and they plan to seize and then destroy (usually by burning) the Virgin's body. When they approach the Virgin's funeral procession, all the Jews are struck blind, except Jephonius; he rushes to the Virgin's bier and either his hands stick or an angel appears brandishing a sword, cutting off Jephonius' hand or hands. In what would prove to be the climactic and defining image of the story, Jephonius the Jew is left writhing in pain, whilst his hands are attached to the bier. Jephonius falls to the ground, in a swoon under Mary's body which parodies her swoon at her son's crucifixion. The apostles tell Jephonius that he can only be healed by praying to the Virgin, which he duly does: on being healed he becomes a Christian and goes back to the other Jews, healing them of their blindness and converting them to Christianity.[15]

The story given by Jacobus de Voragine (*c.* 1230–98) is representative of the Western European tradition. Here, John, having been preaching in Ephesus, goes to Mary's house, and finds her near death. She tells him that she has

> heard some Jews [who] have conspired together, saying, 'Men and brothers, let us wait until the woman who bore Jesus dies. Then we will seize her body, throw it into the fire, and burn it up!'[16]

Therefore, she urges John, he must carry a palm branch in front of the funeral procession. Mary dies and the day of her funeral comes; Peter and Paul lift the bier and sing from Psalm 113, *Exiit Israel de Aegypto, alleluia*: 'When Israel went out of Egypt'. The apostles join in, and then the angels start to sing sweetly too.

> The populace was excited by such dulcet sound and melody, and came rushing out of the city to see what was going on. Then someone said: 'The disciples of Jesus are carrying Mary away dead, and singing around her the melody you hear.' At once they hurried to take arms and exhorted each other, saying, 'Come on, let us kill all those disciples and burn the body that

bore the seducer.' The chief priest, seeing what was happening, was astounded and filled with rage, and said: 'Look at the tabernacle of that man who disturbed us and our people so much! Look at the glory that is now paid to that woman!' After saying this he put his hands on the litter, intending to overturn it and throw the corpse to the ground. But suddenly his hands withered and stuck to the bier, so that he was hanging by his hands; and he moaned and cried in great pain, while the rest of the people were stricken with blindness by angels who were in the cloud.[17]

Peter tells the Jews that they must believe in Christ if they are to be remedied: the Chief Priest says he believes that Jesus is the Son of God and the Jew's hands are loosed, but remain withered. Peter tells the suspended Jew that he must kiss the bier and state his belief in the virginity of Mary: he does this, and 'was cured instantly'. Other, earlier versions of the story have an angel (sometimes the archangel Michael) cut off the Jew's hands, whilst other narratives pay more attention to the punishment and miraculous healing of the Jews.[18]

The story, as given in these accounts, is one of interruption: the Jews interrupt both the Virgin's funeral and the reader/viewer's devotion. Like so many medieval exemplary stories, it is replete with allusive meanings and functions as a kind of mnemonic cue to other examples of veneration and respectful touching. The story calls to mind the Old Testament figures of Moses, whose hand was made leprous and then healed (Exodus 4:6–7), and Oza, struck down by God for touching the Ark (2 Samuel 6:6–8: 'the indignation of the Lord was enkindled against Oza, and he struck him for his rashness . . .').[19] The story also alludes to 'doubting' Thomas and his manual examination of Christ's resurrected body: 'bring hither thy hand, and put it into my side' (John 20:24–9). Indeed in some sources Thomas reappears at the Virgin's funeral, still doubting, incredulous about her Assumption, playing an analogous role to Jephonius.[20] The Jew's hand acts as a kind of opposite to the medieval culture of relics, touching what it should not touch and treating the relic of Mary's body with violence, not veneration.[21] However, perhaps the most powerful meaning of the Jews' interruption is as a kind of inversion of the Assumption: the Jews want to drag the body to the ground and burn its physical essence, whereas the Assumption shows the ascending spirit and soul of the Virgin. And it was this interruptive moment which Jacobus makes much of, when the Jew's hand sticks, a moment of grotesque farce and physical stasis, which became, literally, the shorthand for the episode.

The Jew and the Virgin at Chalgrove: Strip-Art, Liturgy, *Ductus*

Images of sacramental religion and of affective piety were approached through mnemonic cognition rather than simple recognition: the religious and aesthetic *ductus* of an image or narrative – its composition, flow and movement, its *way* of *leading* or *conducting* the viewer – would call to mind a larger set of narratives, which the viewer/reader then directs, arranges, combines. There is little sense, in medieval culture, of an actual 'recollection' in Christian images of Judaism, of something seen and then re-presented in specific detail. Current historicist critical fashions dictate that we find something actual animating something imaginary, but to do so is to neglect the role of the imagination in perceiving and reconstituting things it has never 'actually' encountered. A medieval poem or picture did not provide its audience with anything like a photograph; rather, it solicited the imaginations of its audience, to fit its images into (previously encountered) schemata.[22] The church walls at Chalgrove provide a good example of what this means in terms of the narrative of the Jew at the Virgin's funeral.[23]

The parish church of St Mary the Virgin in the village of Chalgrove, a few miles to the east of Oxford, has some of the most splendid murals surviving from medieval England. In the church's chancel is a three-tiered scheme of paintings, showing the Life and Death of the Virgin together with scenes from the Life and Passion of Christ and an Apocalypse. The Chalgrove frescoes, probably commissioned for the Barantyn family of Chalgrove, date from around 1350.[24] The frescoes bring together several important themes and forms in the way medieval Christians represented Judaism, using excerpted moments of dramatic narrative and contrast, an emphasis on physical drama, the deployment of cartoons and frames to give a kind of accretive montage, and a format which weaves biblical history and religious conflict into the everyday life of the medieval village. The frescoes at Chalgrove demonstrate how within an understanding of emotional *ductus* (from the Latin, *ducere*, to lead) – conducting, educating – we can see the image of the Jew at the Virgin's funeral as part of the

EAST WALL

16. Ascension	St Peter holding the keys to Heaven in window-splay [facing St Paul] ⇔	[East Window]	St Paul holding a sword in window-splay [facing St Peter] ⇔	13. Coronation of the Virgin
15. Resurrection ⇧				12. Assumption of the Virgin ⇧
14. Harrowing of Hell ⇧				11. Thomas receiving the Girdle ⇧

NORTH WALL

- 11. Crucifixion ⇧
- 10. Christ Carrying the Cross ⇧
- 9. Flagellation of Christ ⇧
- 8. Mocking of Christ by two figures ⇧
- 7. Trial before Pilate [?Annas or Caiaphas?] ⇦
- 6. Betrayal of Jesus (Judas in profile to left, Jesus right) ⇦
- 5. ?Judas receiving the silver; St Peter cuts off Malchus' ear ⇦

- 12. Descent from the Cross ⇧
- North-East Window [St Helena and St Mary Magdalene in window-splay, facing St John the Baptist and St John the Evangelist]
- 4. Presentation in the Temple & [to Judas]
- 3. Massacre of the Innocents ⇦
- Annunciation Window [Gabriel and Mary, facing St Laurence and St Bartholomew] {⟷}
- Jesse Tree in three tiers (or boughs?), with Virgin and Child at centre [facing Last Judgement] {⟷}

- 13. Anointing of the Body & [to 14 - Harrowing of Hell, East Wall]
- 2. Adoration of the Magi &
- 1. ♫ Nativity ⇦

SOUTH WALL

- 8. Burial of the Virgin ⇧
- 9. The Apostles at Table with Thomas showing the Virgin's Girdle ⇧
- 10. Apostles at Empty Tomb ⇐ [to 11 - Thomas receiving the Girdle, East Wal] ⇧

- 7. Conversion and Healing of the Jews ⇧
- [St John the Baptist and St John the Evangelist in window-splay] {⟷}

- 6. St Peter converts the Jewish High Priest by sprinkling holy water on him ⇧
- 4. Death of the Virgin, with Christ receiving the Virgin's soul &
- 2. The Virgin at Prayer [and a further obscured scene involving the Virgin] &

- 5. The Jew Attacks the Virgin's Bier; the bier is held by six Apostles. ⇧
- 3. The Apostles and the Virgin's Neighbours Gathered at the Virgin's Door ⇧
- ♫ 1. The Angel Presents the Palm of Paradise to the Virgin ⇧

- South-West Window [St Laurence with gridiron holding book and St Bartholomew holding flaying knife in window-splay] {⟷}

- Last Judgement in three tiers, with Christ enthroned and Mary Mediatrix (Mary kneeling in intercession); in the lower tiers, souls, including clerics, rise from their graves [facing Jesse Tree] {⟷}

17 Diagrammatic layout of the frescoes at Chalgrove (Oxfordshire), showing the west-east 'route' of the narrative.

cultural memory-work being performed and thus we can understand that surprising and exaggerated images are part of a larger Christian drama of learning and salvation.

The frescoes, now faint and partly obscured by later monuments, follow a route (illus. 17). The North Wall of the Chancel is 'read' left to right and shows scenes from the Life and Passion of Christ, starting with a Jesse Tree, the 'root' of Christ's genealogy. The South Wall is read right to left (apart from the Last Judgment), and shows the Virgin's Death and Funeral, as narrated in Jacobus de Voragine's *Golden Legend*. The East Wall has parallel tiered scenes of the Ascension of Christ and the Coronation of the Virgin.

The images are laid out in a 'trinitarian' structure of three tiers and, within these tiers, the Jesse Tree and Last Judgment are subdivided into segments of three. The scenes 'correspond to the feast days and liturgical celebrations that punctuate the church year'.[25] Broadly, the narrative is orientated towards the East, to heaven and the Heavenly Jerusalem. Whilst the 'sequence' of reading is West to East, culminating in the Ascension, it also demands that one reads upwards, downwards, and through facing parallelism (for example, in the image of the Jesse Tree which faces the Last Judgment, 'framing' the scheme with the first and last moments in the Life of Christ).[26] Each of the 'stories' on the North and South walls, of Christ and Mary respectively, start at corresponding points, first moving upwards through the centre then along the top tier, then down to the corresponding scenes on the North Wall. Moreover, the North and South walls are markedly designed to be read in conversation with each other in such a way as to make the Life of the Virgin parallel to that of Christ: a divine order of similitudes, a kind of visual *oppositio* making a cogent statement of Jewish violence against Christian bodies.[27] So the Mocking of Christ faces the Jew grabbing the Virgin's bier; the Crucifixion faces the Burial of the Virgin; the Jew's torn hand is answered opposite in Peter's cutting of Malchus' ear; there are two miracles of St Peter (the servant's ear and the Jew's hand), two of St Thomas (his doubting of Christ, his doubting of Mary); the Assumption becomes cognate with the Resurrection, the Coronation with the Ascension. Far from offering a 'simple' picture book for the unlettered, the frescoes, with their patterns of narrative and parallelism, demand of the viewer a sophisticated knowledge of *how* to read, of how to direct, and 'move' with, one's reading. One moves with and within the fabric of the building – for example, one goes down to the

Harrowing of Hell with Christ but goes up with Christ to his Ascension and with Mary to her Coronation. Whilst certainly providing a coherent sequence, this is a complicated set of images and it is clear that one would have to know from previous reading or to learn from the sequence how to follow it correctly.[28]

We are familiar from stational liturgy – the place or stations of the Cross – with the idea that space inside a church, monastery or city could be organized according to an imagined sacred landscape.[29] Moreover, 'elaborate, journey-like processions' by monks and in some place congregants could take place, 'visiting' these stations around the church or city.[30] To visit these places (*loci*) was not just to recognize the narrative content of each station, but to make a personal performance, in which one was aesthetically and emotionally embedded, of the biblical narrative. One could, therefore, stand near the altar at Chalgrove and, in the quiet of the Oxfordshire countryside, experience the lives and deaths of Christ and the Virgin by becoming an active participant in its narrative. In its manifestation at Chalgrove, this kind of pious comic-strip organizes well-known stimuli which lead, within the established story given in *The Golden Legend*, to an affective response through accretive montage.

A comparison with modern cartoon strips is apt here:[31] symbolic rather than natural, heavily invested in violent contrast and the grotesque, delineating and defining good and evil, focusing on physical violence and moral contrast, all through the uses of frames and, literally, 'strips' of narrative. Moreover, like strip-art, sequences like the wall paintings at Chalgrove gains its audience's participation through the recognition of its generic nature, as a cue to stories encountered previously and elsewhere, with an established moral and narrative end-point. Such strip-art is similar to other medieval devotional schemata which appeal to vision, touch, memory and pain through an intense materiality. A good example is a fifteenth-century 'grid' of the *Arma Christi* (London, British Library Royal MS 6.E.vi, f. 15r, illus. 18), in which the reader/viewer moves from one torture to the next. The order of this image is unclear: how the torturous jumble was organized relies on a learned memory of the Passion, encountered previously, but this image does contain patterns – for instance the two flails either side of Christ, the central row which includes only 'embodied', fleshly figures (the Eucharist, the Jew, the cock, and Christ) – in a kind of devotional game of 'snakes and ladders'. Alongside is a prayer for an indulgence.

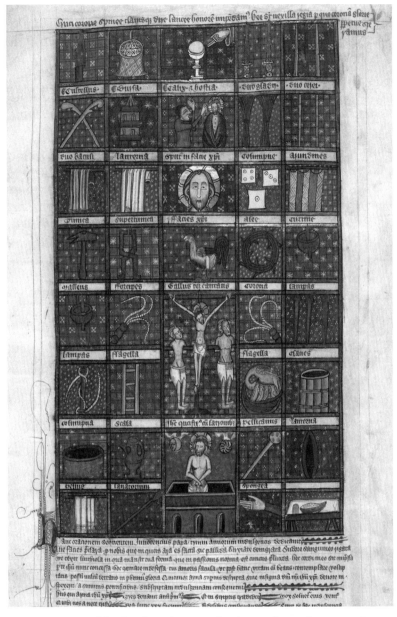

18 Instruments of the Passion; the central column shows, from top, the Host; the Jew spitting in Christ's face; Christ's face; the cock that crowed; Christ crucified between thieves; the Resurrection. BL Royal MS 6.E.vi, f. 15r, England, fourteenth century.

19 The Jew and the Virgin's bier, Chalgrove (Oxfordshire). The Jew attacks the bier [r.] and, after conversion, ministers to the other Jews [l.]. Wall painting, mid-fourteenth century.

The Chalgrove frescoes include a wonderfully vigorous and expressive image of the Jew jumping on the Virgin's bier (illus. 19). The 'rationale' for the inclusion of this story is that it complements and parallels the betrayal, interrogation, mocking, scourging and cruci-fixion of Christ in the same place on the facing wall which, likewise, displays the Christian body under vigorous attack from Jews. But the funeral procession image also nearly encapsulates the way in which the Jewish image engaged, violently, with Christian *ductus*: the funeral procession moves from right to left (and thus towards Mary's Assumption) whereas the Jewish figures attacking the bier move from left to right, thus obstructing the passage to Assumption and demon-strating their powerfully retrospective pull. Thus these Jews enact a condensed perceptual *passio*, tugging to the right when the sequence marches to the left, bringing disorder and disruption into this orderly and immersive sequence of paintings.[32]

The Jewish figures around the bier at Chalgrove are three Jews (on first sight they look identical and seem to show the Jew leaping from the left, adhering to the bier, and then falling under the bier to the right). They are, however, the same the three assailants as in the N-Town play (discussed below): one is struck blind (at Chalgrove the left-hand Jew who gestures to his eyes); another is made mad (the right-hand Jew who twists and turns under the bier); the third dares to carry out his attack on the Virgin's bier (the one who hangs from it at Chalgrove). Other images, such as those from the Taymouth Hours (illus. 16) and Luttrell Psalter (illus. 20), simplify the scene, entirely representing the episode as one Jew hanging from the bier in the op-posite direction to the apostles, with disruption made central. At Chalgrove, the healing of the Jewish priest effects an aesthetic heal-ing. The Jews' high-priest, once converted, can face the east, and

20 The Jew at the Virgin's Funeral, Luttrell Psalter. England, *c.* 1350. BL Add. MS 42130, f. 99r.

join the narrative correctly. Likewise, the Jew grasps for the bier with his left hand, but, once converted, the Jewish priest ministers to the Jews with his right hand.

'Are ye ferd of a ded body?': Jewish Touch at N-Town

A version of the Funeral of the Virgin was performed in the English N-Town plays, pageants from eastern England performed at 'N-Town' – possibly Bury St Edmunds (Suffolk) – written down before 1468.[33] These plays furnish a memorable example of the story as it was performed by the people of late medieval England. The Marian plays from N-Town have been described as 'iconographical' drama and the plays' indebtness to picture cycles has been noted, but the plays might better be described as affective satires.[34] The N-Town plays are noteworthy for their emphasis on apocryphal episodes of Mary's life which contrast incorrect, over-literal understandings of Mary and correct, spiritual/figurative understandings of her. The plays include a 'Joachim and Anna' play (in which the Virgin's parents are put in conflict with the priest Ysakar and his literal understanding of fertility and sacrifice), an unusual 'Marriage of Mary and Joseph' play (which contrasts spiritual and carnal versions of marriage), the 'Trial of Mary and Joseph' play (in which Jewish detractors called Reysesclaundyr ('Raise Slander') and Bakbytere ('Backbiter') accuse the holy couple of adultery) and the play of the 'Assumption of Mary', which includes the Jews' attack on the Virgin's funeral and is the penultimate episode in the cycle, before 'Judgement Day'.[35] The 'Trial of Mary and Joseph' play acts in particular as a counterpart to the Virgin's funeral, showing the groping examination of the Virgin by a midwife named

Zelomye, who, like the Jew at the funeral, brings a literalism of touch to the Virgin's body which misunderstands its miraculous nature.

When 'Jewish' detractors focus excessively on Mary's appearance, they treat her as an object and enact the concerns of iconoclasts about the use of images by making Mary a means of indulging their lustful imaginings, rather than a way to achieve spiritual understanding.[36] The detractors' accusations and legalistic diction is 'based on a misreading of Mary's body', as at the Assumption, a theme carried through to the play of the Virgin's funeral.[37] The N-Town play of the Virgin's funeral shows how the episode of the Jew's hand could be useful, especially in a performance reliant on spectacle and music.[38]

The N-Town play opens with a 'Doctor' summarizing Mary's pious biography, conventionally retold from *The Golden Legend*: the Virgin conceived Christ at fourteen, gave birth at fifteen, died at sixty, when she 'assumpte above the ierarchye' ('was taken to heaven higher than the angels', line 11). The Doctor's solemn speech is then interrupted by a soldier, who barks

Pes now youre blabering, in the develis name!	*Stop*
What, lousy *begchis, mow* ye not se,	*bitches, can*
Owre worthy *prynsis*, lo, are gaderid *in-same*	*princes, together*
That are *statis* of this lond, *hye* men of degré.	*lords, lofty*
By there hye wisdam they schal now attaine	
How alle *Juré* beste governyd may be.[39]	*Judea*
(lines 27–32)	

The play sets up a contrast between the apostles ('pilled' or tonsured 'prechouris', line 33) and the princes of Judea who repeatedly threaten violence. This threat of violence is then turned to the audience, as the soldier menacingly warns

Wherfore in *pes* be ye,	*Therefore, quiet*
And herkenyth onto *hem* moste stilly.	*them* [i.e. the Judean princes]
For what boy bragge outh, *hym spille I!*	*I will kill him!*
As *knave* with this *craggyd knag* hym kille I!	a *rogue, pointed rock*
Now herkenyth oure pryncis alle	
kneland on kne.	*kneeling on knees*
(lines 35–9)	

The soldier's threat to kill the boys in the audience recalls the Massacre of the Innocents, as the Virgin's Assumption becomes yet another Christian arena of Jewish violence and Christian passivity. So, on one hand, the play depicts Christian preachers, respectful keepers of Mary's biography and guardians of a spiritual realm. On the other hand, the Judean princes speak violently, threaten violence, and are concerned with worldly power. In fact, the play is coherently and subtly structured through this violent contrast, which culminates in the attack on the Virgin's bier. The contrast is sustained through the careful modulation of the Judeans' language, to include shocking physical coarseness, as the Judean 'bishop' plots:

But *be that seustere ded, Mary, that fise,*	*once that sister, Mary, that fart, is dead*
We shal *brenne here* body and *the aschis hide,*	*burn her, hide the ashes*
And *don here all the dispith* we can here devise,	*do to her all the humiliation*
And *than sle tho* disciplis that walkyn so *wyde,*	*then slay those, widely*
And *here bodyes devyde.*	*dismember their bodies*

(lines 83–7)

So, proleptically, the spirit of the Jews' assault of the Virgin and their own dismemberment inheres not only in their intentions but also in their jarring, disruptive and over-embodied language, of violence and murder. The Jews' language alliterates ('gnaggyd vp by the gomys tyl deuyl doth hem grone!', 'hanged up by the gums until the devil moans for them!', line 47), is full of exclamations, questions, repeated oaths, physical insults to Mary and fantasies of her dismemberment ('the devyl smite of here hed!', line 91). In contrast, Mary's speech is dignified by Latinate vocabulary ('salvacion . . . gratulacion . . . desideracion . . . excitacion . . . dominacion . . . formacion') and her dialogue with the angels is marked by its diction of courtesy ('excellent princes', 'radiant sterre', 'graciows aungyl', 'swete aungyl').

In the N-Town play, Mary meets again with the apostles, and, in a passage closely modelled on the Latin liturgy of the Assumption, Mary's soul ascends (lines 310–29). In a further proleptic example, two virgins 'wesche and worschepe' ('wash and worship', line 353) Mary's body as they prepare it for the funeral, speaking in tones of reverence ('myn hol affyaunce' ('my total faith'), line 352) and kissing the corpse (lines 355–6), an image of correct relic veneration.

The funeral procession then commences, with the apostles singing 'Exiit Israel de Egipto' and angels accompanying, singing 'Alleluia!'; but this 'noyse' (lines 371, 373, 381) of 'yon lousy doggys' (line 388) enrages the Jews; they swear by 'Mahound' ('Mohammed', line 391) to demonstrate their allegiance to a non-Christian God and the three Judean princes pledge 'We schal don schame to that body and to tho prechours' (line 398) and approach the funeral procession. Two of the princes start to have second thoughts about their plan to attack Mary's body – one saying that he cannot see (line 411), the other becoming frenzied (line 416), as depicted at Chalgrove. The third Jew mockingly asks 'Are ye ferd of a ded body?' – 'Are you afraid of a dead body?' (line 420) – and jumps onto the shrine of Mary. Here, in the script, is the Latin stage direction *'Hic saltat insanus ad feretrum Marie et pendet per manus'* – 'Here the madman jumps to the bier of Mary and hangs by the hand'.[40]

How this moment was performed is unclear but the spectacle or *tableau vivant* of the Jew hanging from the bier is a dramatic climax: the episode occurs not only through words but through the striking of an affective and memorable pose, via the familiar visual cue of the Jew hanging from the bier. Liturgical music performs a similar mnemonic role in the play (and the N-Town play of the Assumption is unusually exact in its liturgical correspondences):[41] directly quoting the appropriate liturgical sections ('Assumpta est Maria', 'De terra', 'Exiit Israel') from the liturgy of the Assumption, added to the account given by Jacobus, the N-Town performance called to mind the audience's larger, extra-dramatic experience of the liturgy in other settings.

The scene of the Jew hanging from the bier corresponds with, through violent visual contrast, the play's closing 'special effect', for which Assumption plays were famous, of the raising of an image of the Virgin to the accompaniment of celestial music. Hanging from the bier, the Judean prince screams out:

Allas, my body is ful of *peyne*!	*pain*
I am fastened sore to this bere!	
Myn handys are ser	*Both my two hands are*
bothe twenye.	*withered*

> O, Peter, now prey thy God for
> me here.
> In Cayfas halle when thou
> were *seyne*   *seen*
> And *of the, Peter, a mayde*   *a maiden accused you, Peter*
> *acusid* there,
> I *halpe the tho; now*   *helped you then*
> helpe me ageyne,
> That I were hol, *outh of this fere –*   *out of this frightening situation*
> *Sum medycyn me lere.*   *teach me some medicine.*
>
> (lines 423–31)

That the Jew has become stuck to the bier and his hands withered has to be declared (perhaps because of the difficulty in performing this with only rudimentary special effects!). However, the rest of the prince's speech complements his getting 'fastened sore' in being retrospective, backwards: he arrests the narrative both by attacking the bier and becoming attached to it; he disturbs the atmosphere and progress of the funeral, presenting to the audience his unruly body of pain and his jarring withered hands; but he also explicitly recalls the incident (described in the gospels) in which Peter denied Christ to a servant-girl before the cock crowed, thereby dragging the narrative back to a time before the establishment of the Christian ministry.[42] The other reference of hindsight, to Caiaphas' hall, recalls to the audience the Jews' role at the Crucifixion, underscoring the maxim that, in Anselm's words, 'When I have sinned against the son,/ I have alienated the mother,/ nor can I offend the mother without hurting the son'.[43]

The Jewish prince converts and Peter commands him to take his holy palm, go to his people and touch them with it. The Virgin's funeral then continues, with the body carried to the sepulchre; but, there are yet futher interruptions. One prince takes the palm and is healed of his blindness but the other refuses to forsake his Law: he is then struck down, crying in distress:

> I deye! Outh, outh! Harro!
> The wilde develys *mot me to-drawe!*   *must pull me away!*
>
> (lines 475–6)

The Virgin's funeral thus descends into a diabolical farce, returning again to images of pain and dismemberment, as two demons appear, repeating the graphically violent language earlier associated with the Jews (e.g. lines 484–8).

These repeated interjections by Jews and demons in the Virgin's funeral do, of course, articulate a conventional and simple doctrinal lesson: belief in Christ and the Virgin will spare one from hell. But such episodes also stimulate the audience's *compunctio cordis*, their emotional, heartfelt engagement, as would be appropriate at a funeral. Given the synaesthetic impetus of the play, uniting speech, pageant, music, liturgy, it is not surprising to find also a countervailing emphasis on the senses of pain and touch. In the background of this play of diabolical dismemberment is the Virgin's bier and the lamenting apostles; the play effectively moves between the two images and registers of lament and disrespect, buffeting the audience between two kinds of performance. The play's aim, the assumption of Mary, her passage to celestial perpetuity, is deferred by the Jews' fooling, through contrasting scenes of decorous Christian grief and grotesque 'Jewish' antipathy, and contrasts between the 'now' of the Virgin's funeral and the Jews' 'then' of the Crucifixion. Finally, the overblown language, gruesome violence and egregious special effects associated with the Jewish and demonic characters delays the most special of sequences in the play: the final scene in which the voice of Mary's soul speaks and she is assumed to heaven to a musical accompaniment.[44] The successful execution of the Assumption would have been achieved, in part, through its contrast with the earlier theatrical violence of the Jews.

Fergus the Jew, York, 1432

As well as the N-Town version, the Dormition was performed dramatically throughout Europe, including in plays at Brussels, Innsbruck, Lille, Paris, Ripoll, Valencia and Valenciennes, and in liturgical processions at Rome and Cluny;[45] from the 1370s to this day, the Dormition is performed in August at Elche/Elx in Spain, in which 'a crowd of interrupting Jews', to use a contemporary journalist's words, plays a key part.[46] In 2001 the Elche play was declared a UNESCO 'Masterpiece of World Oral and Intangible Heritage', an ironic moniker as the play is concerned with what is and is not tangible. Moreover, the story gained its own fifteenth-century pilgrimage site, on Jerusalem's Mount Zion, at the 'howse of cursyd cunsel . . . the furste plase wher Jues wold have brennyd/ Owre lady['s] body when hit scholde be buried'.[47]

21 Funeral of the Virgin, stained glass, York Minster, *c.* 1400.

By 1432, in the large and wealthy northern English city of York, the celebration of the Dormition of the Virgin had become a grotesque farce, the nature of celebration and theology changed utterly. The story formed one of the episodes of the well-known York 'mystery plays' as the 'Transitus' or 'Funeral of the Virgin', the play-text for which unfortunately no longer survives. The 'Transitus' – the 'passing on' or 'crossing over' of the Virgin – was performed within York's dramatic cycle of Corpus Christi plays. The play was known in York as the '*arrêt*' (arrest) or 'pageant of Fergus' or 'Vergus' (suggesting that its Jewish anti-hero was the focus rather than the Virgin's assumption) and seems to have been performed by different craft guilds and was not performed continuously. In 1415 it appears to have been performed by the Linen-weavers (when it was described as the pageant of 'Mary and Fergus hanging from the bier' ('*Marie et fergus pendens super feretrum*')). In the early 1430s the Masons were responsible for the play and in the 1470s the Linen-weavers were playing *Fergus*. In 1485 controversy raged again about the play, then performed by either the Sawyers or the Wrights (or both). The Linen-weavers were again responsible in 1486, when they were fined for failing to perform the play. The play still existed in 1518, apparently resurrected by the Linen-weavers.[48] Around 1330, a stained-glass window was made for York Minster of a monkeys' funeral procession which seems to represent the story; a slightly later window at York certainly includes the story, with a foreshortened, twisted Jew hanging, screaming, from the bier (illus. 21).[49] The reason we know of the existence of the play of *Fergus* is because of its difficult, interrupted history, because it passed discontinuously between guilds; in particular, the Masons complained, in the 1430s, of having to perform it. Within a petition from the Goldsmiths' Guild to reduce their dramatic burden, the York Masons raised a complaint:

> the Masons of this city have been accustomed to murmur among themselves about their pageant in the Corpus Christi Play in which Fergus was beaten because the subject of this pageant is not contained in the sacred scripture and used to produce more noise and laughter than devotion [*& magis risum & clamorem causabat quam deuocionem*]. And whenever quarrels, disagreements, and fights used to arise among the people from this, they have rarely or never been able to produce their pageant and to play in daylight as the preceding pageants do.[50]

So the play of the Jew jumping on the Virgin's bier caused laughter and 'noise' (*clamor* can encompass loud shouting or riot, but truly suggests a noisy *public* expression, a scandal); the play failed to stimulate devotion. It is easy to see how the arresting image of the Jew hanging on the Virgin's bier could become not only funny but also how it could eclipse the *true* subject of the play, the Virgin's Assumption.

On one level, the York Masons' complaint profoundly troubles the popular notion that medieval people simply had a 'popular culture' which rambunctiously defamed and parodied Jews. The York Masons wanted to be part of an elegant and canonical story of redemption, grace and mystery. Their complaint shows us that this kind of story was not received uncritically by its medieval audiences, and, in demonstrating the abiding role of the grotesque and the comic within the medieval Christian representation of Jewry, shows how disruptive, interruptive, this story could be. The point of the story – ostensibly, the Jews' conversion – was eclipsed by that image of Christianity persecuted by Judaism (which can then be persecuted by Christianity) to which medieval culture insistently returned time and again.

Rosemary Woolf, often a sensitive reader of medieval English literature, called the medieval Dormition plays featuring the Jew's hand 'strange'; Woolf went on to wish away the *Fergus* play, stating that the York cycle 'appears the more dignified without' it.[51] If the image of the Jew's hand is 'strange' it is because it is unclear how it is to be read, whether it is frightening or funny. As Quintilian explained, 'laughter is not far from derision', and, following Cicero, laughter 'has its basis in a certain deformity and ugliness'.[52] The *Fergus* episode is both frightening and funny and so, like a marginal wyvern or hybrid, it is conspicuous and strange both in form and purpose: it is *illustrative*, it *elucidates*, by being memorable and stirring. The reaction at York to the play – of hilarity and of worries about heresy – show how the subject-matter was funny and disruptive, but also shows the kind of 'reality' constructed in this egregiously theatrical performance. The play did not urge action against Jews, but caused a crisis in the Christian polity, for the medieval audience had a 'spiritual dependency' on the events being played in the drama.[53] Medieval (and modern) anxieties about the undignified level of the York *Fergus* play are borne out in the appearance of a doggerel fifteenth-century English verse on the Assumption, 'Assumpcioun de Notre Dame'. This long poem tells a predictable, if intensified, version of the last days, death, funeral and Assumption of Mary (adding the piquant detail that the Jews plan to throw Mary's corpse 'in-to a foule pitt', 'a foule sloo', using a scatological image of degradation-by-sewer to counterpoint the coming Assumption).[54] In its manuscripts, this poem sits alongside formulaic and sentimental romances, bearing out the irreligious appeal of the story: even its own author calls it a 'tale' rather than a miracle or legend.

The Croxton Play: Dismemberment and the Affective Memory-Image

The English grammarian and memory-theorist Thomas Bradwardine wrote that one of the 'wondrous and intense' ways to impress something on the memory might be to imagine

> a person who has been injured with an enormous open wound flowing with a remarkable river of blood, or in some other way made ugly, having strange clothing and every bizarre embellishment . . . the whole image also should have some other quality such as movement, that thus it may be commended to memory more effectively than through tranquillity or repose.[55]

The open wound, the river of blood, the bizarre embellishment, the quality of movement contrasted with repose: the very hallmarks of the drama of the Jew at the Virgin's funeral. The Jew's hand, as an eloquent and shocking metonym of the incorrect engagement with Christian symbols, is central to the well-known late fifteenth-century Croxton *Play of the Sacrament*. This miracle play, a farce about all the different ways one can misunderstand the Christian sacraments, has become much studied recently on account of its burlesque Jews defined by their ruptured and over-determined bodies;[56] it would be easy to forget, from the solemn and sincere tone of much recent criticism, that the Croxton *Play* is partly a comedy, at the same time that it asks serious and profound questions about sacramental efficacy and religious affiliation.

The Croxton *Play* is set in Aragon in 1461 (a specific locale and date it recalls repeatedly) but was performed, probably in Suffolk, in the early sixteenth century. The play presents and parodies 'false' and inefficacious remedies by repeatedly placing incongruous obstacles in the way of true Christian salvation: the Presbiter's immoderate enjoyment of red wine (line 269), Master Brundyche's silly medicine (line

567), and, most memorably, the Jews' misunderstanding of the real presence of the eucharistic wafer, the thing they call a 'cake' (line 120).[57] It is true that the play sets up 'analogous' version of the sacraments, but more apt is a description of these analogies as 'parody'.[58] In keeping with its generic classification as a miracle rather than morality play, the Croxton *Play* seeks to articulate the miracle of Christianity through display and performance rather than through suasion or doctrinal explication.

The Croxton *Play of the Sacrament* remains a potent and memorable piece of drama on account of its two key moments of memorable visual and performative stasis, in which the audience is shown moral tableaux constituted by affective stereotypes.[59] First, the Jew Jonathas loses his hand, when it adheres to the Eucharistic wafer which he has abused; the stage direction explicitly says that the Jew's hand should 'hang still with the Sacrament' (lines 435–7). This moment of contrived grotesquery is designed to jar, to shock, forcefully to assert body rather than spirit; like in the Jewish profile, the Jew's body acts as a part, a metonym, which demands our attention and halts the narrative. Whilst the play's Jews are insistently conspicuous and embodied they themselves are unable to read or see properly; such a Jew is thus both utterly representable and yet unable to read correctly.

A little later in the play the doctor Master Brundyche and his boy Colle are introduced and the audience's progress towards proper and pious salvation is further delayed, by scurrilous and foolish quackery. When proper faith is shown, upon the conversion of the Jews, it is again at a moment of 'dramatic stasis', the display of the Christ-Child's speaking 'image' which should 'appere owt [of an oven] with woundys bleding' (632–3). This second image in effect answers and corrects that of Jonathas' hand, contrasting and replacing one bloodied icon with another, though both devices are 'frankly outrageous' and 'egregious' moments of 'theatrical illusion'.[60] One critic has described how the play moves from 'private atrocity to public spectacle', cognate with Michel Foucault's suggestion of the need for a viewed performance of punishment.[61] However, the play's moments of violence are those at which religious identification, and conversion, take place, as the Croxton play vividly portrays the transformative and edifying powers of violence. Both the Jew's severed hand and the Christ-Child are iconic bloodied bodies which frighten their audience into penance.

Such violent contrast is then manifested in the speech delivered by the image of 'Jhesu', in which the *contentio* rhetorical *topos* again

sets up stark antitheses between the 'onkind' Jews and Jesus' 'blisse'
(lines 640–41):

Why fare ye thus *fule* with yowre frende?	*foully*
Why *peyne* you Me and *straytly Me pynde*,	*hurt, forcefully*
	tormented me
And I your love so derely have *bowght*?	*redeemed*
Why are ye so unstedfast in your minde?	
Why *wrath ye* Me? *I greve you nought.*	*are you angry with,*
(642–6)	*I did not injure you*

'Fule' counters 'frende', 'peyne' begets 'love'; the Jews cannot answer
Christ's questions, which culminate in his definitive answer 'I greve
you nought'. Like images and dramas of the Dormition, the Croxton
Play does 'invoke a mode of viewing that is itself painful'.[62] Critics
have highlighted the play's disruptive nature and its focus on conflicting emotions as, throughout the play, the evocation and performance
of precious mnemonic symbols (not least that of the Christ-Child)
and their un-Christian adversaries prevent an uninterrupted immersive relationship with Christ.[63] Both the key symbols at the heart of
the play – the Jew's hand and the Christ-Child – are emotive and in
them seeing and feeling come together, but oscillate between pleasure
and pain; in such cultural productions we thus need not concern ourselves with the 'historical' absence of Jews from England as the Jewish
stereotype in all its fantastical grotesquery could be enabling and
meaningful in its interaction with Christian symbols. In all the materials we have surveyed, the 'likeness' of Judaism derives from a moral
or religious sense of representation, not from an actual recollection.
In this way, the interruptive hand is like the miraculous bread/body of
the Eucharist – an ever-present touch from the past, disrupting time.

Such a representation of the obstinate, interruptive Jew mirrors
Christian exegesis which describes the eternal obstinacy of the Jews.[64]
This obstinacy frequently takes the form of the Jews' perceived inabil-
ity, as in the Croxton *Play*, to read and interact correctly with Christian
texts and images, a failed legible practice in and of themselves. The
Jew's hand, like the Jew in profile or the red-haired Judas, is out of place,
and profoundly, haltingly, swiftly, *recognizable*. As Ronald Schechter
writes of the image of the 'obstinate Hebrew', 'the famed obstinacy of
the Jews, their alleged hostility to change, their apparently eternal
nature made them, more than any other group, ideal figures in the

discussion of what was perhaps the greatest question of the day: the possibility of human perfectibility.'[65] These words about revolutionary France are no less true of medieval Europe. This Jew was part of a visual and cultural environment in which any representation might be convincing not because it is like its actual signified but because it produces an authentic affective and/or moral response in the viewer.

Thus we see an aesthetics of dismemberment emerging, often configured around the spectacular wounding and healing of the Jew's body; to 'condemn' or 'excuse' texts like the N-Town or Croxton plays is a product of our own moral positioning and shows an approach to medieval culture as something to be *explained away*, on our terms, rather than understood on the aesthetic terms with which medieval people approached such artefacts.[66] Whether we identify a perverse sadism, anxiety or alterity in the way such Christian productions dismember Jewish bodies, we explain away the intellectual and mnemonic sense that they made.

'Does God Hate Amputees?'

A contemporary Christian internet forum has a section devoted to it called 'Why Does God Hate Amputees?' One writer states: 'Suffering serves a purpose. Without suffering, we would not know compassion'; another that '[f]aith, like a muscle, needs to be exercised'; another that 'God does not grow limbs back although he could. God heals broken hearts instead, and He does this through imperfect human beings just like you and me'; yet another writes that '[t]hose that are healed are healed for the glory of God and those who are not healed are also for the glory of God.' Most of the (Christian) users of this forum seem unaware that the Christian God does heal amputees, as shown in the parable of Christ restoring the servant's severed ear (Luke 22:51). These twenty-first-century correspondents are, whether they know it or not, taking part in a very ancient dispute, about what good and holy bodies should and should not look like, and what the nature of divine punishment and miraculous divine intervention means for the human body. It is the same debate which animated St Augustine who, in *The City of God*, wrote a famous discussion of 'monstrous races' and outlandish bodies, arguing that '[t]he man who cannot view the whole is offended by what he takes to be the deformity of a part; but this is because he does not know how it is adapted or related to the whole.'[67] Augustine's maxim can be seen to be a motif of this study, in as much as medieval representations of Jews make 'proper', devotional sense in their larger Christian context.

Both the Old and New Testaments are replete with amputees and sufferers of withered hands and broken arms: Jeroboam, a haughty king, has his hand withered (3 Kings 13:4); Pharoah's arm is broken as a divine punishment (Ezechiel 30:21; the other arm breaks in the next verse); 'a man who had a withered hand' asks Jesus in the synagogue if it is lawful to be healed on the Sabbath; Jesus heals him, causing the Pharisees to plot his murder (Matthew 12:10, Mark 3:1–4, Luke 6:6–8). To have a limb withered (and therefore able to be miraculously restored) is temporarily to lose those things – martial skill, temporal power, public coherence – which make one whole and masculine but it is the bloodied stump of a limb that speaks most eloquently.[68]

The image of the Jew's hand cut off and restored might be seen as a perfect complement to the late medieval fascination with Christ's suffering and those perverse desires which are features particularly of Franciscan piety: 'replacing health with sickness, embracing the leprous and the maimed, the high with the low, its embrace of filth and flesh, its emphatic fetishizing of Christ's torn and bleeding body as the object, indeed subject, of compassion and passion, were simultaneously strategies of profanation and sacralisation.'[69] The dismembered limb, and its restoration, was translated into a remarkably wide range of preachers' stories. On the positive side, King Oswald's almsgiving hand remained incorrupt after his death;[70] St John of Damascus had a severed limb miraculously restored by the Virgin;[71] one reads the story of three thieves, of whom one became an honest man: to save his ham from being stolen by his two companions, he struck off their hands as they reached for the meat;[72] a lustful man's hand withers after being kissed by a woman, but is restored by the Virgin so he can honour her.[73] More often, however, the body dismembered is a sinful body, and to lose a hand is to lose good, Christian reason: a peasant violated the Sabbath by repairing his plough on Sunday and his hands became paralyzed;[74] Christ appears to a woman who concealed a sin from her confessor: she touches Christ's wound and her hand is stained with blood until she confesses;[75] a girl's hand withers when she breaks an oath to God;[76] the mother of St Clement goes into exile in Athens in order to avoid temptation with her husband's brother, and her hands become numb and useless until St Clement appears and restores them; a perjurer holds out his right hand (with which he had sworn on the bible) and claims it is as sound as the other, but the hand and arm immediately shrivel up.[77] The cutting off of a thief's hand is today considered representative of the harsh literalness of *sharia* law, although it was common legal punishment in medieval Europe and appears in Old English and skaldic poetry.[78] The Jew at the Virgin's dormition would have been fecund with this punitive imagery, and indeed Jephonius' grabbing is a kind of *furta sacra*, the inappropriate, criminal moment of *touch* which demonstrates the relic's desirability and the power.

However, the isolated, withered limb, the shocking violence of it and its memorable grotesquery is not so different from other ornaments in medieval visual culture:

> the basic features of . . . ornaments are also elementary principles of mnemonics: surprise and strangeness (for example, *metaphora*, metonymy, *allegoria*, oxymoron, and, in art, grotesquery), exaggeration, orderliness and pattern, brevity, copiousness, similarity, opposition, contrast.[79]

The cut-off hand as a haptic memory image is most obviously and frequently seen in the manicule, the pointing hand, which reach from the margins of medieval texts, drawing our attention to important points, a gestural 'nota bene'. The Hand of God appears out of the margin of pages, reaching down from heaven.[80] Ubiquitous Jewish hands slap Christ and pull at his hair at the Passion, hands which appear, disembodied, in *Arma Christi* artefacts (see illus. 18). Christ's hands and feet, bearers of his Wounds, appear in the later medieval period, venerated separate from the rest of His body. The Guidonian Hand was a kind of musical map of the left hand used for instruction in different tones, in which expression, corporeality and inventional memory were located.[81] Islamic and Jewish cultures have their counterparts in the omnipresent symbols of the Hands of Fatima and Miriam.

The Jew's hand is within the logic of 'gesture-rich occasions' which, in the Middle Ages, used bodily elevation to establish 'relative status positions, or in providing a code (a "vocabulary") in which status relations can be expressed'.[82] Jephonius' body falls downwards, under the Virgin's bier, to mark a fallen status, but, perhaps more powerfully, the Jew's touch perverts some of the key symbolic acts and gestures in medieval culture: to touch with a hand could be to make a deal, to make a friend, to demonstrate intimacy but, most pertinently, relics were touched with the right hand and sacred books were touched by hand in order to make an oath at once formal, binding, public, ceremonial and pious.[83] Thus the episode of the Jew touching the Virgin's bier vividly represents a fundamentally transgressive and violent gesture, even as it contains within it the stimulus for the Jew's miraculous healing.

Whilst the Jew's hand is a widespread subject in medieval art, the subsequent miracle of the Jews' healing rarely features in visual representations of the Dormition; this does not necessarily mean that the 'point' of the story was the Jews' gruesome suffering rather than their conversion – however, the image of the Jew's hand, static, shocking and conspicuous, is a mnemonic cue, the starting-point for remembering the entire episode (in the sense that medieval mnemotechnic does not seek to stop one from forgetting, but rather to call things to mind in particular patterns and orders). From this Jew the audience can remember, in microcosm, the context and establishment of the early Church, the Assumption of the Virgin, the works of the Apostles, as well as the conversion of the Jews – and, crucially, as with the other narratives considered in these pages, one can recreate an aesthetic narrative of Christian victimhood, the eruption of the enduring, moving miracle of Christlike sacrifice at Jewish hands.

CHAPTER 5

Visiting Calvary: Contrition, Intimacy and Virtual Persecution

King Henry IV:
Doth any name particular belong
Unto the lodging where I first did swoon?
Warwick:
'Tis call'd Jerusalem, my noble lord.
William Shakespeare, *Henry IV Part 2* (IV:iii:361–3)

At the Jerusalem Chamber

On 20 March 1413, Henry IV, king of England, fulfilled a prophecy that he should die at Jerusalem. He did not die at the 'actual' Jerusalem, the Mameluk metropolis conquered by Saladin in 1189 and in 1413 ruled by Al-Muayad Saif Addin Shaykh, but at a more potent, more intimate version: the 'Jerusalem Chamber' at Westminster Abbey (illus. 22). The room seems to have been named after now-lost decorations, either wall-hangings or frescoes, depicting scenes of Jerusalem and inscribed with biblical verses about Jerusalem; thus Jerusalem's sacred landscape was remade at Westminster, England's royal and political centre. Next door are medieval chambers called Jericho and Samaria, so, in medieval Westminster, one could progress through a holy 'landscape' (a complex of gothic rooms). The medieval designers of the building – its crenellations recalling Jerusalem's battlements, its polygonal tower suggesting the Holy Sepulchre – wanted to make a domestic Jerusalem in Westminster. The Jerusalem chamber was built in the fourteenth century, by abbot Nicholas Litlyngton (d. 1386; his device and initials appear on the roof), and it was originally part of the abbot's lodgings; the chamber still stands, although its interior is much altered.[1] It was here in 1882 that Elizabeth Finn, an energetic Christian Zionist, held the first meeting of a relief committee for Jews to buy land in Palestine, the chamber's name singularly appropriate to projects of pilgrimage, conquest, nation-building and religious fantasy.[2]

In Shakespeare's dramatization of Henry IV's career, Jerusalem is a nebulous object of desire dogging the king's life. Henry vows to make a penitential crusade, guilt-ridden after his role in Richard II's

22 The Jerusalem Chamber, Westminster Abbey, built *c.* 1380 for abbot
Nicholas Litlyngton.

death;[3] Henry had visited Jerusalem as a crusader-pilgrim in his youth,
and the city becomes the destination, the *telos*, to which he craves to
return. But parallel to this penitential pilgrimage is Henry's desire to
launch a new crusade to recapture the Holy Sepulchre, as a distraction
from his domestic worries. Henry falls ill before the crusade can start
and, raving on his deathbed, he believes himself to have reached
Jerusalem. This, however, is a Jerusalem of his fantasy and annihila-
tion rather than of conquest or expiation.

The story of Henry's death in 'Jerusalem' at Westminster was cur-
rent well before Shakespeare: the legend seems to originate with the
French chronicler Enguerrand de Monstrelet (d. 1453), who wrote that
Henry hubristically planned to conquer Jerusalem after conquering
France.[4] The English *Cronycles* of Robert Fabyan (d. 1513) state that
the king

> [felt] himself so sike he comaunded to aske if that Chambre had
> any special name, wherunto it was answerid that it was named
> Jherusalem. Than said the kinge 'lovynge be to the Fader of
> Heuen for nowe I knowe I shall die in this Chambre according

to the prophecie of me beforesaid that I shulde die in Jherusalem', and so after he made himself Redy & died shortly after . . .[5]

Henry IV's piety in this case calls to mind an earlier king, Robert 'the
Bruce' of Scotland (d. 1329), who, on *his* deathbed, had longed for
his heart to be buried at the Holy Sepulchre in Jerusalem.[6] Before
him, Edward I (d. 1307) had foretold his own death in the 'burgh' of
Jerusalem, but died instead at Burgh-by-Sands near Carlisle.[7] From
even earlier, an *exemplum* said that Pope Sylvester II (d. 1003) had his
death at Jerusalem foretold by the devil; he was then struck down in
Rome's church of Santa Croce in Gerusalemme.[8] From the thirteenth century, lives of St Edmund described king Offa dying on his
way back from Jerusalem.[9] These stories say much about Christian
eschatological desires to return to Jerusalem, both the Heavenly City
and the centre of the religious world, and about the sentiments of
crusade: to die the good death is to wish to die at Jerusalem.

The very notion of the Jerusalem Chamber at Westminster also
reveals the mobility of Jerusalem, and the vogue, in the later Middle
Ages, of making material copies of Jerusalem, of bringing Jerusalem
home. Shakespeare, writing in newly Protestant sixteenth-century
England, implies that Henry's longed-for death in Jerusalem is a hal-
lucination, both unreal and unrealistic, with the medieval king fooled
by his counsellors and by the devices on the chamber's walls into
thinking that he has reached the Heavenly City. Henry had used the
idea of crusading to Jerusalem first as penance for his complicity in
the murder of Richard II, then in a Machiavellian way as a means of
distracting his Court from strife in England, but, Shakespeare suggests, conflict returns and translates; conflict cannot be translated
abroad, but rather Calvary is at the heart of Westminster.

From antique times and throughout the Middle Ages, Jerusalem,
a city sacred to Jews, Christians and Muslims, was known and depicted as the *omphalos* (Greek), *umbilicus* (Latin) or *tabur* (Hebrew), that
is, navel, of the world: the point of Creation, from which Christian
time and space emanated.[10] Medieval world maps, like the famous
Hereford *mappa mundi*, usually make Jerusalem central. It is, perhaps,
curious then that Jerusalem was so mobile, indeed motile – not only
utterly translatable, but also endlessly representable away from and
outside of itself. Late medieval people 'made' many artificial versions
of Jerusalem and in particular of Calvary, which brought the Passion
and its re-performance into one's familiar world. The Jerusalem of

Christ's Passion was brought into medieval intimate and cultural lives, in order to be re-experienced as a personal, domestic Calvary, as in the Jerusalem Chamber. That is to say, medieval people made recreations, simulacra and models of Calvary in order to experience the Passion on their own terms and on their own turf, a Jerusalem involving a sense of the self imperilled. The violence said to have been committed to Christ by Jews at Calvary became a remarkably versatile and translatable system of images; throughout the Middle Ages, the 'location' of the Passion came to have a kind of aesthetic geography of its own. In particular, medieval Christians sought to experience Christ's Passion through empathy and imitation, through staging their own suffering.

We have repeatedly seen how medieval culture made an abiding and usually edifying connection between memory/remembering and terror/pain; one of the central images of this connection was the body of Christ and its suffering at the hands of the Jews, whose violence was recalled in order to help medieval Christians undergo their own personal version of the Passion. Thus the thoughts of medieval kings turned on their deathbeds to Jerusalem. Indeed, we might say that amongst the pre-eminent medieval memory systems was Christ's Passion and the forms in which it was narrated: schemata like the Stations of the Cross and the *Via Dolorosa*, the Five Wounds of Christ, the Five Joys, Seven Sorrows and Fifteen Oos of the Virgin, the Instruments of the Passion, the Fifteen Tokens of the Doom. As Mary Carruthers writes about the fourth-century pilgrim Egeria, who visited the Holy Land,

> [t]he holy sites were embedded within liturgical processions, in which the pilgrims moved from site (and sight) to site across a correlated map grid made up from both topographical and calendrical features . . . Egeria's descriptions of the sites she visited are fully embedded within a liturgical journey which she enacted among them, with appropriate readings, hymns, and processions timed to visit the sites at the optimal moments . . . The narrative of the Bible as a whole was conceived as a 'way' among 'places' – in short, as a map.[11]

In such narratives the valorized pain of the Passion was ordered into a memorably painful set of images and moments. In the later Middle Ages, the idea of pilgrimage 'combined the traditional mnemonic practices of monastic *meditatio* with emphasis on a human Christ and his suffering' and 'demanded the visual and physical expression of piety through action and movement'.[12] Naturally, at the centre of these narratives was the unique and specific memory-site of Jerusalem and in particular Calvary/Golgotha, the scene of Christ's Passion, the principal place in which we find violently debased images of Jews within an affective spectacle of pain. In thus constructing one's own religious experience, biblical history was made into 'digestible' pieces of memorable moments, potent cues and emotive, affective fearful incidents, often 'using' the Jewish image within Christian devotional aesthetics. Jerusalem, encompassing Calvary and Golgotha, became familiar and omnipresent in the Latin Christian imagination as the site of Christ's Passion. To be experienced emotionally and remembered in personal terms, Jerusalem was effectively *remade* by European culture and figures repeatedly as the place one might imagine oneself to be to have an ardent and individuated experience of religious suffering.[13]

Jerusalem was, and remains so today, an inherently translatable idea, a set of images rather than a place, of 'remarkably generative . . . saturated sanctity'.[14] As Mary Carruthers has pithily suggested, medieval pilgrimage was imagined, represented and mediated as 'a map for remembering'; 'Calvary' did not refer to a place as such but rather a scene with a standard narrative and a specific cast of characters.[15] The landscape of Palestine became the Holy Land, both legible landscape and relic, which was made to accord with the biblical text. Walls, ruins and rocks were identified as key sites in Christ's life; 'all one had to do was to think of a text, and the authentic spot could be provided.'[16] As Carruthers observes, there was little concern with the city as 'an authentic, validated historical object'.[17] In particular, Jewish and Roman monuments were treated as if they were not there, as a Christian understanding of the landscape overlaid previous histories.[18] The large number of surviving medieval maps of Jerusalem show an over-determined and excessively *represented* place: from exegetical diagrams of the tabernacle to pilgrimage route-maps, such maps do not seek to show Jerusalem as a contemporary site; instead, they 'map' Jerusalem as a series of Christian holy sites, manifesting biblical places and times, and, not unlike a cartoon strip, form an image-text narrative with its own established schema.[19] The landscape of Jerusalem became a liturgical map too, through which the pilgrim or worshipper moved about to visit the holy places, with 'the topography of Jerusalem . . .

experienced liturgically as a historical narrative of the Passion'.[20] The fifteenth-century European pilgrim John Poloner called this the 'order of pilgrimage', detailing the number of steps from one site to another and the sequence in which sites should be approached.[21] The focus of this topography was the Church of the Holy Sepulchre, the round basilica which held the tomb at which the *anastasis* (resurrection) occurred, marking Christ's divinity, nearby the site of Calvary/ Golgotha, marking Christ's humanity.

This kind of 'map for remembering' inheres in the earliest pilgrims' itineraries: early accounts, such as Jerome's description of Paula's journey, conjoin a Christian landscape with intense emotional response:

> On entering the Tomb of the Resurrection she kissed the stone which the angel removed from the sepulchre door; then like a thirsty man who has waited long, and at last comes to water, she faithfully kissed the very shelf on which the Lord's body had lain. Her tears and lamentations there are known to all Jerusalem – or rather to the Lord himself to whom she was praying.[22]

Jerome emphasizes the authenticity of Paula's experience – 'the stone which the angel removed', 'the very shelf'. But the stone and the sepulchre allow Paula to transcend space and materiality to pray 'to the Lord himself'. This was also clearly a highly public performance of piety, both in the symbolic kissing and in the tears and lamentations broadcast 'to all Jerusalem'. Likewise, the sixth-century 'Piacenza Pilgrim' emphasizes the enactment of something both personal and formulaic when visiting Golgotha:

> In the courtyard of the basilica is a small room where they keep the Wood of the Cross. We venerated it with a kiss. The title is also there which they placed over the Lord's head, on which they wrote 'This is the King of the Jews'. This I have seen, and had it in my hand and kissed it. The Wood of the Cross comes from the nut-tree.[23]

To put oneself in the site of Christ's Passion was to revive not just the spirit of the Passion but its bloodied, actual, material whole, the most precious sites being those of Christ's greatest suffering.

Jerusalem as Schema: The Stasyons of Jerusalem

The Middle English poem *The Stasyons of Jersualem* provides a neat case-study of the ways in which Jerusalem was imagined as schematized and subject to memory, together with an aesthetic landscape of torture and empathy. In this way representations of Jerusalem and of Jews go hand in hand. The poem is a complaint ('mone', line 2) to God, describing, in the first person, 'the pilgrimeage that I have gone' (4).[24]

The poem describes the journey from Venice, 'a cité of grete renoune' (7), 'so rownd, riche & stoute' (13), via Cyprus and Emmaus to Jerusalem and other holy sites there. At Venice the pilgrim sees various saints' shrines: 'Seint Marke & seinte Nicholas' (17), 'Seinte Elyne, that fonde the cros' (19), 'seint Jeorge, oure lady knight' (20; i.e. the Virgin's knight), 'Seinte Paule, the first hermite that was' (23), saints Simeon (24), Lucy (27) and Christopher (31). The poem thus opens with the galaxy of saints, Christ's representatives of martyrdom, witnesses to the repeated conjunction of humanity, suffering and divinity. Even in Venice, the pilgrim-narrator tells us that he is rendered speechless on seeing St Christopher's relics:

> Fore ther is the *whyrlbone* of his kne,   *patella*
> And his *toth closyd* in crystall to se (33–4).   *tooth enclosed*

The pilgrim then moves on to Rhodes, where he sees many relics, including 'A crosse, made of the basyne suete / That oure lord wessch in hys postyllus fete' (47–8) (the sweet basin in which the lord washed the apostles' feet, citing John 13), and 'a thorne of the crowne/ That styked in hys hede aboune,/ That blomys euery gode-frydey' (52–4).

This is not a subtle or sophisticated poem, but it is clear that the poem moves from the post-figurations of Christ in his saints through relics of the life of Christ until it reaches the Holy Land, the *actuality* and scene of Christ's life – that is, the poem is structured as a return to the ongoing present of the past. The pilgrim visits Cyprus, and sees a chapel, 'Where seynte Kateryne was borne' (70), receiving many years' pardon for the visit. He then reaches Jaffa, and repeats the popular derivation of the port's name from Japhet, son of Noah (Genesis 5:31), and quickly reaches Emmaus, 'Theere Jhesu spake to Cleophas' (90, referring to Luke 24:18).

On seeing the walls of Jerusalem the pilgrim feels great joy. On taking his first step inside the city,

We were delivered of all oure sinne
And *reseyved* indulgens "*a pena & culpa*",[25]   *received*
And at other many places *mo* also.   *more*

(94–6)

So the pilgrim receives an indulgence in that place, as physical space
has spiritual consequences. In narrative terms, the poem gives the
game away pretty quickly: within its first 100 lines (of an 848-line
poem) the pious purpose of the pilgrimage, the gaining of an indulgence, has been realized. But this is to misunderstand the poem, for
the rest of it is about holy sites, enumerative stational veneration, the
emphasis of key moments of torture and pain. Throughout the poem,
there is almost no information about the contemporaneity of
Jerusalem, other than that the pilgrims simply stay in a hospital (a
Christian lodging-house), they are shown round by Saracens, and,
whilst locked overnight in the Holy Sepulchre, they sing the litany with
local clerks.

Instead, the poem explains and moralizes the holy sites: this
includes the pillar of the flagellation, ('a pylere/ Where-to was bond
hys body bare', line 130) and the 'prison of Christ' or Holy Prison (illus.
23), an apocryphal site, near the Holy Sepulchre, which became a popular pilgrimage location in the later Middle Ages. This tour around the
scenes of Christ's trials is followed by an extended, graphic account
of the Jews' attack on Christ:

We fond the *holys* in the stone   *holes*
There-in they *Joddyd* him onne the gronde   *stabbed*
And gave him many a blody wonde.   140
And ther they *spolyd* him of his clothys   *despoiled*
And swore his deth with grete *othes*,   *oaths*
And ther at the *dyfe* they *gane* pleye   *death, began*
Who schuld bere his clothys aweye.
And whene he sufferd all this scorne,   145
On his hede they sete a *crone* of thorne   *crown*
And after askyd him of that thinge
If that he were *Jues*' kinge.   *the Jews'*
Behind that is a *pylere* also   *pillar*
There that he sufferd *mekyll wo*:   *great woe* 150
They bonde his *hondys* & his fete   *hands*
And rollyd his body in the strete,

125

That erth & gravell onne the grounde
Hade filled full *ilke a wounde*;   *each wound*
And under an *auter* betwene the stones   *altar*   155
They made him crepe all at-ones.
When he was so sore *Ibonde*,   *fettered*
With ther fete they spurned him as a *hunde*,   *cur*
And he ley as a babe stille
And sufferd them to do ther wille.   160
                    (138–60)

So far, so rigidly conventional: key moments (not all of them canon-ical) of Christ's tortures are linked to sites/sights for the pilgrim. The poet gives us a graphic and sensational account of the Passion, merg-ing the 'then' of Christ's Passion with the 'now' afforded by the relics of his suffering. But the poem then moves into a different key:

All cristen kingys, with one assente
Fore godys *luffe* giffe this Jugemente: *love*
What cursyde Jue cum to youre ground,
Spurne ye his body as a hounde,
And, *bote* he wille 'mersy' crye,   *even though*   165
Honge him up on galow-tre,   *hang*
Fore-why thei dide him all this wo!   *Because*
                    (138–67)

The poet appeals in the present tense to 'crysten kyngys' – Christian kings – to spurn and persecute any Jew that comes into his territory, to mistreat a Jew 'as a hounde' as the Jews had spurned Christ 'as a hunde'. As well as being un-Christian in its sentiments of vengeance and lack of 'mersy', it asserts ongoing, contemporary Jewry into the poem. This is particularly hard to read in the context of late fif-teenth-century England where no Jew was likely to 'cum to youre ground'. The Jews thus interrupt the poem in two ways – first, in their painful and grotesque tortures of Christ, and second in their ongoing, present-tense diaspora, troubling lands ruled by Christian kings.[26]

The Stasyons of Jerusalem goes on to cover a wide range of holy sites, from the Mount of Olives to Bethphage. The route taken by the poem is conventional of the scenes of Christ's life, and mirrors that taken by pilgrims from all over Europe; moreover, the accounts are retrospective, and tell the audience what *happened* in the Bible in each of the places. The poem would allow a reader who had never visited the Holy Land to mimic, imaginatively, the pilgrimage. In the present context, there are two important points to be taken from the poem. First, that Jews provide a kind of typological fault-line in Christian history, both facilitating the Passion and asserting themselves as obstacles to Christian progression. Second, that, Jewry aside, there was almost no contemporary detail involved for medieval people when thinking about Jerusalem: the poem is, largely, a retrospective mental map of Christian sites. The stated aim of the poem, in its closing lines, is 'to teche a man the weye' (line 830). So a simple poem like this served to evoke the biblical landscape for medieval readers at home, whilst at the same time presenting the Passion, and its element of Jewish–Christian animosity, as an ongoing, Christ-like persecution.

One image from late medieval England speaks clearly for the proximity of the idea of Jerusalem to the idea of home. An image from the famous and unique manuscript of the Middle English poems *Pearl* and *Sir Gawain and the Green Knight* shows the dreamer in *Pearl* catching a glimpse of the Heavenly Jerusalem (illus. 23). This rudimentary Heavenly Jerusalem is represented by just three worldly motifs: the first, the round tower with its hexagonal crenellated top, with a window in the form of a crucifix, which suggests the Holy Sepulchre (in a relationship with polygonal, crenellated buildings which will become clear); second, the crenellated walls over which the Pearl-Maiden reaches; third, a timber-framed Heavenly Mansion, looking very much like an English manor-house, looms over the image. A river, the water of life, runs through the centre of the image, dividing the dreamer from the Pearl-Maiden. The first two elements, the polygonal Holy Sepulchre and the walled city's battlements, are the fundamental shorthand images in medieval culture for both worldly and heavenly Jerusalems (and are the same motifs used in the exterior of the Jerusalem Chamber at Westminster).

This particular version of Jerusalem diverges from the accompanying poem, for the Jerusalem described is the Heavenly Jerusalem of the apocalypse, the extraordinary vision of the lamb on Mount Zion with 144,000 virgins (*Pearl,* lines 865–76, quoting Revelation 14:1).[27] The built elements described in the poem's vision of New Jerusalem are the gates to the city and a jewel-encrusted tower which forms the city itself:

Wyth bantelez twelue on basyng boun,
Þe foundementez twelue of riche tenoun.

With twelve arches of masonry arranged on the foundations, the
twelve tiers of fine joinery. (lines 992–3)[28]

Twelve is a theme of the poem's imagery and form: the city is described
as being twelve furlongs long, and the poem, at 1212 lines, plays with
this dodecahedral structure.[29] This is the city as image, at once representing heaven and the idealized journey of the soul, the ideal city and
the ideal church or communion, and the poet makes it clear that this
is not the same as the earthly Jerusalem where Jesus was slain (line
805). But the polygonal building described in *Pearl* is important too
in suggesting a relationship with the *anastasis*, always depicted as a
polygonal tower by the city wall and often described as having twelve
main pillars. The artist, in depicting the Heavenly Jerusalem, relies on
a visual shorthand of the earthly wall and tower. The image barely accords with that depicted in the poem, and instead suggests the image
of Jerusalem from pilgrimage accounts and from self-referential
ideas of Jerusalem as home.[30]

The point I want to make most forcefully regarding poems like
The Stasyons of Jerusalem, *Pearl* and later medieval plans and maps of
Jerusalem is simply that such artefacts familiarize the city in logical
and easily learned Passional symbols and schema. Jerusalem was
reduced to key devotional *loci* (as in stational liturgy) and made concordant for Christian experience, an atavistic cue to Christ's Passion.[31]
In this way such images complement the replication of Judaism in
Western Europe in as much as they themselves thoroughly replicate
Western European ideas and ideals. Medieval Christian memory
remade places according to how they were to be best remembered,
rather than what they looked like and it did the same with Jews. The
'real' Jerusalem was inauthentic because it was not like the maps and
images and poems through which medieval people had memorized
and memorialized the Passion; maps, plans, replications of Jerusalem,
on the other hand, allowed for a pure site in which one could be persecuted *like Christ*, one could *feel* an aesthetic pain, one could be
edified through fantasies of fear, torture and persecution. In this way
this kind of Jerusalem literally sets the scene for us to reject a strictly
historicist reading of Christian–Jewish relations, which sees in an
image of violence the report or potential for actual violence, in order

23 The Heavenly Jerusalem, accompanying the poem *Pearl*. England, *c.* 1400. BL Cotton MS Nero A. X, f. 42v.

to rediscover, to recover, an aesthetic world in things are understood because they are felt.

In Prison with Christ

The 'Prison of Christ' shows one such 'invention' of violence. The Gospels are full of information about the ordeals to which Jesus was

subjected at Calvary; later 'apocryphal' Gospels and religious traditions added to these torments. What we do not know, however, is
where Jesus was held between the events of his Passion, and the Bible
never explicitly mentions his imprisonment. Nonetheless, in the later
Middle Ages 'The Prison of Christ' became a well-known site; one
can still visit the Prison, a quiet, dark chapel, with barred windows,
in a corner at the north of the Church of the Holy Sepulchre in
Jerusalem (illus. 24).

The Prison of Christ is a fake: it alludes to an apocryphal place
and the building dates from the eleventh century. Three further sites
vie with the Holy Sepulchre for the Prison: the Convent of the Sisters
of Zion in the Via Dolorosa; the 'House of Caiaphas' on Mount Zion;
and the 'Chapel of the Repose', which was identified in the Middle
Ages 'as the prison to which Jesus was taken after his arrest in Geth-
semane'.[32] Meanwhile, one can visit later Italian copies of the Prison,
at Bologna's 'Jerusalem' complex and at San Vivaldo ('la Gerusalemme di Toscana').

The Prison of Christ is a small chapel, but is probably on the site
of an ancient cistern or tomb, once separate from the Church of the
Holy Sepulchre itself.[33] From the ninth century, the Prison became
known as the place in which Christ was held as the Cross was prepared, eventually becoming a pilgrimage site in its own right (to this
day, the Prison retains a fundamental importance in Greek Orthodox
liturgy, in which it is the First Station of the Cross).[34] Such places
reflect an imaginative preference, characteristic of medieval spirituality, for particularizing and materializing the Passion, humanizing and
personalizing Christ's role in it, and focusing on the persecutory,
frightening and difficult nature of the religious landscape. In particular, the Prison allowed pilgrims to empathize individually with Christ's
status as victim, his assumption of human infirmity. The Prison is a
compact example of how medieval culture developed an additional
episode of Christ's suffering, specifically finding authority and power
in feeling persecuted.

Christ's imprisonment is first described in the Latin Gospel of
Nicodemus (or *Acta Pilati*), the 'apocryphal gospel' which greatly
increases the role of the Jews in the persecution and death of Christ,
effectively seeking to exonerate Pilate. The prison seems to have been
extrapolated from the story of the two thieves Dysmas and Gestas
and the imprisonment of Barabbas (Matthew 27:15–17). The Gospel
of Nicodemus states that Pilate 'commanded Jesus to be set apart'

24 The Prison of Christ, Church of the Holy Sepulchre, Jerusalem.

and he later removed to a 'place' with Dysmas and Gestas; here Jesus is stripped and crowned with thorns.[35] A prison is not explicitly mentioned. However, Pseudo-Bonaventure's *Meditations* (*c.* 1300) described 'a kind of prison . . . remains of which can still be seen', and the Middle English version of the Gospel of Nicodemus reports that the 'Jewes . . . put him in-to a stronge prisoun where no window nor light was in' (line 80), and a further northern European tradition described Jesus being plunging into two filthy privies there.[36] The imprisonment of Christ places him in a tradition of biblical and saintly prisoners (Daniel, Paul, John the Baptist, Margaret, Leonard, Roch), whilst, from Seneca to Malory via Boethius and Marco Polo, the idea of imprisonment was a powerful symbolic pose of grace in victimhood, and intellectual and spiritual development in adversity.[37] The medieval idea of imprisonment was not focused on exclusion but rather corrective punishment and redemption, a place of spiritual growth; indeed, Purgatory was itself described as a prison, and later medieval representations of Christ often show him in chains.[38] Following the establishment of the Crusader Kingdom of Jerusalem in 1099, the Prison of Christ rapidly gained recognition, providing pilgrims with a literal, material space in which to celebrate penal, edifying suffering.

Visitors' accounts of the Prison multiply from the mid-twelfth century, when it seems to have gained considerable status as a pilgrimage site. The Prison was probably (re)built in or around the 1140s, by settlers in the newly Christian kingdom; the site had been outside the Church, but at this point was brought into the main precinct, as the liminal place – a prison which was on the edge, unofficial – became established and recognized. The Prison in part functioned typologically, as indicated by a decorated Crusader-era Romanesque capital there, which shows the story of Daniel imprisoned in the lion's den;[39] the Prison of Christ comes to fulfil and surpass Hebrew scripture. Many pilgrims – such as Fetullus (visiting around 1130), al-Idrīsī (1154), John of Würzburg (c. 1160), Othmar (c. 1165), Thedoric (1172) and an anonymous Icelandic pilgrim – give only the barest details, some identifying it with the 'House of Pilate', others mentioning a small incised cross which served as a focus for prayer, some mentioning iron chains in which Christ was fettered. The Prison is a part of the late-medieval multiplication of semi-canonical *loci* (places) at the Holy Sepulchre, based around increasingly sensational moments of Christ's Passion – such as the altar at which the three nails of the Passion were forged, or the place where Jesus was stripped – as well as new, often apocryphal sites in the Crusader Kingdom (1099–1291). These included 'Condemnation' and 'Flagellation' chapels founded in Jerusalem, the thirteenth-century Church of St Mary of the Spasm (where Mary swooned at seeing her son carrying the Cross), and the pilgrimage site of St Mary in the Marshes, near Caesarea, where the exhausted Virgin Mary putatively rested amongst crocodile-infested marshes.[40] The Crusaders' short-lived territorial gains, followed by the Franciscans' successful establishment of a pilgrimage industry in the fourteenth century, were accompanied by the proliferation of aesthetic sites of vulnerability: conquest and expansion veiled as, or even experienced as, victimhood. The Seigneur de Caumont, a French pilgrim travelling in 1419, visited 'all' the sites at which Jesus was treated 'so cruelly' by 'the false Jews'; however, Caumont also tartly described the Holy Sepulchre as 'almost full of Saracens', as Christ's vulnerability amongst the Jews shades into Caumont's amongst the Saracens.[41]

John of Würzburg, a twelfth-century visitor, was unsure of the Prison's authenticity:

> while the rock was being prepared to receive the Cross, our Lord was kept bound as it were in prison in a certain place which

there was in the fields, which place is now formed into a chapel, and is to this day called 'The Prison of the Lord', and is exactly opposite to Calvary, in the left-hand apse of the church. Others, however, have other opinions about this place, as I heard on the spot.[42]

John's description of his visit is underwhelming, with the pilgrims grumbling about the sanctity of the place. Moreover, his account suggests a tension between sites learned about at home, from books, and the 'on the spot' experience of these sites.

The Prison of Christ remained on the itinerary for late medieval pilgrims and indeed came into its own in the affective, somatic devotional habits of the later period, particularly those fostered by the Franciscans which focused on penitential suffering. The author of the *Stasyons of Jerusalem* includes the Prison in his account of Jerusalem, stating that this is where Christ was held whilst the Cross was being made:

Than *kepyd* thei him in presone stille,	*kept*
To the crosse was ordeynd at *ther* wille.	*their*
That presone is *hold* a welle of grace	*held to be*
Fore all that comys in that place,	
And it is callyd of olde & *yenge*	*young*
The prisone of oure heven kinge.	
(171–6)	

The idea of a 'prison' for a king, a penitentiary that was also a well of grace, evidently held great appeal in later medieval religious culture which so highly valued abjection and debasement. Felix Fabri, an ebullient fifteenth-century German Dominican pilgrim visiting in the early 1480s, gives a vivid description of his visit which is worth quoting at length:

we went on our way singing in procession, and entered a darksome chapel hewn out of the rock, which has no windows, but contains one altar within it, and has two small doors. This chapel in the time of Christ was a prison or lock-up near the Mount Calvary, built to the intent that condemned criminals appointed to die might be locked up therein while the instruments of their torture were being made ready, such as crosses, gallows, wheels, wood for fires, and the like, and also that they might drink and make themselves drunk therein, for it was the custom that those who were to be punished with death should first be made drunk with the strongest wine, that they might fear death less, and endure their torments with greater courage: so that they might drink the more deeply, they were shut in here with wine, that they might do so without shame. Wherefore when the Lord Jesus was brought out hither with His cross, they shut Him up in this cell, while the three holes were being made in the rock of Calvary for the three crosses, that in the meantime He might drink. They gave the Lord 'wine mingled with myrrh' [Mark 15:23], which was exceeding bitter, wherefore He refused the proffered drink, as we are told in the same passage.

In this venerable cell we reflected, not without sorrow, how the Lord Jesus wept therein, and awaited the torture of the Cross with *equal dread and desire*. We therefore entered it one by one, with sighs and groans, and each in turn bowed himself to the earth, and kissed the footprints of our Saviour, and there we received indulgences.[43]

Fabri's account shows how a rich set of rituals and beliefs had developed around the Prison, how it had become a full, indeed 'venerable', part of the pilgrims' emotional and religious experience (and, possibly, gave pilgrims an excuse for their frequent drunkenness!). But, more than this, Fabri's joining together of 'dread' with 'desire' is utterly in keeping with the persecutory aesthetic through which a memory – of Christ's imprisonment – was literally invented. The pilgrims entered the prison 'one by one' in an individualized but highly formal *imitatio Christi*, in which they placed themselves in a literal, constructed and idealized memory-event. The 'sighs and groans' of the pained, imperilled pilgrim give way to the receiving of an indulgence, a remission from sin. By Fabri's time, the sacrament of penance was well established, especially amongst the Franciscans, with their focus on contrite penitential *acts*, who controlled the Jerusalem pilgrimage industry. The Prison of Christ, effectively building on the sense that the Crucifixion involved a shameful penal incident between Christ and the Jews added to the self-authorizing image of prison and fortitude in the face of injustice, acted as a powerful stage for a performative act of contrition.

At Ramle: Pilgrimage as Persecution

Following Chaucer's Canterbury pilgrims it would be easy to portray medieval pilgrimage as a kind of early version of the contemporary package-holiday and visits to a theme-park:[44] 'cattle-class' travel, all-inclusive, familiar places crowded with people from home, the menus and itineraries geared to tourists, annoying companions drawn from different social classes, excessive alcohol, regrettable sexual encounters, perplexing foreigners hawking souvenirs. 'Popular' pilgrimages came to rely less on contemplation and more on gaining indulgences, relics and souvenirs.[45] However, beyond this characterization, much medieval travel was defined by friction, persecution and aggression. On the one hand, pilgrimage-related travel stemmed from the wars of faith and territory of the Crusades; later medieval Christian pilgrims to Palestine would have seen signs of the Crusaders' defeat all around them, as at Jaffa and Ramle, and can perhaps be connected to a much bigger connection between tourism and terrorism which has reached its zenith in our own day.[46] Moreover, medieval pilgrimage was increasingly used as an instrument of justice and punishment and for individual penance, with pilgrimages ordered for serious crimes; indeed, Henry iv's plans for a penitential journey to Jerusalem, and his failure to make the journey, must be seen in the light of the murder of Richard ii for which Henry felt responsible. Compulsory pilgrimages were imposed on murderers, making the criminal atone whilst benefitting the deceased soul.[47] Physical pilgrimage alone did not provide salvation: one had to make an internal, spiritual pilgrimage too.[48] Pilgrimage gave remission from sin, but was arduous, uncomfortable and risky; we should see no contradiction in a journey to Jerusalem being at once a leisure activity and a form of punishment, both pleasure and pain, as this is representative of medieval religious aesthetics, in which self-sacrifice and auto-abnegation were amongst the most valorized forms of pious activity: for both the voluntary and penitential pilgrim, as for the martyr, 'pain [is] the condition that will bring about future pleasure'.[49]

The medieval pilgrim's experience of Palestine was exceptionally formulaic: the routes were predetermined, the most popular being sailing to Jaffa (also known as Port of Jerusalem), with a short stay at the town of Ramle (Ramlah), followed by a trip to Emmaus, then to Jerusalem. The culmination of the journey was, for most pilgrims, to visit to the Church of the Holy Sepulchre in Jerusalem,

25 Crucifix graffiti left by pilgrims, Church of the Holy Sepulchre, Jerusalem.

where, as described in *The Stasyons of Jerusalem*, pilgrims usually spent several nights locked inside the Church and where they could engage with a variety of material artefacts (some more apocryphal than others) associated with the death of Christ: they could touch the rock of Golgotha, kiss the Slab of Unction, see Christ's tomb, enter the Prison of Christ, and visit the Chapel of St Helena. It was at this last place where pilgrims carved a small crucifix into the wall (see illus. 25), joining Helena – the first Jerusalem pilgrim as well as the first Christian archaeologist – in an affective relationship of place and spirituality. The crosses – Maltese or Amalfi crosses of the Crusaders, Coptic ankh crosses, saltires, three-bar Slavonic crosses, Tau crosses like that usually held by St Helena – celebrate, within the fabric of the building, the pilgrim's presence and, through etching, the pilgrim leaves their mark on the sacred landscape. Just as the crucifix is a sign of Calvary, pilgrims brought their sign *back* to Calvary: each cross marks the pilgrim's own private Calvary in the site of Christ's Passion and Helena's discovery of it.

With the expansion of pilgrimage under Franciscan auspices within the Mameluk state came regulation, the 'discipline and authorization of movement', 'surveillance and control', and, inevitably, a greater focus on 'radical transgressions directed against that very logic of regulation':[50] tour guides, limits on movement, the control of where pilgrims could stay. At all times the Western pilgrims were expected to carry a *bulletta*, a letter of introduction and paper of safe passage.[51] On arrival at Jaffa, with its treacherous rocky harbour, the pilgrims would have not seen an inspirational biblical landscape but rather fortified buildings, mostly falling into decay and ruin; writing in 1419 the French pilgrim de Caumont noted on his arrival at Jaffa how 'in times past the said city was conquered for the Christians and destroyed; at the present time nobody lives there', and he describes how his party had to wait until a friar, a 'consol', came to give them safe passage past the 'sarrazins' and miscreants.[52] By Jaffa, many pilgrims had already succumbed to the rigours of the journey; accounts of pilgrims' deaths at Candia (Heraklion), the Venetian port on Crete, and Ramle are particularly common.[53] The pilgrims would have travelled from Jaffa to the major pilgrimage hostel at Ramle which was, for most pilgrims, the first place of rest after the long sea-voyage through the Mediterranean. But Ramle was, paradoxically, an emphatically non-Christian place. Founded by Arabs in the eighth century, Ramle had no authentic connection with biblical, Christian or Christological history; moreover, its enormous, barn-like twelfth-century Crusader cathedral or parish church at the centre of the town

26 The mosque at Ramle (Israel), formerly a Crusader-era church.

had been turned, in the thirteenth century, into a mosque (see illus. 26).[54] The magnificent thirteenth-century White Mosque at Ramle, with its huge tower (showing the clear influence of Western architectural styles), dominated, as it does now, the town's skyline. Later medieval Ramle was a wealthy and cosmopolitan place, a centre for the spice industry and the capital of the Filastin district, but it was also a place where the superfluity and redundancy of Christianity was etched in every part of the town's aspect. In the pilgrims' hostel in Ramle, run by the Franciscans, the pilgrims were told exactly what hazards they faced from the locals, and what rules they must obey.

Felix Fabri made two journeys to the Holy Land: the first was a disappointment, full of diversions and obstacles. He returned to Germany, read widely to prepare for his return; on his second trip, he largely avoided apocryphal sites, and focused instead on visiting the Temple and the Holy Sepulchre.[55] The chronology of Fabri's journeys shows him turning from his experience of an actual place back to books in order to find a more rewarding Jerusalem. Travelling from Jaffa to Ramle Fabri's group was met three times by hostile Arabs, who did not intend violence 'but secretly joined our host by the side of the pilgrims, and tried to steal scrips, clothes, and the like'.[56] Fabri reports that 'had we not travelled with so great a force, they would have fallen upon us and beaten us with stones, sticks and staves, as often befalls pilgrims'.[57] Likewise, Bertrandon de la Brocquière, travelling in 1432, describes how he was ill and cared for in Gaza by a kindly Arab; here, he was laid on a mattress and massaged. 'During this time', he says,

> no one did me the least harm, nor took any thing from me. It would, however, have been very easy for them to do so; and I must have been tempting prey for I had with me two hundred ducats, and two camels, laden with provision and wine.[58]

Whilst he was unwell, de la Brocquière's pilgrim-companions left him for Jerusalem – but another kindly stranger, a Sicilian Jew, sets him on the route again. Both Fabri and de la Brocquière describe an intuition, rather than an actuality, of persecution.

Fabri and his group reached Ramle but could enter only by dark, because 'the infidels' would not let Christians enter their cities on beasts; here, the pilgrims rented mats to put on the bare ground, there being no other facilities apart from empty chambers. Fabri reports that then the 'Father Guardian' of the pilgrims' hostel gave a 'beautiful sermon in Latin', the contents of which are not included in Fabri's account. Instead, Fabri describes in great detail the various rules of the Holy Places. These include injunctions that 'no pilgrim ought to wander alone about the holy places without a Saracen guide, because this is dangerous and unsafe'; that 'the pilgrim should beware of stepping over the sepulchres of the Saracens, because they are greatly vexed when they see this done, and pelt with stones anyone who steps over them'; that 'chipping off fragments from the holy sepulchre, and from the buildings at other places, and spoiling the hewn stones thereof … is forbidden under pain of excommunication'; that 'pilgrims must beware of laughing together as they walk about Jerusalem to see the holy places, but they must be grave and devout'; that 'the pilgrims [should] beware of gazing upon any women whom they may meet, because all Saracens are exceedingly jealous'; and that 'every pilgrim beware of giving a Saracen wine when he asks for drink, whether on the roadside or elsewhere, because straightaway after one single draught thereof he becomes mad, and the first man who he attacks is the pilgrim who gave it him.'[59] Whilst at Ramle, Fabri ventures into buying food from 'Saracens, Jews, Heretics, and Eastern Christians' and goes to a hot bath, bathing with Saracens.[60] Throughout, Fabri's account suggests very strongly the limits, dangers, extortions and disappointments of the Holy Land, especially the 'vexatious tricks' of the Saracens who accompany him everywhere.[61]

Likewise, the disappointment and frustration of arrival in the Holy Land is clear in other late medieval pilgrims' accounts. William Wey (d. 1476) of Eton College describes spending his first night of his 1462 journey to the Holy Land in a cave under Jaffa, and the subsequent two nights sleeping on the ground at Ramle (which he calls Ram, Ramath, Ramys and Ramatha); as Wey and his party entered Jerusalem, he says children threw stones at them, a painful inversion of Christ's triumphant entry into the city.[62] Anselmo Adorno, from Bruges, said of his 1471 journey that he lacked every necessity and that staying in Ramle was like being in prison.[63] Richard Torkington, writing in 1517, describes the 'stynking Stable grounde' on which the pilgrims were made to sleep, as they were 'ryght evyll intretyd by the seyd Turkes'; Torkington notes, characteristically laconically, that 'This Jaff[a] was sumtyme a grett citee, as it appereth by the Ruyne of the same, but nowe ther standeth never an howse but oonly ıı towers.'[64] Torkington visits the site of St George's martyrdom, but draws our attention too to the privations of the pilgrimage hostel at Ramle, 'bar walles and bar florethes' (bare walls and bare floors), with 'feinyd Cristen Peple of Sonndry Sectis' selling food – boiled eggs, grapes, apples – and hiring out mats for sleeping.[65] Such journeys were neither transcendent nor peaceful, but the presence of 'feinyd Cristen Peple of Sonndry Sectis', presumably Eastern Orthodox Christians, does imply the spiritual authority of Torkington's own Christian pilgrimage. The privations of the journey did not deter pilgrims: the harsh conditions could parallel Christ's ordeals which the pilgrims were ardently, and painfully, re-enacting. Several accounts record how, whilst horses and camels were offered, many pilgrims preferred to walk barefoot, suffering as had Christ.[66]

The difficulties of travelling in Mameluk Palestine perhaps led to another transformation, which occurred in the cases of both Jaffa and Ramle: a kind of 're-historicization', in which the landscape was made concordant with Christian sacred (invented) traditions.[67] Both Jaffa and Ramle were manufactured through the pilgrims' aesthetic memory, often at odds with the less-than-dignified surroundings in which the pilgrims found themselves. Thus the port of Jaffa was etymologically linked with Noah's son Japhet; the House of Simon the Tanner and Tabitha (Acts 9:36) was identified there and became a pilgrimage site in itself. The Friars Minor established at Jaffa a tradition that it had been the home of SS Peter, Paul and Andrew and the site of St James's execution.[68] At Ramle, meanwhile, the town was identified as the home of Joseph of Arimathea and relics of St George became a popular attraction.[69] Mandeville's *Travels* (*c.* 1365) claim that near Ramle 'is a fair chirche of oure lady wheyre oure lorde schewyed him to here in thre liknes that bytokenyde the trinité'.[70] The Seigneur de Caumont describes Ramle as a merchant town, but notes that it was the birthplace of the early Christian martyr St Martial, whose head Caumont had worshipped in a reliquary at Limoges; Caumont then describes the 'false dogs', the Saracens, who mar his trip to Lydda.[71] The nearby town of Lydda, identified as the site of St George's martyrdom, made for a religious, rather than practical, stopping-off point on the way to Jerusalem (or, rather, the practical stopping-off point of Ramle was made into a religious one at Lydda). Anselmo Adorno records how, at Lydda, he went with his pilgrimage group to see the site of St George's martyrdom, but found only a ruined church ('ecclesia rupta'); the journey became even less spiritually rewarding as, on the way back to Ramle, Adorno was attacked by two Arabs.[72] The Jewish traveller Benjamin of Tudela (*fl.* 1159–73) also visited Ramle and claimed it, equally erroneously, as a Jewish historical site.[73] Meshullam of Volterra, travelling in 1481, was sure that Ramle was a post-biblical city, but notes how sacred traditions were invented for it:

> Several persons have assured me that Ramleh was Modin; others maintain that it is Timna. In one author I have found that this city is called Palestine, in another writer that its name is Rama. God alone knows what the truth of the matter is.[74]

Medieval pilgrims travelled as anachronists, making a journey of feeling and memory, not of fact. The layering of sites like Jaffa and Ramle with new spiritual associations shows how more anecdotal and personalized religious sites were made to mediate the pilgrims' experience. Such sites also articulate powerfully the changing nature of sacral landscape: like any product of the imagination, they underwent transformations, mutating with new details and characters: ostensibly places of the past, sites like Jaffa and Ramle were very much places of the pilgrimage's present. But, perhaps most importantly, these places show how pilgrims travelled to Palestine not only for an experience of the authentic *via crucis* but for a journey which brought and developed Latin religion and Western European devotional culture, especially concerning the saints, to Palestine.

CHAPTER 6

Making Calvary

Suppose they came along one morning and said 'Right! To-day we're
going to crucify you!' It would come as a shock, to say the least; and
particularly if they had already set up a brand new wooden cross, hand-
made, in your back garden, and had the hammers and high quality nails
ready, no expense spared, to do the thing in style. After the first numbness
of the shock, who would be able to resist shouting and screaming,
completely hysterical or even technically mad?
Gavin Ewart, 'Crucifixion'

St Helena and Memories of Persecution

Suffering and persecution were made material as a physical site in
which pain could be remembered and re-experienced: Jerusalem and,
especially, Calvary. The earthly Jerusalem, the Jerusalem of the biblical past, the Heavenly Jerusalem and the New Jerusalem were not
thought of as entirely separate, or identical: Jerusalem was a shifting
signifier, from the historical, regal and political site, Jewish and
Roman, of the Old Testament and Christ's Passion to the apocalyptic
Jerusalem, 'coming down out of heaven from God, prepared as a
bride adorned for her husband' (Apocalypse [Revelation] 21:2–10).
The literal, physical site of Jerusalem was exceptionally important to
the Western European view of the world – seen most egregiously in
the Crusades and the foundation of the Latin kingdom of Jerusalem
and then in pilgrimage, which proliferated in the later Middle Ages.
The monastic idea of Jerusalem, however, conceptualized two Jerusalems: the Jerusalem above, the Heavenly City, and the Jerusalem
below, that is the monastic life and the monastery or church itself: 'As
the holy soul strives to return to God, it travels to Jerusalem, the
beginning and end of the quest for God'.[1]

The foundation of the remaking of Jerusalem, configured around
valorized suffering and mnemonic geography, is the Jerusalem of St
Helena of Constantinople (*c.* 250 – *c.* 330), mother of Constantine the
Great. Helena was celebrated throughout the Middle Ages for finding the True Cross on which Christ was crucified and for locating the
holy sites (*loci sancti*) of the Passion; in particular, the Church of the
Holy Sepulchre was built at the places identified by Helena. Helena's
inventio – both discovery, 'bringing into view', and also the term for

textual and imaginative composition – of the True Cross provided the stimulus for a range of remade Calvary landscapes in Western Europe.

Helena returned home with a range of relics which went on to be the centrepiece of the church at Santa Croce in Gerusalemme, Rome.[2] Throughout the Middle Ages, pieces of the True Cross multiplied, with fragments enshrined and worshipped across Europe; following the sack of Constantinople in 1204, yet more relics of the True Cross came into the western European devotional arena.[3] The wood of doors, beams and splinters said to be from the True Cross was used in church decoration.[4] More intimately, fragments of the True Cross became multiplied as miracle-working jewellery and pilgrimage souvenirs.[5] Little pewter *ampullae* (souvenir bottles) of 'oil of the wood of life' – oil which had touched the True Cross – were widespread in the Mediterranean from the sixth century and glass pilgrims' vessels circulated even earlier.[6] Such souvenirs featured schematic images of the holy places, at once indicating divinity and the specific places and buildings of Christ's human and earthly suffering.

Not only did Helena invest enormous spiritual power in specific places and things – pieces of stone, bits of wood, fragments which demonstrated the actuality and humanity of Christ – but she herself became a sainted symbol of Christian duration, conquest and conversion. The story of her finding and identifying the holy sites suggested a making authentic, in place and object, of the spiritual message of the Passion and Resurrection as souvenirs proliferated throughout Europe. Susan Stewart, in her discussion of souvenirs, suggests that the souvenir is an 'authenticating sign of origin', 'external experience internalized'; Stewart rightly observes that 'the closing pitch of the freak show is often manifested by the souvenir', a comment as relevant to the Middle Ages and its culture of gory relics as to the twentieth century.[7] Souvenirs may be seen to represent an authenticity which is always past, foreign and therefore lost and, paradoxically, inauthentic;[8] likewise, '[a] relic is a sign of previous power, real or imagined. It promises to put that power back to work. A relic is a fragment that evokes a lost fullness.'[9] Such a 'lost fullness' eloquently describes that Christian interrelationship with Jews and Judaism, oscillating between desire and repudiation, past foundations and present rejection, and speaks incisively for medieval Christianity's relationship with Jerusalem, at once intimate and lost.

The legend of St Helena took for granted that the holy sites had been correctly identified;[10] what the legend makes clear, however, is that the ownership and *belief* in these sites was an ongoing encounter with conquest, conversion and violence. In particular, the medieval legend of St Helena foregrounded Jewish hostility to Helena's mission, for the medieval legend made her central miracle the conversion of Jerusalem's Jews, in particular a significantly named Judas who was hostile, then converted, and eventually assisted Helena in finding and identifying the True Cross. The legend of Judas the Jew (sometimes called Judas Cyriacus) spread throughout medieval Christendom in the *Acta Cyriaci*, developed from Eastern Christian sources of the fifth century.[11] The legend circulated in the early Middle Ages in Syriac, Greek and Latin and Helena's story appears in the early ninth-century Anglo-Saxon poem *Elene* by Cynewulf.[12] It was repeated in widespread accounts by Gregory of Tours (sixth century) and by Jacobus de Voragine (*fl.* 1261–6) in his *Golden Legend*, which in turn supplied the template for Piero della Francesca's famous frescoes of the *Legend of the True Cross* in the church of San Francesco in Arezzo.[13]

The basic story is as follows: Helena, upon arriving in Jerusalem, gathers 3,000 Jews of the city. She reproaches them for their lack of faith and their blindness and demands of them a learned representative who can help her in her researches. Five hundred Jews are produced who have a good knowledge of the Law, but they are again reproved by Helena for their lack of Christian faith. The Jews are confused by Helena, but one of them, Judas (in later Latin texts, described as brother to St Stephen), discerns that she is searching for the True Cross.[14] Judas retells a story he had been told by his father that once the True Cross had been asked for, its whereabouts should be disclosed. Judas goes to Helena and tells her various lies, for which he is thrown by Helena into a well for seven days (and threatened with other tortures). On the seventh day in the well, Judas agrees to show Helena the True Cross. Having been led by Judas to Calvary, Helena digs and finds three crosses. Helena prays to God that the True Cross be revealed. The three crosses are taken to Jerusalem, and a dead or sick man placed against each of them. On touching the third cross, the dead man is revived: Helena knows that she has found the True Cross. Judas converts from Judaism to Christianity, takes the name Cyriacus, and, eventually, becomes bishop of Jerusalem. Helena establishes a church on the spot where the Cross was found, puts the True Cross in a reliquary, expels the Jews from Jerusalem and Judea and orders that the Invention of the

True Cross be celebrated on 3 May. Judas Cyriacus subsequently finds the nails that were hammered into Christ's hands; the nails are then used to make a bridle for Constantine's horse, fulfilling the prophecy of Zacharias 14:20: 'In that day that which is upon the bridle of the horse shall be holy to the Lord.'

This fanciful, exemplary narrative casts Helena as intrepid, lone explorer, facing a hostile, threatening community of Jews. The narrative uses the Jews and their dogged and obstructive presence to make Helena's journey into both a quest and a battle of faith. Like Christ, Helena is in Jerusalem alone amongst Jews, hindered and persecuted. Like Christ, Helena triumphs over Judaism at Calvary. Unlike Christ, however, Helena can persecute back: throughout the narrative she argues that the Jews are blind, she extracts the location of the Cross from Judas through a trial by ordeal, and, at the end of the story, the Jews disappear as Jews – either through conversion (Judas) or expulsion (the other Jews). The Anglo-Saxon poem *Elene* makes anachronism and violence the defining motifs of Helena's enterprise: the poem merges Helena's journey with Roman, Hun, Frankish and Viking conquests. Her sea journey to Palestine resonates with Anglo-Saxon and Viking seafaring and, on reaching Palestine, Helena performs the role of warrior-queen as the diction of Helena's conquest transplants that of Christ's passive martyrdom: here Helena is a battle-queen commanding her troops, come to rule over the Jewish kingdom with might and force.[15]

The story of Helena and Judas Cyriacus became very popular in Byzantine and late medieval Western European culture, veiling acquisition and expansion in pious terms of victimhood and hostility. Santo Toribio de Liébana (Spain) became a significant pilgrimage centre on account of its *Lignum Crucis*; a piece of the Cross, acquired in 1241, was one of the relics for which the Sainte-Chapelle in Paris was built (consecrated 1248). The Benedictines of Hautvillers, near Reims, claimed Helena's body, as relic-hunter became relic; in 1095 the corpse was translated into the abbey, which became a pilgrimage centre where miracles were performed.[16] St Helena became an exceptionally popular saint in northern Europe, in England in particular. She was usually represented as an empress holding a crucifix, but she was also commonly shown with Judas. One fifteenth-century Italian image of Helena and Judas (illus. 27) is broadly representative of the western European iconographic tradition. This image shows Helena, clad in a blue shift possibly to recall the Virgin Mary, and her female

27 St Helena, Cyriacus and the True Cross. Italy, fifteenth century. BL Add.
MS 30038, f. 237r.

assistant watching over the moment of the revelation of the crosses.
Judas stands next to the Christian women, gesturing to the place
where the crosses have been hidden. Judas is emphatically represented
in a different register, as a Jew: not only in profile, bearded, sunken-
eyed and altogether drab (as opposed to the bright red of Helena's
gown and blue of her assistant), but also short and marginal. In fact,
within the figures of Judas and Helena are articulated the contrast

146

between old and new laws, the false way and the True Way, in much the same vein as in images of Ecclesia and Synagoga.

Such images, which alert the medieval Christian to the discovery of the True Cross, emphasize the difficult but successful foundation of Helena's Jerusalem and with it the proof of Christianity's supersession of both Judaism and Jewish space. The elaboration of the story of Judas the Jew within the legend of St Helena signals the central trend of the artefacts studied in this book: that medieval Christians repeatedly subjected their most cherished and fundamental symbols and bodies to a symbolic, imagined assault from Jewry. A further strand of the story, the *Exultatio crucis*, placed the Cross under another non-Christian assault, that of the Persians.[17] Helena's story, and the masses and feasts associated with it, celebrated the fiction of the precarious establishment of Christianity, revealing the importance of the Jews' active antagonism within this founding myth, just as saints' lives imagined a dissident, minority Christianity forever under the threat of martyrdom. The Christian relic of the True Cross was celebrated at the same time as it was doubted, the triumph of the relic being not its actuality but its possession in the face of rival claimants and disbelievers. Perhaps we should see the elaboration of the myth of St Helena as the passage of the True Cross from relic (literally, a vestige or remainder) to souvenir (something remembered): the difficulty of identifying and owning the True Cross in the legend of St Helena is mirrored in the late medieval desire to remember, through active and painful confrontation, the process of Passion, foundation and authentic possession.

In terms of more intimate and domestic memory, there are at least forty-three holy wells in the British Isles alone that are dedicated to St Helena (or Helen/Elen), clearly referring to the well in which Judas was tortured.[18] In these wells we encounter the first of many physical replicas of Jerusalem and especially Calvary which would have been familiar and practical in the daily lives of many medieval people. Helena was the most popular non-biblical dedicatee of English holy wells and devotion at these wells, which often took the form of an offering of linen or ribbon, is attested into the nineteenth century. Each of these wells of St Helena – fecund with multivalent images of Jewish well-poisoning, baptism and ascension as well as to the story of Judas – domesticates and memorializes Helena's persecution and defeat of Judas Cyriacus in Jerusalem. At wells dedicated to Helena at Brindle (Lancashire) and Sefton (Lancashire), a popular

28 St Helen's well, Rushton Spencer (Staffordshire).

custom was the throwing of a bent pin into the well (a pagan symbol of attack) whilst saying an *ave*.[19] The well dedicated to St Helen at Stainland (Yorkshire), established as a holy site by the 1270s, had a chapel attached to it, and a large stone known as 'The Cross' lodged in its walls.[20] At St Helen's well at Gargrave (Yorkshire), ribbons were left and the water was thought to be a cure for sore and weak eyes, possibly recalling Helena's success at making Judas perceive correctly.[21] The wells of St Helena demonstrate the intense popularity of her story but, more than this, they demonstrate how the *sentiment* of Jerusalem could be copied and translated into local and personal surroundings. In the medieval hamlet of Rushton Spencer (Staffordshire) St Helen's well (illus. 28), recalling Calvary on a green hill outside the village, was the focus of a procession each St Helen's Day.[22] Similarly, at the town of Beverley (Yorkshire) the Guild of St Helena [Elene] performed a kind of dumb-show of the finding of the cross each year:

> a fair youth, the fairest they can find, is picked out, and is clad
> as a queen, like to St Elene [i.e. Helena]. And an old man goes

before this youth, carrying a cross, and another old man carrying a shovel, in token of the finding of the Holy Cross.[23]

At Beverley the townspeople re-enacted this story of origins, apparently with local old men playing Judas Cyriacus and the Jerusalem-
mite excavator. Throughout Europe pilgrimage badges of the True
Cross are common, bearing legends such as 'Hail, O Cross Our Only
Hope' or 'By the wood of the Cross we are saved', as the Cross proved
remarkably mobile.

The story of St Helena was subjected to a further turn, and a further domesticization, in that later medieval English culture named
and claimed her as an English or British-born saint. An invention of
imaginative histories, the *Historia anglorum* by Henry of Huntingdon (*c.* 1088–*c.* 1157) and *Historia regum Britanniae* of Geoffrey of
Monmouth (d. 1154–5), this Helena was claimed as the daughter of
'old' King Coel of Colchester (the city of which she remains patron
saint).[24] This legend, which attempts to knit English history with that
of Jerusalem, is obviously an apocryphal one, but it does signal the
ways in which Helena was useful in supplanting non-Christian beliefs
and sites. St Helen's well at Burnsall (Yorkshire) had been a pagan
pre-Christian site, and, even though formally rededicated to Helena,
remained known as Thor's Well. Likewise, several important pagan
sites and buildings seem to have been dedicated, after the Norman
Conquest of 1066, to St Helena (as at St Helen's-on-the-Walls, York,
and St Helen's, Colchester, both of which were important Roman
buildings).[25] In sum, St Helena was a particularly appropriate saint of
conquest and re-dedicatory supersession, her legend calling to mind
both the elimination of non-Christians and the original struggle of
Christian foundation.

Calvary in Norfolk

Medieval Europe could boast many replicas and versions of Jerusalem. Perhaps the best known of such copies of Jerusalem's Holy
Sepulchre are the round Templar churches (built by the military
orders of the Knights Templar and the Knights Hospitaller), said to
be modelled on the rotunda of the *anastasis* ('resurrection'),
believed to have been the site of Calvary and of Christ's burial.[26]
However, many early and non-Templar examples of copies of the
anastasis existed across Europe, built between the eighth and twelfth

centuries, from Italy to Orkney. These churches and chapels were distinctively circular/polygonal in plan, usually eight- or twelve-sided, and can be seen as 'analogous in concept to the smaller, portable pilgrims' souvenirs' like *ampullae*, relics, maps and plans.[27] In one case, at Bologna, a wide-ranging complex was laid out to resemble not just the Holy Sepulchre but also the entire city of Jerusalem, with monuments *in similitudine* (simulation) such as the column of the flagellation of Christ, the site of the Annunciation, the Mount of Olives and the Field of Haceldama.[28] Several further European pilgrimage churches were laid out as copies of the Holy Sepulchre, again independent of the Templars: at Cambrai and Piacenza, Holy Sepulchre chapels were constructed explicitly for those unable to visit the Holy Land, whilst those visiting the church of San Sepolcro in Milan 'received an indulgence equivalent to one-third of that given for visiting Jerusalem'.[29] The Templars' circular replicas of the *anastasis* are thus part of a wide-ranging tradition of simulated Jerusalems: this was a kind of 'centrifugal' Jerusalem, an image taken by the travellers and Crusaders and spread throughout the Christian world. Indeed, at Chastiau Pélerin ('Atlit) and Safed (Tzfat) in the Holy Land, near to Jerusalem, the Templars built polygonal churches in imitation of the Holy Sepulchre, probably in 'response to the loss of the Templar headquarters at Jerusalem'.[30] There can be little doubt that the Crusades, from the late eleventh century, and the Templars in particular, were in part responsible for this multiplication of representations of the Holy Sepulchre. But, in particular in the context of the later medieval development of lay piety, these buildings were meaningful too in other ways: sometimes as the results of pilgrimages to Jerusalem, sometimes as replacements or proxies for pilgrimages to Jerusalem, sometimes as appropriate homes for relics from Jerusalem, and sometimes as the setting for liturgical or devotional ceremonies, especially at Easter, in which a copied 'Jerusalem' and Calvary set the stage. In all such buildings, we must acknowledge not just an architectural or stylistic copy of Jerusalem but also an aesthetic Jerusalem which knitted conflict, conquest, empathy and devotion.

Later Jerusalem replications survive in the northern Italian *sacri monti*, Calvary theme-parks in which the devout could imitate the route of Christ through an aesthetic, replica landscape. Such sites became popular from the later fifteenth century, with the ambitious project at Varallo begun in 1480.[31] These *sacri monti* or *monti di pietà*

29 Waxworks of
the Nailing of
Christ to the
Cross, Varallo.
Sixteenth century.

were usually established by Franciscans; as Ariel Toaff has shown, their establishment could stimulate other local acts of anti-Jewish social piety, for they were often accompanied by banning Jews from lending money, expelling Jews from towns and, consequently, the establishment of Christian financial institutions in their place.[32] Along-side these local and financial projects, the *sacri monti* reflect key trends in Franciscan spirituality: in these landscapes one could take *imitatio* to its logical conclusion, collapsing time so the past became present, feeling oneself to be at Calvary, walking the route of Calvary as Christ had done, being a participant in the bible, without any of the inconvenience and inauthenticity of doing it in the real Jerusalem. At some of these parks there were waxworks, hideously malformed, poised to persecute the pilgrim (illus. 29).[33] The Italian *sacri monti* were very obvious and explicit models of Jerusalem and offered idealized and easily accessible Calvary parklands for visitors. The *sacri monti* are probably the most complete Jerusalem simulations in western Europe, but they should be considered alongside a number of

30 Red Mount
Chapel, King's
Lynn (Norfolk).
Built 1482–5.

similar structures, productions and landscapes: churches and chapels which claim (or are claimed) to copy the Church of the Holy Sepulchre; buildings and places with layouts or imputed associations with Jerusalem and Calvary; spaces, including taverns, wells, roads and hills, which are imagined as part of a pilgrimage or crusade to Jerusalem;[34] relics of the rock of Calvary and Christ's sepulchre;[35] the elaborate *calvaires* of northern France;[36] dramatic productions which represent the Crucifixion within the medieval European city; and pilgrimages to other shrines (especially Rome) as a substitute for visiting Jerusalem.[37] All such places and images sought to bring meditation on the Passion into the one's intimate or domestic experience.

The fifteenth-century Red Mount Chapel (see illus. 30), or 'Chapel of Our Lady', at King's Lynn (Norfolk), is a copy of a copy of a simulacrum, an aesthetic idea of Calvary. At the very end of this 'tradition', if it can be so called, and likely via several other buildings, the Red Mount Chapel has long been neglected. It was started in

1482 and finished by 1485, and was dedicated to the Virgin. It is an octagonal, three-storey chapel, with a room on each storey, built in red brick on an artificial mound outside the East Anglian port of King's Lynn.[38] In the fifteenth-century this was one of the wealthiest and best-connected of English towns, its coffers swollen in particular by the wool trade and its connections with the Low Countries and the Baltic.[39]

The Chapel lies east of the town, between the two gates of the thirteenth-century town wall. At the time at which it was built, the chapel would have been outside the wall but within the town ditch, in rural common land. An earlier chapel owned by the Lynn Guild of Our Lady probably stood on this site (called 'Ladye Hylle'), but the Red Mount Chapel was built under the auspices of William Spynk, prior of St Margaret's (Lynn's main church), and a local burgess, Robert Currance (*fl.* 1482).[40] The conventional explanation for the Red Mount Chapel has been that it was a lucrative way-station, a stopping-off point, for pilgrims to the nearby shrine of the Our Lady of Walsingham, an important English pilgrimage site. However, the Red Mount seems too to embody a Passion narrative:[41] located on a mount outside the city walls (like Calvary), and polygonal (like the 'round' *anastasis* at Jerusalem), entered through the basement to a tomb, after which one ascended to a chapel of the Virgin. The location accords with the description of Calvary extrapolated from the Gospels, a garden on a hill (John 19:41) outside the city walls (Hebrews 13:12), fulfilling the description of Jeremias 31:40, 'the whole valley of dead bodies and of ashes, and all the country of death, even to the torrent Cedron, and the corner of the horse gate towards the east'.[42] The Red Mount Chapel likely has further, possibly irretrievable, forms within its design: two niches by its north door may have been for statues or offerings; a long-lost crenellated surrounding wall may have called to mind the battlements of Jerusalem.[43] The now inaccessible interior was of a cruciform chapel inside an octagon, with worshippers apparently entering at the base of the building and working their way up; the setting may have been used for devotional drama or for the ceremonies of the Guild of Our Lady or local guilds devoted to the True Cross.[44]

What seems certain is that the Red Mount Chapel was designed to enhance, by providing a memorable setting, the *via crucis* of the people of this corner of medieval Norfolk. If the chapel was used by pilgrims on their way to Walsingham, the resonance of the building, *as* Calvary, would become all the more powerful. But, perhaps even more powerfully than this, the Red Mount Chapel would have called to mind, to some (if not all) of its medieval visitors, a range of other structures which 'looked like Jerusalem', including the round Templar churches. At London, the Mercers' Guild or the adjacent Chapel of the Holy Cross (founded by 1424) may have had some kind of monumental Calvary, based on a painted statue of Christ in agony found in the rubble of the building following bomb damage.[45] The most obvious counterpart to the Red Mount is the Holy House at Walsingham itself, a small wooden cottage which was a copy of the house in which the Virgin received the Annunciation. Walsingham was a pre-eminent English pilgrimage site and is situated about twenty-five miles east of Lynn. The legend of the Holy House is that, in 1061, the Virgin appeared to a local woman, Richeldis, and instructed her build the Holy House according to plans revealed in the vision; in the later Middle Ages, the Holy House was enclosed by a fourteenth-century chapel, and the visit to the Holy House was the culmination of one's Walsingham pilgrimage.[46] The Holy House has an Italian counterpart at Loreto, where 'the story developed that in 1296 the house of Mary herself had miraculously been transported from Nazareth by the hand of angels'.[47]

A fascinating poem by the printer Richard Pynson, dating from about 1496, shows how later medieval Walsingham became a 'New' and improved Nazareth: 'O Englonde! Great cause thou haste glad for to be/ Compared to the londe of promyssyon' (i.e. the Promised Land). Pynson addresses Walsingham thus:

In thee is *belded* newe nazareth a *mancyon*	*built, mansion*
To the honoure of the hevenly empresse	
And of *hir* moste glorious salutacion	*her*
Chief principill and *grounde* of oure salvacion.	*basis*
Whan Gabriell said at olde Nazareth 'Ave'	
This joy here daily remembred for to be.[48]	

In Pynson's poem England has inherited the mantle of 'promised land', a 'newe Nazareth' through simulation, as Old becomes New and Walsingham supersedes 'olde antiquité'. The Holy Land is thus turned to 'oure salvacion' in Pynson's England.

The form of such replicas can be understood through the description of one such building, William Wey's 'chapel made to the liknes of the sepulkyr of owre Lorde at Jerusalem' at Edington (Wiltshire; illus. 31).[49] The chapel does not survive, but one manuscript of Wey's journeys to the Holy Land includes a detailed account of the chapel's furnishing and decoration.[50] This included numerous hangings and painted-cloths, showing bible scenes ('owre Lorde with a spade in his hande', 'the tempyl of Jerusalem', 'the Mounte of Olyvete, and Beth-leem', 'thre Maryes and thre pilgremys', the 'apering of owre Lord Criste Jhesu unto his moder'); relics ('a ston of the Mownte of Calvery, a stone of sepulkyr, a stone of the hil of Tabor, a stone of the piler that oure Lord was stowrchyd [*scourged*] too, a stone of the plase wher the crosse was hid and funde, also a stone of the holy cave of Bethleem'); and liturgical furniture (candles and candlesticks, a 'paxbrede' – an osculatory – decorated with a Crucifix, dishes and chalices). There was also a 'mappa Mundy' (a world map), rich vestments in green and red velvet and silk, and various books: Wey's own *Itineraries*, St Anselm's *Meditations*, the *Vitae Patrum* (the lives of the 'Desert Fathers', the ascetics of the early church), and various things made 'in bordys' – that is, planks or panelling: lengths showing the measurements of Christ's sepulchre, the height and width of its door, Christ's foot, and the deepness and roundness of the mortice of the Cross. But, perhaps most arrestingly, also described are several structures in the Eding-ton Chapter House: a Calvary chapel, the Church of Bethlehem, the

31 Site of Calvary chapel, Edington (Wiltshire). The Chapter House stood to the left of the current building.

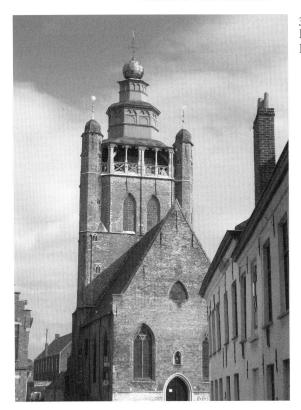

32 Jeruzalemkerk,
Bruges (Belgium).
Built 1471–83.

Mount of Olivet and the Valley of Jehoshaphat. Moreover, there was
'the sepulker of oure Lorde with too howses', apparently by the 'clokke
howse'.[51] This description of an impressive and expensive project
sounds like a dramatic set, a kind of stage against which to play and
replay the trip to Jerusalem and the Passion of Christ, but it was also
an imaginative and aesthetic recreation of several different Passional
landscapes: the site of Calvary, the archaeologized Jerusalem (stones),
the Jerusalem of biblical narrative, a liturgical Jerusalem (vestments,
bell, Mass paraphernalia), a place at once of imagination, empathy and
the hard facts of relics, measurements and fabric.[52] In the 'sepulkyr'
was a quire of 'paper with the peinting of owre Lorde[']s passiun' on
it, depicting the Passion at the centre of this luxurious and busy
mediation. Nothing in the surviving account of the chapel suggests it
was only for Easter, or unique; indeed it was a 'permanent' structure, as
the closing lines of Wey's accompanying 'will' state that the buildings
should never be removed. The actualization of Calvary at Edington is
in conversation with the Calvary of Wey's written account, and the

other actualization of Calvary, Wey's two journeys to the Holy Land itself. Finally, the Edington Calvary chapel gives us some idea what the Red Mount might have looked like, and the rich 'setting' it provided. A further analogue might be seen in the octagonal Chapel of Our Lady in Oxford (built 1521), very similar to the Red Mount, just inside the medieval city wall.[53]

Perhaps closer than Wiltshire, culturally, to Lynn is the Low Countries: just across the North Sea, Lynn had many trading links there, including those through its Hansard colony. Bruges has its own monumental Calvary structure, the Jeruzalemkerk, built by the Flemish-Genoese Adorno merchant family just a few years before the Red Mount.[54] The Bruges Jeruzalemkerk was complete by 1483, when Anselmo Adorno's corpse was moved from Scotland, where he had died, to Bruges for burial there. The church (illus. 32) is situated at the eastern edge of the city, and was built on the site of a convent; it is made up as a Calvary chapel, with a massive polygonal tower (half a dodecagon) behind it and, below, a vaulted crypt which leads through

33 Calvary, Jeruzalemkerk, Bruges (Belgium). Mid-fifteenth century.

to a tiny 'tomb of Christ', entered through a miniature portal. At the centre of the main chapel is the giant replica of Calvary (illus. 33), said to have been built by Pietro and Jacopo Adorno on their return from the Holy Land in 1427, which now forms the first altar of the church. Anselmo Adorno had also visited Jerusalem in 1471, and wrote a wonderful account of his journey; the Jeruzalemkerk is thus, at some level, a version of something Adorno had seen and visited.

The Jeruzalemkerk is, however, made up of 'inauthentic' liturgical tags and references: the octagonal tower and series of polygons which form the exterior of the tower and interior of the vaulted tower;[55] the giant Calvary decorated with the *Arma Christi*; the motto, 'para tutum' (citing the Marian prayer, 'Iter para tutum', 'prepare a safe way'), which decorates the beams and outside walls; and, from the 1520s, the version of the Holy Sepulchre itself, a tiny tomb at the back of the church with an effigy of the naked Christ. Around this time a fraternity of Jerusalem pilgrims had been established at the building, as the Flemish chapel supplanted the foreign site of Jerusalem. As Anselmo Adorno himself wrote of the Jerusalem Holy Sepulchre, 'This is the place of our redemption and of the entire fulfilment of ancient Scripture';[56] Adorno described the church in Jerusalem as an inexpressible place of marvellous devotion, whilst picking out key features for his family chapel at Bruges: the small covered vault in which Christ was buried, with a low door and no windows; the high, rounded tower of the main church; and the eminence of Calvary, a lone white rock.[57] The family church at Bruges thus replayed and inherited these features, and Bruges became an accessible and homely Jerusalem. And, indeed, the Jeruzalemkerk, or a structure based on this, figures as the Jerusalem skyline in the background of Gerard David's *Baptism of Christ* (Flanders, 1502–18).

The structures at Lynn, Edington and Bruges had distinctive, if now cryptic, *ductus* encoded in their design: one is led through these buildings in a contemplative exercise which is directed by tags, mottoes, pictures, texts as well as architectural design. We know that similar pious and meditative exercises were performed throughout Europe, in which 'armchair' travellers and enclosed monks and nuns remade Jerusalem, combining abstraction and empathy, in their own setting.[58] The Red Mount Chapel and the Edington Calvary share a similar sense of literalizing the death of Christ in an aesthetic and highly mediated landscape which was in fact safe and comfortable; in all cases, luxurious domestic environments imaginatively remade as places of suffering.

These buildings are indebted to the living, rising buildings we find in biblical portrayals of the apocalyptic Temple (Ezekiel 40, Esdras [Ezra] 3), but they replace the New Jerusalem with an empathic pilgrimage to a Calvary of Christ's personal, human suffering.

These buildings re-remember the Passion in domestic familiar ways and imbue the provincial with the spirit and form of the central (Jerusalem). In this regard, Sabine MacCormack usefully suggests that 'doublethink' is a representative thought-system of the Middle Ages, in which 'the symbol and the prototype were regarded as equal'.[59] One might go further than this, to suggest that, by the later Middle Ages, Calvary had become akin to home, not distant in time or place at all, and 'Jerusalem' was easily concordant, easily transferable, with local copies being more useful, more familiar, than the distant 'original' they called to mind.[60] But, strictly speaking, buildings like those at Lynn, Edington and Bruges were not copies, replicas or relics but, like the 'Prison of Christ', simulacra, copies of something for which there is no original. Their resemblance to the physical Jerusalem was slight, perverse, and cannot be measured in empirical terms. In his discussion of 'the culture of the copy', Hillel Schwartz argues that '[a]nything unique is at risk of vanishing', that copies and originals certify each other in a bewildering relationship of mutual inauthenticity. Schwartz goes on to suggest that

> [an] object uncopied is under perpetual siege, valued less for itself than for the struggle to prevent its being copied. The more adept the West has become at the making of copies, the more we have exalted uniqueness. It is within an exuberant world of copies that we arrive at our experience of originality.[61]

Schwartz's theory of the self-defeating copy is particularly relevant in considering medieval Christian responses to Jerusalem, which had at its core a 'lost' original of its biblical landscape, which had become first Jewish and Roman then foreign, conquered and Islamic; 'even if a country such as England had slim hopes of ever owning the Terrestrial Jerusalem, they were assured of inhabiting its space in their mind's eye'.[62] After the crusaders' loss of Jerusalem in the late twelfth century, European Christians might be seen to besiege Jerusalem with copies and imaginative artefacts (including the exponential development of pilgrimage to Rome and Santiago), rather than with weapons and aggression. But whereas Schwartz laments the lost original, one might posit a pleasure in the copy: Jerusalem at Westminster was more emotionally resonant, and certainly more Christian, than Mameluk Jerusalem. If we can acknowledge the role of thought, emotion and religious ardour, Westminster does not just *pass as* Jerusalem, but surpasses Jerusalem *as* Jerusalem.[63] Schwartz argues that '[t]he more we attempt to tell things apart, the more we end up defending our skills at replication';[64] this is undoubtedly true if we take a rational, empirical approach to knowledge. However, we should understand feeling, aesthetics, emotion and affect, rather than fact and proof, to be the dominant modes in the Middle Ages for discerning true spirit from false, authentic experience from hollow acting. Thus I see in the Westminster Jerusalem Chamber and other occidental versions of Jerusalem a status between the souvenir (a memory-cue, something remembered, necessarily separate from that which it claims to depict, bridging the material and spiritual) and the replica (a practical thing, representing displacement). Such reproductions are fundamentally different from relics, which 'travel well', act miraculously and spiritually, and are identical to and part of what they represent.[65] 'Palm Sunday processions could now be realized much better in Augsburg or Siena (or almost anywhere else) than in Jerusalem itself':[66] this was not just because of the difficulties of going to Palestine, but because, from the start, the idea of Jerusalem was a familiar, solipsistic one and, in keeping with late medieval spirituality, was better experienced on one's own terms, in one's own space and in one's own body.

Margery Kempe's Calvary: Norfolk and Jerusalem

Margery Kempe (*c.* 1373 – *c.* 1440), mystic, pilgrim and controversialist of Lynn (Norfolk), left a long account of her spiritual visions, her sexual temptations, her trials and her many pilgrimages.[67] More than one hundred years after the Jews' expulsion, *The Book of Margery Kempe* describes Jews throughout fifteenth-century England; Kempe's neighbours are cast as Jews, Kempe is accused of being a Jew, she prays for the Jews, Christ's torments at the Jews' hands are re-enacted in Kempe's mystical visions and in her imitative manner of living. On Kempe's many opportunities to meet Jews, during trips through Europe and the Levant, she does not. 'Jews', as seen by Kempe, could be fabricated, as if drawn or 'built' in mnemotechnical terms, from biblical and popular religious experiences. *The Book of Margery Kempe* is a useful document in this regard because Kempe also visited Jerusalem and the Holy Land. *The Book of Margery Kempe* thus allows us to compare and contrast Kempe's religious experience in England (a land emptied of Jews but replete with Jewish images) with that in the Holy Land, where she is likely to have encountered Jews. Inevitably, this was a Jerusalem of European aesthetics and devotional fashions.

Kempe's Jews are part of her *imitatio Christi*. When 'many' people around her believe Kempe to be possessed by a tear-inducing devil, Kempe invokes the Jews thus:

> And al she toke paciently for owr Lordys love, for she wist wel that the Jewys seid meche wers of his owyn persone than men dede of hir. And therfor she toke it the mor meekly. (3471–4)[68]

Kempe, in keeping with her *imitatio*, presents her patience under trial as a parallel, if lesser, Passion. This reference to Kempe's fellow Englishmen and Englishwomen as Jews is continued, as she describes how the 'folke spitted at hir' (line 3478), as they think her epileptic and diabolical. This spitting recalls the characteristic 'unclean' behaviour of the Jews at the Passion.[69]

Strikingly, as she is undergoing clerical examination for heresy in York, Kempe, with her disruptive and violent devotional style, is mistaken for a Jew: 'Sum of the pepil askyd whedyr she wer a Cristen woman er a Jewe? Sum seid she was a good-woman and sum seid "nay"' (4146–89). 'Jewe' here seems really to mean 'Loller' (i.e. Lollard) and 'heretike' (4116) for the ecclesiastics seek to determine the extent, if any, of Kempe's heresy rather than Judaism.[70] 'Jewe' does not mean Jewish, but rather that which is disruptive to Christianity; elsewhere Kempe prays for 'Jewys, Sarazinys and alle fals heretikys' (4733) and their 'blindnes'. Indeed, the Archbishop of York and his 'many worthy clerkys' (4142–3), trained in Scripture, can hardly have taken Kempe for a Jew; instead, here Kempe characteristically casts herself as a Christlike figure, tried, like Christ, before an illegitimate court.[71] Kempe manipulates martyrological tropes, recreating popular images of Christ tried before the Sanhedrin, Annas and Caiaphas. Throughout her book, Kempe repeatedly places herself in the martyr's persecuted position.[72] It is significant that Kempe little attempts to counter accusations of Lollardy, heresy or Judaism with reason or argument, instead crying (4154), screaming out (4154–6), praying to herself (4138) and mystically conversing with Christ (4204–7): a performance of feeling persecuted.

Kempe's most extended passage on the Jews occurs in the 'glori-ows sight in hir sowle' (6332), an interaction with Christ's trial and Passion (chapter 79). This takes the form of a witnessing of several key moments of the Passion. Kempe follows the biblical narrative but her visions are profoundly inflected by popular religion, in particular her emphasis on gory and sensational violence. Kempe starts as spectator, viewing the Virgin 'swowning befor hir sone' (6287). The dialogue between the Virgin and Christ is given in *The Book of Margery Kempe* in reported speech and emphasizes Kempe's passive role. Kempe assumes an active role in her 'thowt' – 'the seid creatur thowt she toke our Lord Jhesu Christ by the clothys and fel down at his feet . . .' (6333–7). Christ commands Kempe to stay with the Virgin and comfort her. The account becomes progressively less concerned with communication through speech and more ekphrastic, as Kempe and the Virgin follow Christ through the torments of his Passion.

Kempe describes her vision of 'many armyd men with stavys, swedys, and polexis' (i.e. staves, swords and poleaxes, 6364–5) who turn out to be the gang of Jews who fall to the ground (as described in John 18:1–19:42). Kempe's detailed account of the Passion is largely faithful to gospel account whilst including non-scriptural addition (for instance the Jews' tearing of Christ's beard (6389), the description of the whiteness of Christ's body (6396)). It is, however, remarkable as a kind of gathering-up of Passion *topoi* in which Christ's tortures are laboriously compiled: the Jews spit in Christ's face, 'in the most schamful *wise* [*manner*] that they cowde', they pull at his 'blisful' ears, tug his beard, draw off his clothes and leave him naked, as if he's 'the *most malefactowr* in al the worlde' (i.e. 'the *greatest malefac-tor*', 6385–92). And so it goes on, an exhaustive enumeration ('And than . . . and anon . . . And than . . .') of grim tortures. Kempe's tableaux of the Passion owes a great deal to visual images, in partic-ular Passion cycles, likewise framed and rigidly schematized;[73] these tableaux return us to the perceptual *passio*, a visual experience of pleasurable pain, an ocular suffering *imitatio*, a 'salubrious' violence, presented as a series of key moments which build the correct *memo-ria passionis*.[74] The strip-art format, with its schematization, enumeration and bold contrasts, delineates Christian redemption partly through its easily identifiable villain, the spitting, violent Jew-ish grotesque.

Kempe's *memoria passionis* can be set against her pilgrimage to the sites of the Passion in Jerusalem, where she herself performs as persecuted victim.[75] Kempe sailed from Venice for Jaffa in the spring of 1414, proceeding to Jerusalem, including Calvary, Mount Zion and Kidron. Her journey was funded by gifts, including one from the Bishop of Lincoln, Philip Repyngdon, of twenty-six shillings and eight pence, to support Kempe's prayers.[76] She then went by ass to Bethlehem (2382) and on to the Jordan Valley, Jericho and Bethany, in the conventional Christlike route;[77] Kempe returned to Jaffa via Ramle. Her account of her trip includes no visits to Old Testament sites. The daunting itinerary and the preceding journey through Europe is described in *The Book of Margery Kempe* in some detail but the account of the destination is strangely bare: it is mostly devoid of people and here, when Kempe's *imitatio Christi* seems to reach its zenith, the Holy Land is largely empty. Whilst it is on her pilgrimage to Jerusalem that Kempe first finds herself 'krying and roring' (2216) in compassion for 'owyr Lordys pein' (2215), the remainder of the journey was a standard group tour, organized by Franciscans and led by 'Sarazyn' guides, around key biblical sites. Conspicuously absent from Kempe's Holy Land is a sense of Jerusalem as a fifteenth-century Mameluk metropolis; the only indication of this is in the Saracen guides who receive Kempe. Kempe visited Jerusalem as a pilgrim, not a tourist or anthropologist, but her Jerusalem is a paradoxical landscape of Christian fantasy and memory, not least in its being free of Jews, both biblical and contemporary. In travelling to Jerusalem, Kempe was going 'home' to that most well-remembered of painful mental places.

The voyage to Jerusalem is fraught with persecutory friction between Kempe and the other pilgrims: this is her *via crucis*. Shortly after setting off, the other pilgrims are irked at Kempe's refusal to eat meat (1973) and by her constant talk of God (1975). At Constance, they tell her that she is a 'strumpet' (1994) and ridicule her by cutting her gown short and making her wear a canvas shirt like sackcloth, 'for she shuld ben holdyn a fool and the pepyl schuld not makyn of hir ne han hir reputacion' ('so she should be thought a fool and the people should not have regard for her or esteem her', 2007–8). She's ejected from the pilgrimage with just one noble (a gold coin) and her money is stolen not once but twice (1995; 2075). After rejoining the pilgrims, she is memorably bullied at Venice (2149), where her companions refuse to eat with her, putting commensality and its associated religious images into crisis; Kempe is thus ejected from normative social and fraternal bonds, just as Christ, on his way to Calvary, was ogled by 'citesenes & strangers . . . the foulest Ribawdes & wine drinkers, not to have compassion of him, bot to wondre upon him, & scorne him.'[78] Then, the pilgrims order boats, wine and bedding but none for Kempe (2152), and a priest steals her sheet (2167) in an unedifying episode in which Kempe 'toke God to witnesse that it was hire schete!' (2170). Kempe does find the comfort of strangers during her pilgrimage, notably a kindly Devonshire man called William Weaver who prays with her (2100), a papal legate at Constance who tries to restore her money to her (2074) and the hunchbacked Irishman Richard (2496), who leads Kempe from Jerusalem to Rome.[79] Upon finally seeing Jerusalem, Kempe nearly falls off her ass, 'for she myth not beryn the swetnesse and grace that God wrowte in hir sowle' ('for she could not bear the sweetness and grace that God wrought in her soul', 2189); two German pilgrims come to help and give her spices to comfort her, but her English companions are notably absent.

These social interactions are described in the language of Christ's Passion: the 'felaschep' is angry with her (1982), they do her 'schame and gret grevawns' ('grievance', 1987), Kempe suffers 'mech tribulacion til she cam to Jherusalem' (2173), and the cut gown and the one gold coin she is left with recall the rent purple coat and the Judas pence of Christ's Passion. Richard of Ireland makes this martyrological and Christ-like persecuting rhetoric clear when he says to Kempe that her countrymen have 'forsakyn' her (2497) and threaten them with 'bothyn bowys and arwys' ('both bows and arrows', 2500) whereas Richard 'with the broke bak' (2522) has only 'a cloke ful of clowtys' ('a patchy cloak', 2502). Their 'enmys' ('enemies', 2502), says Richard, seek to rob them, 'peraventur takyn the awey from me and defowlyn thy body' ('perhaps to take you away from me and rape you', 2503).

The Mameluk Jerusalem visited by Kempe had a thriving Jewish population: both Arabic-speaking Palestinian Jews and immigrant Jews from all over Europe, North Africa and the Levant and they were involved in the Christian pilgrimage industry, of which Kempe was a part. Examples of fourteenth- and fifteenth-century Jewish guides are abundant; an Italian monk, writing in 1335, described how the Jews can 'explain all the ancient sites, for they are very erudite in their Holy Scriptures and in the locations mentioned in the tales of their forefathers and sages'.[80] But, to her mind, Kempe met more Jews in England than in the Holy Land; the Palestinian Jews were of no interest to Kempe and her self-reflexive experience of the Holy Land.

However, the 'Sarasyn' Jerusalemites are more amenable to Kempe's pilgrimage experience; by the term 'Sarasyn' – that is, Saracen – it is assumed that *The Book of Margery Kempe* means a Muslim, although it might mean something akin too to 'non-Christian', 'non-European' or 'non-white'.[81] Kempe employs a Saracen guide, a 'welfaring' man (i.e. handsome, 2410) and at Jerusalem 'she fond alle pepyl good onto hir and gentyl, saf only hir owyn cuntremen' ('she found all people good and gentle towards her, apart only from her country-men', 2443–4).[82] The tone of *The Book of Margery Kempe* is strikingly accommodating here, for it is 'hir owyn cuntremen' in the pilgrimage group who have turned against her.[83]

Kempe's 'empty' Holy Land has a source and precedent in the pilgrimage account left by Bridget of Sweden (1303–73), which is 'almost entirely devoid of any reference to the physical conditions of her pilgrimage and the *realia* of Jerusalem'.[84] The pilgrim focuses on what is seen with the 'eye of faith' rather than the 'eye of the body', usually collapsing biblical time into the pilgrim's experience.[85] So the devotional landscape becomes an aesthetic projection of the pilgrim's own making (rather than a reflection of the pilgrim's experience). One cannot approach *The Book of Margery Kempe* for a historical portrait of the landscape which greeted the pilgrim to Jerusalem. Kempe's 'blinkers' might be attributed to her wish to represent *sapientia* and *scientia* (worthy wisdom and knowledge) rather than *curiositas* (forbidden mental and physical wandering);[86] *imitatio* was to be achieved not through scenery but through persecution by one's fellow pilgrims. Again, Kempe is the medium here, marking herself, the 'text' with which the Christological precedent is etched. One suspects that, for Kempe, Jerusalem was not as potent in reality as it was as a fiction. As Annabel Wharton comments, '[t]he sites associated with Jesus's life and death in fifteenth-century Jerusalem were empty by comparison with those of Varallo [near Milan]'.[87] Similarly, the most potent Calvary for Kempe was not in Jerusalem but in Canterbury, Leicester, Lynn or York, where she underwent spectacular and public trials framed as versions of the Passion. Wharton notes how the Italian recreation of Calvary made 'real' or manifest, through a simulacrum, 'a Jew-free Jerusalem';[88] at the same time, violent Jewish caricatures, gurning in devotional tableaux, could endlessly repeat their Passional crimes.

'If I forget thee, O Jerusalem . . .' (Psalm 136)

At Wells Cathedral (Somerset), the thirteenth-century West Front, representing the Heavenly Jerusalem, was transformed into Jerusalem each Palm Sunday. The deacon would read the story of Christ's Entry into Jerusalem (Matthew 21) to the congregants assembled outside the cathedral. From a hidden choir passage behind the facade a boy chorister sang out to the congregation the '*Gloria laus*', the address to Christ on his Entry into the city. The effect would have been of the statues of the saints singing out, and the Heavenly Jerusalem coming to life. The procession moved into the cathedral, the people singing together,

> As the Lord was entering the Holy City the children of the Hebrews proclaimed the resurrection of life, and with the branches of palms, cried out: Hosanna in the highest.[89]

Thus, once a year, was Wells made into concordant, expressive and familiar Jerusalem, seamlessly uniting time, space and divinity, both Jerusalem and the New Jerusalem. The people of Wells fulfilled typology, becoming 'the children of the Hebrews' as they entered 'the Heavenly Jerusalem'. Physical activity came to mirror mental activity, utterly representative of the mnemonic impetus to make ideas familiar (*domesticare*), the Passion contemplated and re-experienced most acutely as part of one's own experience.

Yet the tavern, as well as the cathedral, could be Jerusalem. It is fitting then that 'the oldest pub in England' is (reputedly) Nottingham's Trip to Jerusalem, a tiny touristy booth set beneath Nottingham Castle just off 'Maid Marian Way', and dated (spuriously) to 1189; local lore says that the pub was founded for the crusaders accompanying Richard I on his ill-fated journey in this year to the Holy Land.

The Nottingham Trip to Jerusalem pretends, through its name and status as a pilgrimage and crusader tavern, to be the point of departure but it is, and probably always was, the destination. To the Trip to Jerusalem could be added more common inn names: The Pilgrim, The Lamb and Flag (recalling the symbol of the Knights Templar, whom we have seen as key proponents of an aestheticized replicated Jerusalem), The Rising Sun, The Saracen's Head, The Turk's Head and so on, all of which locate eastern fantasies of both conquest and devotion in the medieval tavern. Such sites called to mind the routes and spaces associated with contemporary pilgrimage and/or crusade, but also acted as retrospective memory-tags of the life and Passion of Christ and the places associated with His life. At some time before the putative founding of the Trip to Jerusalem tavern the Augustinian hospital of the Holy Sepulchre had been established in Nottingham (*c.* 1170) just outside the city's walls. The ideas of Jerusalem constructed at Nottingham supplant Jerusalem with the key processes associated with it – crusade, pilgrimage, and, in the later Middle Ages especially, lamentation. The *realia* of Jerusalem is similarly lost in many of the medieval artefacts which represent the city. Through an aesthetics of virtuality and intimacy, Jerusalem became a kind of translatable and endlessly portable stage on which the drama of salvation and the contrast of good and evil could be played out. Conversely, the urban landscape of Jerusalem, which endures to this day, was itself inflected by these Western versions to the extent that one might suggest that Jerusalem is a true simulacrum, a copy without an original, a copy of a Western European idea of Jerusalem. Jerusalem was itself a learned *and* sentimental map of a Western idea of Jerusalem which itself referred to an imagined biblical Jerusalem.

In Christian culture, the desire to witness and be part of the Passion required the ongoing, aestheticized evocation of Jewish violence: '[f]or medieval people, the experience of seeing and imagining a body that was ravaged and bleeding from tortures inflicted upon it lay at the centre of a constellation of religious doctrines, beliefs and devotional practices'.[90] The spectacle of redemptive, valorized pain was to be sought everywhere. New formats, new media, new spaces, were developed which gave medieval people greater access to this pain: it could be gazed on, in both private and corporate settings, and, as for Margery Kempe, repeated to the extent that it structured and suffused one's life. There is little that is frightening or terrifying to us about these artefacts; rather, they made from Christ's distant and abstract death at Calvary something domestic, familiar and painful.

CHAPTER 7

Cultures in Pain

Taste is context, and the context has changed.
—Susan Sontag, *Fascinating Fascism*

'A Jew Asked a Monk . . .'

Two stories from the *Sefer Chasidim* (*The Book of the Righteous*), the didactic twelfth-century book on Jewish ethics by Yehudah Ha-Chasid (Judah ben Samuel) of Regensburg (*c.* 1150–1217), provide contradictory information about Jewish-Christian relations in terms of literary and devotional culture. The first is about a bookbinder's apprentice:

> A Jew asked a monk to teach him the art of bookbinding. The monk told him, 'I'll start by letting you bind one of my ecclesiastical manuscripts, and I'll correct your mistakes and teach you as you go.'
> When the Jew consulted the rabbi, the rabbi said, 'Don't bind even one section, and don't assist him in binding his books.'[1]

This little story demonstrates how the means of book production, at least in central and northern Europe, were in the hands of Christians, and might also be evidence of a Jew's ability to approach a monk in terms of craftsmanship and trade, rather than religious difference. The rabbi's reaction, however, confirms the popular impression that Jews and Christians lived largely incompatible, separate lives in the Middle Ages, reminding us that such separation could be as much a consequence of Jewish piety as it was Christian persecution.

The next story in *Sefer Chasidim*, about two bookbinders, deals with a similar situation rather differently:

> Two devout Jews had books that needed binding. There were two bookbinders in town, one a monk who was a master craftsman, the other a Jew who was less proficient than the monk.

One Jew gave his books to the Jewish bookbinder to bind. He reasoned, 'How can I let a monk touch my *sefarim* [holy books]? He will treat them with disdain. Besides, he may use the remnants to repair his ecclesiastical manuscripts.'

The other Jew handed his books to the monk for binding. He argued, 'Of course, a monk is not allowed to write or sew the parchments of a *sefer Torah*, but it is not forbidden to bind or replace the covers of sefarim in which you learn.' But he did watch the monk to make sure that he did not use the remnants for one of his church books.[2]

The Jews' anxiety about remnants of their books being used in Christian binding was real, as revealed in several thirteenth-century European books.[3] The first Jew's distrust of the monastic bookbinder brings him into conflict with the *Sefer Chasidim*'s many rules and exhortations about showing proper respect for one's books, because he is not doing the best for his precious books.[4] An altogether happier commerce between Christian and Jew is described in the case of the second Jew, who takes the sensible, and more pious, course of action: he ultimately treats his books with respect and gets them bound in the best possible way, whilst also bearing in mind what is 'allowed' rather than letting his prejudice against the monk determine his decision.

These two stories show emphatically that books, learning and cultural artefacts were key areas of interpenetration and shared prestige between Christian and Jew in medieval Europe.[5] Yet both stories gloss this interpenetration with an anxious, proleptic perception of persecution, a troubled feeling that Jews and Christians might come into conflict or that such contact may infringe one's doctrines.

In medieval Christianity, to engage one's senses was to gain a more profound and more individual relationship with religion. Jews too engaged in somatic, emotional and physical devotional practices, often based around feeling persecuted. For all its stated aniconic dogma – encapsulated in the Second Commandment which prohibits the making of idols – later medieval Judaism generally respected the powers of images, books and objects to move and engage one's senses. Jews too knew standard rhetorical models, including, via Averroës, Aristotle's *Rhetoric*. Averroës describes, in his commentary to the *Rhetoric*, several modes of persuasion which do not occur by (forensic, syllogistic) argument, including 'bringing the listener around to assent by means of the passions . . . so that he must assent because of fanaticism, mercy, fear, or anger.'[6] Similarly, 'challenging and beating', 'awakening a desire for, or apprehension about, something', and 'distorting speeches and . . . putting them into a form in which their repulsiveness appears' are all, for the Aristotelian Arab Averroës as for Quintilian or Prudentius, amongst the best methods of making something persuasive, memorable and affective.[7] Jews too had an agency in the production of images which were designed to help them *feel* persecuted; such images have subsequently been labelled 'anti-Semitic', thus showing the inadequacy and totalizing force of a critical debate focused around 'anti-Semitism' and 'Jew-hatred'. Medieval Jewish culture had its own 'sensory underpinnings' and culturally interpenetrated Christian and Islamic spheres, and this section alights on some germane examples, which involve grotes-query and the memory of pain, contrast and feeling.[8]

Clifford's Tower in the English city of York is a potent emblem of the persecution of medieval Jewry by its neighbours and, more generally, a metonym of medieval violence, cruelty and bloodiness. It is, in the words of Barrie Dobson, 'the supreme example on English soil of the evils of anti-semitism and of the need for recon-ciliation between Christians and Jews.'[9] The massacre of York's Jews in 1190 combined money and indebtedness, crusading zeal and regal power, religious and local tensions, written and devotional models of martyrdom, as seen in the main Christian account, by William of Newburgh (*c.* 1136 – *c.* 1198).

At the climax of his account, Newburgh describes how 'a certain elder', a very famous religious man from overseas, addressed the besieged Jews, urging them to die 'willingly and devoutly'; 'God, to whom we ought not to say, Why dost Thou this? commands us now to die for His Law – and behold our death is at the doors, as you see'.[10] His speech is full of biblical allusions to persecution, in particular to Job 9:2: 'or who can say, "Why dost thou so?"' and Ecclesiastes 8:4, 'And his word is full of power: neither can any man say to him: "Why dost thou so?"' This desperate question – '*Cur ita facis?*' – was also the stimulus for many patristic considerations of why bad things happen to good people.[11] Moreover, both the shape of the account and the speeches of the leader of the Jews are highly imitative of Eleazar, the leader of the suicidal zealots at Masada (73 CE), as narrated by Josephus (*c.* 37–100 CE) in *De bello Judaico*.[12]

Newburgh describes the grand houses and furniture of the York Jews, just as Josephus describes the lavish furnishings Eleazar brought to Masada; both vividly describe the spoliation of these riches. The speeches of the York Jew and Eleazar are far from identical, but both explain why death is less disgraceful than life under one's enemies. Indeed Newburgh refers us to Josephus, drawing an explicit parallel between York and Masada: 'whoever reads the History of the Jewish War, by Josephus, understands well enough, that madness of this kind, arising from their ancient superstition, has continued down to our own times, whenever any very heavy misfortune fell upon them.'[13]

Newburgh's account has been called 'well-informed and emotionally involved' yet also 'comparatively impartial and well-balanced if sometimes over-calculated'.[14] It is important to remember that this is a section of Newburgh's chronicle – beginning with the massacre of the Jews at Richard 1's 1189 coronation and ending with the mass suicide in York – containing what its author describes as 'ambiguous readings' ('*ambigua*'); Newburgh says that such awkward events should be understood 'in the better rather than the worse sense' as well as 'the most appropriate meaning'.[15] In other words, William of Newburgh is alerting the reader to the act of interpretation to which he is subjecting these shocking acts of violence. Other Latin Christian accounts provide additional narrative details, such as that it was the sheriff who besieged the Jews and that 500 Jews perished, and almost all accounts, both Latin and Hebrew, agree that the Jews' leader encouraged the martyrdom and the Jews carried it out. For both Jews and Christians, this was a shared way of making a 'religious' sense – via martyrdom – of the event at York. William of Newburgh concludes his account with a solemn description of the burning of the Jews' bonds, 'those evidences of detestable avarice', in the cathedral, and notes that 'these events . . . occurred at the time of the Passion of our Lord, that is to say, on the day before Palm Sunday', signalling the appropriate liturgical memory to accompany the description of the event. Similarly, Hebrew accounts of the York massacre, by Ephraim of Bonn (d. 1200), Joseph of Chartres (*fl. c.* 1200) and Menahem of Worms (d. 1203), are grounded not in 'reportage' but in Jewish literary conventions of Ashkenazi poets, which exalt martyrdom and make central a poetics of noble death.[16] The accounts of the death of the Jews of York through mass suicide reflect the growing custom of *Kiddush ha-Shem* (literally, 'sanctification of the name', understood as pious sacrifice through suicide) in medieval Ashkenazi Jewry but also the growing valorization of this ideal. *Kiddush ha-Shem* was not just a historical practice but held within it a set of emotional sentiments, memories and texts.[17]

Both Joseph of Chartres and Menahem of Worms used the established poetic form of the Hebrew *piyyut* and a litany of biblical references to persecution, revenge and eternal life in order to frame the incident at York within patterns of sacred martyrdom and the apocalyptic end of exile. Menahem laments those slaughtered at Boppard in 1179 (where the Jews were blamed for the death in the Rhine of a Christian girl) and those killed at York, catastrophes understood as signs of both gentile cruelty ('We were battered in all kinds of religious persecutions . . . we were lost, we were lost') and the precious martyrdom of the Jews, the 'pure ones' who were 'delighted to sanctify God'.[18] Menahem's account of the incident at York describes how the Jews' beautiful clothes were discarded, in fact quoting Ezekiel 26:16 (they 'shall remove their robes and strip off their embroidered garments. They shall clothe themselves with trembling . . .'). Likewise, Joseph of Chartres includes few individuating details of the York assault, his *piyyut* instead directing his 'bitter anger' at the 'King of the Isles' (that is, England), who took the blood of 'innocent souls'.

Ephraim of Bonn's account of the York massacre appears at first to be less liturgically inflected.[19] Ephraim's prose account describes how the Jews fled to the house of prayer ('*beit ha-tefilah*'), where rabbi Yom Tov killed fifty souls and other Jews finished off the self-slaughter. Moving the massacre from the castle to a synagogue probably served to heighten the sense of the martyrs' piety. Ephraim then describes in detail how the Jews' gold, silver and their illuminated books were plundered; he says that the Hebrew books were taken to Cologne, apparently by Christians, and sold there to Jews. Ephraim includes one further striking detail in his account of the York massacre: that one of the Jewish men 'ordered' that 'his only son' be slaughtered, a son so 'tender and dainty' that he 'would never venture to set a foot on the ground'. This at first seems to be an affecting detail, a kind of 'close-up', emphasizing intimate rather than generalized suffering. However, the Hebrew directly quotes a singularly appropriate biblical passage about Jewish child-murder and divinely ordained cannibalistic matricide:

> you shall eat your own issue, the flesh of your sons and daughters that the Lord your God has assigned to you, because of the desperate straits to which your enemy shall reduce you./ He who is most *tender and fastidious* among you shall be too mean to his brother and the wife of his bosom and the children he has

spared / to share with any of them the flesh of the children that he eats, because he has nothing else left as a result of the desperate straits to which your enemy shall reduce you in all your towns. / And she who is most tender and dainty among you, *so tender and dainty that she would never venture to set a foot on the ground*, shall begrudge the husband of her bosom, and her son and her daughter, the afterbirth that issues from between her legs and the babies she bears; she shall eat them secretly, because of utter want, in the desperate straits to which your enemy shall reduce you in your towns. (Deuteronomy 28:53–7; cited text in emphases)

In Ephraim's account of the York massacre the gender of the 'tender and dainty' one is changed from female to male – possibly as a way of recalling also the story of Abraham and Isaac, or possibly to make the sense of loss more effective through the death of a man's only son. This section of Deuteronomy – of sacrificing one's most precious loved ones in a siege – provided a potent template through which the York massacre was described.[20]

It is hard to gauge the extent to which this visceral passage from Deuteronomy would have been read through the lens of ritual-murder allegations in twelfth-century Europe; in the context in which Ephraim was writing, it is hard to imagine that he was not aware that the evocation of Jewish cannibalism against one's children would have confirmed, indeed furthered, allegations of Jewish child-murder being developed amongst Christian writers. However, Ephraim's allusion to Deuteronomy shows that biblical accounts of valorized violence against one's children continued to be powerful templates for the emotional understanding of anti-Jewish violence and Jewish self-representation, at the same time as similar slanders about Jews were being circulated by Christians. Ephraim's history conforms to, and confirms, the rhetoricity of medieval historical writing and is more an affective rendering, helping people to *feel* the past through liturgical memories, than a factual account.[21]

The first audiences of these Hebrew accounts of the York massacre were neither witnesses to the massacre nor inhabitants of York: they were French and Rhenish Jews who identified culturally with the English Jews, reading about the massacre some ten years after it took place. By conjuring feelings of persecution and always linking them to general experience (as distinct from specific lived experience) these texts gave York an importance that transcended time and space, and may even have made such details irrelevant. All the twelfth- and thirteenth-century sources we have with which to read about the York massacre are commemorative in character: Christian chronicles or Jewish laments, in which writing *serves* the audience rather than historical fact, wherein the main concern is an emotionally involving recollection in an authorized and communally recognized form. Indeed, such texts can obscure rather than reveal historical fact through their indebtedness to 'typological, cyclic, and mythic' modes of looking back, and martyrologies tell us more about martyrologists than martyrs.[22] They employ rhetorics of martyrdom, victimhood and pain which transcend a historicist pursuit of 'what actually happened' on 16 March 1190. Is not the prerogative to feel 'recreational' fear, to celebrate victimhood, to feel persecuted, necessarily the prerogative of a relatively secure and empowered group? These texts contained a message that was less urgent than it was involving, less a call to action than a reason for reflection.

Hunting for Meaning: the Prato Haggadah

With reflective reading in mind, I turn to a set of marginal images in a medieval Jewish manuscript, scenes of hunting in the Prato Haggadah (New York, Jewish Theological Seminary MS 9478), a luxurious Jewish devotional book produced in Spain around the year 1300. The Prato Haggadah is from a very different environment from the northern European materials on which I have focused so far, but provides an instructive parallel. The *haggadah*, a decorated festival-book which retells the story of Exodus, was read and sung at the Passover *seder* night celebration; the *haggadah* (literally a 'story', 'narrative', a 'making clear') is used at home and designed for the engagement of all members of the family and would be returned to year after year. The Prato Haggadah, whilst unfinished, is richly decorated and beautifully illustrated: hybrids, grotesques and animals abound; birds' heads, bearded half-men and wimpled dogs emerge from the ascenders of Hebrew letters; dragons link their sinewy bodies around the margins of the pages; stunted colourful figures play bagpipes and blow horns; the legs, necks and tails of strange beasts curl through and about the text. These creatures are very similar to the funny, irreverent and perplexing beasts we are used to seeing as gargoyles on cathedrals or in the marginalia of Gothic manuscripts, grotesques which help readers discern the correct from the distorted, sacred from the profane.[23]

The margins of the Prato Haggadah feature, amongst other things, a sequence of energetic and violent images of hunting. On the book's first folio a hound leaps after a jumping deer (f. 1r, illus. 34); a brown dog pursues a hare perched on the foliage springing from the text (f. 4v); a hunting dog, his jaws open, looks back through his own legs (f. 7v); the running dog pursues the hare again along the *bas-de-page* decoration (f. 9v); the dog jumps attacks the deer from behind, sinking his teeth into the deer's back, whilst the hare (now very feint) watches from the edge of the margin (f. 12r; illus. 35); the dog leaps on after the hare, who springs away (f. 33r); the hare is shot by an archer: an arrow is lodged in its back whilst the archer takes aim again (f. 41v; illus. 36). The hunting imagery is striking on several counts and demands several questions. What has hunting got to do with the Jewish ceremony of the Passover *seder*? Given that we know that medieval European Jews did not, by and large, hunt (at least not in the ritualized, courtly form), why are Jews depicting hunting in their midst?[24] In using the imagery of pursuit, violence, victimization, all those hallmarks of the European Jewish historical experience, is the Jewish community, so often described in terms of a hunted, trapped minority, depicting itself as hunted quarry? And in featuring a hare and dogs, why do 'unclean', non-kosher

34 Starting the hunt, from the Prato Haggadah. Spain, *c.* 1300, Jewish Theological Seminary, MS 9478, f. 1r.

35 Dog savages a deer while a hare (l.) looks on, from the Prato Haggadah. Spain, *c.* 1300, Jewish Theological Seminary, MS 9478, f. 12r.

animals appear throughout a Jewish festival book? Nothing in a laborious and detailed production like a medieval manuscript can be dismissed as 'purely decorative'.[25]

Michael Camille's pioneering work on marginal images urged that we consider margins within the function and interpretation of the whole page; Camille argues, focusing in particular on obscenities such as defecating monks and nuns picking fruit from penis trees, that such marginal images 'play' at subversion, problematizing the text's 'authority', celebrating a 'flux of "becoming" rather than "being"'.[26] Discussions of such images have shown how grotesques might take the form of puns or parts of a text to represent a whole: thus marginal images might

36 Archer shoots hare, from the Prato Haggadah. Spain, *c.* 1300, Jewish Theological Seminary, MS 9478, f. 41v.

show a 'chain' of fish-hooks to suggest the chains (*catenae*) through which memory is made; or designs made from biscuits, or showing grazing animals, reflecting the reader's *ruminatio* of the text.[27] Regarding medieval Hebrew manuscripts, Marc Michael Epstein, following Camille, has explored the subversive potential of marginal imagery, arguing that drollery and grotesquery demands interpretation *as* commentary within an 'ideal shelter for sentiments [that artists] might feel the need to occlude in an environment of persecution, but that would still be accessible to "trustworthy and intelligent readers"', that is, Jews reading against a Christian grain.[28]

The hunting of the deer and hare 'moves', and moves with its readers, through the Prato Haggadah: the chase always moves from right to left in tandem with the book's text, helping the eye to leap from one page to the next (this is especially true between ff. 9v and 10r). These are hunts which reach their violent conclusions: the dog sinking its teeth into the deer and the archer shooting his arrow into the hare's back (illus. 35, 36). The dog assails the deer at precisely the point in the text of the *haggadah* which describes how Israel became a nation in Egypt (*Maggid*, Pharoah's pursuit of the Israelites and Israel's journey to freedom), quoting Ezekiel 16:7 and 6, that Israel 'wast naked and bare': 'I passed over you and *saw you wallowing in your bloods* and I said to you *by your blood you shall live*, and I said to you, By your blood you shall live'.[29] A description of Israel's growth is accompanied by its persecution; the blood of suffering and oppression is also the blood of birth and survival.[30] The deer then disappears from the margins of the Prato Haggadah.

The image of the afflicted stag is informed by the beautiful *locus classicus* of the complaint comparing the soul hungry for God to the thirsting stag: 'As the hart panteth after the water brooks, so panteth my soul after thee, O God'(Psalm 41:2). That this called to mind the children of Israel and the parting of the Red Sea is clear from Augustine's interpretation of these lines, in which he says that 'when deer are walking in single file, or want to swim to a different place to find fresh grazing, they rest their heavy heads on each other . . . They go on like this, carrying the heavy weight for each other; so they make good progress, and do not let each other down.' Augustine draws out the language of exile and homecoming thus:

> Once a deer of this kind is established in faith, but does not yet
> see the object of that faith and yearns to understand what he or

she loves, this deer has to endure other people who are not deer at all, people whose understanding is darkened, who are sunk in their inner murk and blinded by vicious desires.[31]

So, for Augustine, the hart panting after the water is an image, he says, of his soul 'athirst for the living God . . . this is what I am thirsting for, to reach him and to appear before him. *I am thirsty on my pilgrimage, parched in my running, but I will be totally satisfied when I arrive*'.[32] The canonical Bestiary, the ubiquitous medieval encyclopaedia of animal lore, embellished Augustine's notion of the deer, *cervus*, walking across water in a way reminiscent of the parting of the Red Sea for the children of Israel:

> Deer have this characteristic also, that they change their feeding-ground for love of another country, and in doing so, they support each other. When they cross great rivers or large long stretches of water, they place their head on the hindquarters of the deer in front and, following one on the other, do not feel impeded by their weight. When they find such places, they cross them quickly, to avoid sinking in the mire . . . When the young grow strong enough to take flight, the deer train them to run and to leap great distances. When deer hear the dogs barking, they move upwind taking their scent with them.[33]

Changing of the group's 'feeding-ground', its mutual 'support', its miraculous ability to cross stretches of water: all such imagery fits perfectly with the story of the *haggadah*, of pursuit, affliction and escape. Similarly, the rituals of the medieval hunt, with its annual assembly at a designated place, its conjunction of pleasure and pain in desperate flight, its emphasis on 'training' along known and un-known paths, its relay stations posted along the route and its highly ceremonial and ordered trappings resembles through analogy both the *seder* meal for which the *haggadah* was used and the form of the manuscript, with its ordered markers, sections and illuminated 'sign-posts' (images, *tituli*, historiated letters and so on).

Similarly, the hare, 'a speedy animal and quite timid',[34] is caught, wounded with an arrow, at a significant and appropriate place in the text (f. 41v, illus. 36): that is, accompanying the text, quoting Psalm 118:5 (Vulgate 117:5), 'In distress I called on the Lord: the Lord answered me and brought me relief. The Lord is on my side, I have no fear; *what can man do to me?*' (emphasis added). The hare represents the people of Israel as quarry, here in keeping with the text of the *haggadah*.

In Christian exegesis, this psalm was understood in terms which would have resonated with both Jewish and Christian audiences, and made utter sense within the logic of the story of Exodus – as St Augustine says in his exposition of this psalm,

> In our distress we are hemmed into a narrow place, but we are on our way to a wide country that has no bounds . . .[35]

The violent and bloody 'conclusions' can thus be seen as devotional and richly aesthetic, and in keeping with the dramatic points in the *haggadah* text and its explication. Crucially, the spilling of the blood of the quarry, both deer and hare, mirrors Moses' sprinkling of sacrificial blood onto the Israelites:

> Moses took the [other half of the] blood and threw it on the people, saying 'Behold the blood of the covenant that the Lord has made with you concerning all these words'. (Exodus 24:8)

The Prato Haggadah retains the sentiment of this potent narrative via the images of the shedding of the animals' blood; however, it does so in such a way as to avoid showing Moses spattering 'unclean' blood onto people (an element of the Exodus story about which medieval Jewish commentators were uneasy).[36] There is nothing subversive, ironic or even controversial about these particular marginal images of a dog attacking a deer or a man shooting at a hare; the margins of this particular book need not be read as if in conflict with the text. The images make sense, and make a good devotional and aesthetic sense, without us identifying persecution or resistance in the circumstances of the book's production. Rather, the book's images of hunting gather up the key sentiments of the *haggadah* and create a memorable symbolism of both abject persecution and faith: in other words, the key impetus of the *haggadah*, to return to the events of the past in order to remember for the future (which is similar to the impetus of memory-aids more generally), that each participant in the *seder* meal can personally experience both the exodus and the book which narrates this exodus. Just as in Christian sources, the idea of victimhood animated one's devotions.

The Prato Haggadah must also be considered in the context of European book production and decoration around the year 1300. To hunt (*persequor,* to track, trail, persecute, and *venor,* to hunt), in particular the stag hunt, was always replete with symbolism, not only as an allegory of love: the hunt could represent the pursuit of an ideal, the smitten soul of mankind, or the ritualized and ceremonial training of the body or mind. Hunting (with fishing, building and storing) was used as an image of information-gathering, recollection and textual composition.[37] Hugh of St Victor (*c.* 1078–1141) allegorized the pursued hind as the pure soul of mankind afflicted with longings, and this kind of allegorical hunt became one of the most 'noble' images of the individual's yearning, pursuit, questing and the loved one's emotional 'capture'.[38] Similarly, the medieval courtly literature of hunting described the harried hart bathing in water to cool itself and cover its scent as *malmené* (literally 'mistreated', 'misled'), 'a word used just as commonly elsewhere in the figurative sense, of heroes, martyrs, and lovers driven to extremes of suffering or to death.'[39] So the medieval hunt draws together the pursuit of the animal as an image of persecution with the image of the hunt as a painful kind of self-development.

Countless European Christian devotional books, from the same period as the Prato Haggadah, open with a hunting scene on the *bas-de-page* margins of their first folio. The hunting scene is used to provide a sense of 'starting off' in a Parisian copy of the book of Genesis from around 1300 (London, British Library Harley MS 616, f. 1r), in a fashion which is very similar to that used in the Prato Haggadah. It is common in European psalters to show dogs hunting deer or hares on their '*beatus vir*' page (the opening of Psalm 1), again suggesting starting off, dogs leaping after their quarry as the reader leaps into the text. In the Percy Psalter (London, British Library Add. MS 70000), made in northern England around 1300, a huntsman starts off a hunt (f. 16r; illus. 37) on the '*beatus vir*' page, and, as in the Prato Haggadah, images of hunting appear throughout the book at resonant moments: next to the beautiful description of Psalm 53 ('For strangers have risen up against me; and the mighty have sought after my soul: and they have not set God before their eyes') a man spears a bleeding deer (f. 66r). Similarly, some manuscripts show a 'before the hunt' scene on the opening page, of a sleeping or resting stag and an alert hound, as in another psalter, from England around 1340 (London, British Library Harley MS 2888, f. 9, again, the '*beatus vir*' page with which the psalms open). The hunt is an image of setting out',

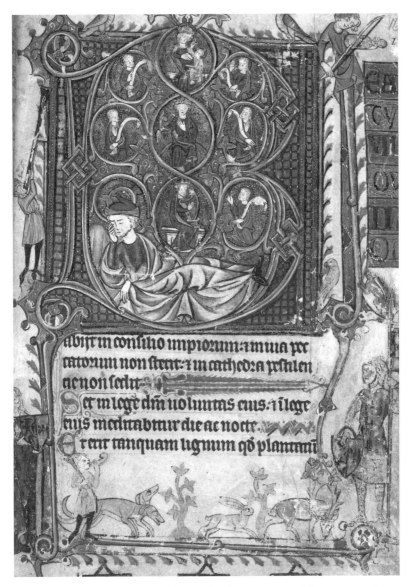

37 Starting the hunt, Percy Psalter. England, *c.* 1300. BL Add. MS 70000, f. 16r.

'starting off', beginning one's 'hunt' along the way of the book and the *loci* of memory, a call to mental action, a meaningful kind of decoration which interacts with how we receive and remember the story and how, through an imagery of violent affliction, the reading experience is made all the more potent. This makes a kind of sense which is neither 'Christian' nor 'Jewish'.

I have so far made no comment about whether the illustrator of the Prato Haggadah was Jewish or Christian, because the book is better seen as a product of the interpenetration of Jewish and Christian cultures. It would be easy to see the book's hunting imagery in terms of Jewish–Christian conflict, but the Jewish patrons of the Prato Haggadah were clearly wealthy and culturally assimilated, and the book's imaginative hunting complements the subject-matter of the *haggadah* in such a way as to purchase also on prestigious Christians models of decoration and interpretation. It would also be easy to make much of the fact that the book is unfinished: were the Jewish patrons the victims of a sudden reversal of fortune, subject to the whims of a cruel ruler or a zealous inquisitorial preacher? Maybe, but unfinished books are not uncommon – they were, after, part of a laborious industrial process – and the artist or scribe might have fallen ill, accepted a more prestigious commission, or had any number of mundane reasons for failing to complete the book.

The comments I have made about the Prato Haggadah apply to that book only: images of hares, deer and hunting mean different things in different books and in different contexts. But the Prato Haggadah is not unique amongst 'Jewish' books in using this kind of imagery. The Barcelona Haggadah (London, British Library Add. MS 14761), produced in Barcelona around 1300, also has a 'decorative' marginal scheme based around the imagery of pursuit: at the illustrated *seder* meal (f. 17v) a hound chases a hare around the margin; on the next folio (f. 18r) an archer shoots a deer, whilst a hound pounces on it; the hare hunt continues on several folios (ff. 19v; 20v; 30v; 31r; 41r; 80r), as do the archers, dogs and deer (ff. 24r; 30v; 82r). Likewise, the interlaced wyverns and hybrids and the marginal birds are followed through the book. In some cases these are anthropomorphic and clearly humorous, such as the image of a hare being served a drink by a dog (f. 30v), a mirror-image drollery of the *seder* meal being undertaken by the book's users.[40] These images hold within them the witticism of the world-turned-upside-down, which could also be seen as a feature of the Exodus story, in which incredible things like the parting of the sea and the appearance of manna transform the fortunes of the hunted victims into a heroic people.

This hunting imagery is then an aesthetic or recreational kind of persecution; books like the Prato Haggadah are de luxe productions, and speak to Jews' cultural and financial confidence and integration rather than their exclusion and communal frailty. Such books are assertions, not anxious repudiations, of confidence and cross-cultural commerce: one of the key aspects of diaspora is that people are alike, that their cultures, habits and ideas of prestige become similar, rather than separate. As Nicholas Mirzoeff cogently observes, 'the diasporic image is necessarily intertextual'.[41] Moreover, in terms of medieval manuscript culture, these books were certainly Christian-Jewish co-productions, in as much as they were influenced by Christian artistic models and devotional fashions and, possibly, produced by monastic scriptoria or commercial workshops and binderies which were mainly producing Christian books. The terms 'Jewish art' or 'Christian interpretation', or an approach to such books in terms of separation rather than miscegenation, are profoundly unhelpful. Whilst we know that the Jewish experience in medieval Europe was an unhappy one, our a priori critical approach to the Jews' books and images cannot be through the lens of 'anti-Semitism' and inter-communal conflict, but through interrogating valued narratives of victimhood, pain and persecution.

'Anti-Semitism', Cause and Affect

In his treatise *On the Soul*, the philosopher Avicenna (980–1037), who fundamentally shaped both medieval Jewish and Christian cultures, addressed the question of what it is to feel afraid and to remember pain. He observed that 'common sense' (or 'picturing') makes us perceive a wolf to be an 'enemy', a child to be a 'darling'; these perceptions, he went on, are not based on any experience of being attacked by the wolf or loved by the child but are merely our ways of reading images and shapes. They rely on reading through the 'mind's eye' which in turn relies on the reports of others: people have been savaged by wolves and have found children adorable, and this is generally known. Avicenna describes this as 'memory' and 'imagination': others have deemed wolves vicious, children adorable, and so, in receiving images of them as such we 'only preserve what another has deemed to be true': all of these images are 'artificial' but also, for Avicenna, have a mysterious and overwhelming power through which one can be terrified by a wolf, or moved by love for a child, without ever having experienced these things.[42] Because emotion does not need to follow experience, the idea of wolf or child can still be terrifying or moving, if one has never encountered a wolf or a baby. What Avicenna suggests is that someone looking on an image of persecution would (or should) not have related this to his own persecution but to an associative range of stories, memories and senses about persecution;[43] indeed, a good and active memory-image could make someone *feel persecuted* without ever having been persecuted.

Medieval Latin Christians repeated a wide range of imaginary slanders against Jews, which were useful to Christian subjects in feeling persecuted for aesthetic, intellectual and devotional reasons. I have avoided, in the preceding pages, using the term 'anti-Semitism' as a critical category by which to understand these slanderous sentiments. The term is not neutral or critically helpful and has become an anti-critical, ahistorical and totalizing term which obscures more than it illuminates. The subject of this book has been the inner world of 'trewe imaginacion & inward compassion' described in medieval Christian mysticism, a world of liturgical memory and individuated feeling encompassing reading, viewing, praying, worshipping, imitating.[44] That this inner world involved public performance – of shared devotions, in literalized, hyper-mediated spaces and luxurious books – was no contradiction in a culture in which the soul was mediated and understood through the body.[45]

Medieval culture often voices an antagonism and aggression towards Judaism: that is axiomatic. The challenge is to understand this cultural antipathy and the forms it took. The lie of Jewish murder of Christian children was partly responsible for the expulsion and execution of Jews at Bury St Edmunds (1190), Lincoln (1255) and Le Puy (1320–21); and yet the same stories, and the resulting cults of Robert of Bury and St Hugh of Lincoln – little boys said to have been slain by Jews – also remained meaningful to English Christians long after the Jews had been expelled from England in 1290 and the possibility of actual violence against Jews had vanished.[46] So texts, images and polemics of hatred can, but do not always, translate into physical violence or political disempowerment and physical and political attacks do not always reflect hatred. For example, we are now well aware that the medieval expulsions of Jewish communities (from England 1290; France 1306; Spain 1492; but also from dozens of towns, counties and principalities throughout the period) which played such a massive role in Jewish lives and Jewish history were not dependent on generalized 'hatred' and 'mob violence' but also required specific, local circumstances, involving politics, finance, internal Christian divisions and other factors.[47]

The common assumption that Christian hatred of Jews moves seamlessly from one generation to another in a relationship of continuous, stable anti-Semitism (the 'longest hatred', the 'generic hatred') underpins much recent scholarly work in this area.[48] However, medieval devotional texts and images are rhetorical records of imaginative desire, not manifestos for direct action. The tendency has been to see medieval religion as symbolic of the social – made of symbols 'through which social worlds are imagined, invented and changed'[49] – but this can make feeling and imagination seem merely weak reflections of the social. The desire to feel persecuted – to imagine fear, to remember repeatedly the pain to which one's community and one's most precious symbols have been subjected, to put oneself in a scene of torture – contrasts with the 'formation of a persecuting society' described as developing from around the year 1100. R. I. Moore has argued that an 'apparatus' was made to persecute Jews, with an associated 'image of the Jew', in which 'persecution became habitual', within 'deliberate and socially sanctioned violence [directed] against groups of people defined by general characteristics such as race, religion or way of life';[50] coterminous with this is the development of a persecuting imaginary, an exculpatory pleasure in feeling oneself to be the victim, not the victor.

So are images like those surveyed here – of Jews torturing Christ, of the Jew interrupting the Virgin's funeral, of Judas's duplicity and his red hair and his shameful end – instances of social persecution? So much of what we understand as Jewish history has been constructed through the lens of the twentieth-century destruction of European Jewry – not just the 'lachrymose conception' of Jewish history which saw diaspora life as inherently miserable but also the larger history of anti-Semitism – that it becomes easy to forget that medieval Christians did not know what catastrophes would eventually befall the Jews of Europe. This hindsight is what Michael André Bernstein has called 'backshadowing', and what George Eliot in *Daniel Deronda* called, more poetically, 'the present causes of past effects'.[51] Equating medieval violence – symbolic or real – with modern persecution is lazy history which reifies 'anti-Semitism' as a constant in which Jews are simply victims of a larger transhistorical 'phenomenon' (the 'anti-Semitic') over which one could have no control because of its inevitability and its foundational role in European, Christian culture. Such logic might be used to exculpate Nazi Germany for its crimes by suggesting the inevitability of the Holocaust, whilst also caricaturing non-Jewish society as inherently violent (and, indeed, much of this writing uses an unpleasant language of contagion, virology, mutation and monstrosity by which to describe not only Nazism and 'anti-Semitism' but also anti-Zionism and contemporary multiculturalism).[52] It is a fundamental misunderstanding to see medieval Christians as 'anti-Semites' according to the conceptions of either racial difference, genocidal ambitions or psychopathology which characterize modern understandings of the term. Likewise, the very many studies of the 'longest hatred' (to use Robert Wistrich's explicitly transhistorical term) merely place a contemporary judgement ('anti-Semitism') onto medieval sources, rather than giving an historically grounded explanation of these sources. Repeatedly, these *longue durée* approaches to the 'anti-Semitic' past negate the medieval audience, presenting medieval Christians as an unthinkingly violent mob, a receptacle for polemic, ever-ready to turn symbolic violence into an endemic, recurring pogrom.

Teasing religious symbols and historical facts from the reports of this violence, David Nirenberg has shown how attacks on Jewish areas of fourteenth-century Spanish towns were clerical and ritual events, in which the town's Jews were the victims of a violence understood by some Christians as ludic jokes, even as childish games; this violence, Nirenberg posits, can be seen as part of a tradition of 'ritualized agonistic events re-enacting and encapsulating the foundational history of Jewish-Christian relations'.[53] Nirenberg explains how actual violence against Jews was not constant, but enriched a virtual, devotional violence which was central to medieval Christian culture. Nirenberg concludes by cautioning us about our understanding of *symbolic* and *ritual* violence in trying to gauge and periodize the 'ebb and flow of intolerance' – that is, the difference or gap between 'ritual-time' and 'actual-time', a 'double-register' in Nirenberg's terms, which may have little to do with each other, or serve quite separate ends.[54] That medieval fantasies of persecution were used in the later persecution of Jewish communities is not the same as saying that medieval stereotypes *caused* this persecution. The fantasies we have seen are not impotent; they may have helped make actual persecution easier, more fulfilling, spiritually rewarding and culturally acceptable. Imaginary violence licenses actual violence by reversing or misremembering its previous imposition.[55]

Since World War II two totemic and inflexible beliefs have been central to most historical writing on 'anti-Semitism': first, an insistence on the unchanging nature of 'Jew-hatred' and, secondly, a description (usually inflected by the language of psychoanalysis) of the irrationality of this hatred. Such writing often takes an aesthetic world and treats it like a factual one, little considering the audience, the imagination or the aesthetic. In a much-cited book, Dan Cohn-Sherbok aimed 'to illustrate that for twenty centuries Christian anti-Semitism has generated hostility toward the Jewish faith and the people of Israel', arguing that 'Christian attacks on Jews were based solely on fear and ignorance'.[56] Not only does Cohn-Sherbok thus construct a Zionist teleology, in which any fearful or ignorant hostility towards Jews equals hostility towards the 'people of Israel', but he links 'fear' with 'ignorance', as if historical cultures of anti-Judaism can described and understood in terms of their stupidity. Similarly, the 'metanarrative' approach has been used by Marvin Perry and Frederick Schweitzer in a series of publications which present an ahistorical and apolitical view of anti-Semitism as 'eternal'.[57] These scholars are not just suggesting the admonitory consequences the past may have for the present; they describe a history which simply keeps repeating itself. Such an approach makes historical subjects utterly passive in their reading and viewing, for such descriptions are a way of dismissing the historical audience and thereby dismissing meaning; because the religious culture of anti-Jewish violence is distasteful, a lexicon of anti-Semitism has been used which cannot accommodate medieval Christians finding meaning in their religious books, their civic drama, their stained glass, their statues and icons. Imaginative and recreational fear, as we have seen, are highly intellectual if self-regarding things which, whilst not dealing with 'truth', were concerned with knowledge and feeling.

Hannah Arendt warned against bringing a rational critique to bear on 'anti-Semitism', which she called 'an outrage against common sense'.[58] 'Common sense' empiricism fails with texts and images of religious violence because of their hazy, indirect relationship to what they purport to represent. 'Anti-Semitism', for Arendt, is an emotion, a feeling, and so resists post-Enlightenment reason. For Arendt, a group that revels in the imagery of its own persecution is often deflecting discussion of 'their share of responsibility' for violence and injustice. This is seen clearly in medieval Christian Europe, where imagined assaults by Jews accompanied actual assaults on Jews, but may also be seen today in Zionist historiography in which victimhood ('eternal' anti-Semitism) is 'eagerly embraced' to disguise current strength.[59] An emotive narrative of a group's past based on historical grievances is unlikely to be an accurate history, even if it is an affecting one that is precious for its readership. One can identify and understand a moment of hatred or oppression without it becoming part of a sub-sequent history to which it was never a part.[60]

In place of the 'longest hatred' model, others have understood Jewish-Christian relations through psychoanalysis, seeing the Jews – and other 'outgroups' – as coded manifestations of Christian anxieties and repressions, immensely useful to a Christian audience in explor-ing and diffusing its deepest fears and its doubts; thus 'spectral' and 'imaginary' Jews have been suggested. Whilst such an approach has brought forth many valuable insights, not least into the discontents of the medieval world, it has often depended on reading symbolic violence as something else (such as doubts about the Eucharist, or conversion, or Christian identity). Is it possible that some medieval Christians and medieval Jews could have a readerly, imaginative world, structured around horror, emotion, affectivity, empathy and aesthetic violence, which is neither seamlessly connected to the terrible violence which punctuates the Jewish historical experience in medieval Europe nor able to be explained away by psychoanalysis? Medieval texts and images frequently returned to fear, violence and persecution as rhetor-ical memories, as violent ideas which served their audiences.

Violence is a powerful agent in shaping and remaking history; what I have sought to foreground instead, in the present study, is the history of solipsistic emotions involved in this history of violence, part of a growing field of the study of subjection. Just as for the oafish boy in the Grimms' tale with which I started, to feel persecuted, to enjoy fear, to seek out victimhood is to deploy, not deny, one's subjectivity. Recreational persecution is an assertion of one's self-development and a celebration of being in the world. This is not to see religious media as sado-masochistic or, as did Freud, connected to a 'universal com-pulsive neurosis'.[61] The media of religion could be seen as offering quite the opposite: empowering, totalizing and joyously sensual media. This has little to do with reality, but everything to do with vengeance and rage, pain and grief, terror and pleasure, those most self-authorizing sensations which are at the centre of Western culture. The horror of fairytales and the sensational imaginings of horror films with which this book opened also provide a good place to close: the medieval media of feeling persecuted, like fairytales and horror films, reveal a pleasure in stock 'special' effects, and a repetitive, creative delight in encountering shock, revulsion, fear and loathing as part of the development of one's recreational subjectivity.

Disturbing though it may be to some modern readers, we must remember that in the religious imagination the image of violence holds within it the image of beauty, as St Augustine made clear in a striking passage. Accompanied by two teenagers, Licentius and Trygetius, the young Augustine set out for the bath-house, a favourite place for the young men to talk about the nature of good and the divine order. On one occasion, they were interrupted before they reached the bath-house:

> All of a sudden we came across a cock fight, and eagerly watched. What wouldn't lovers of truth and beauty be eager to see and search out? Isn't any such occasion good enough to bring the beauty of reason to bear on things known and unknown, and let it attract its followers wherever and however it can? Cannot signs of it be seen anywhere and coming from anywhere? Take that cock fight. We could see their intent heads stretched forward, hackles raised, mighty thrusts of beak and spur, uncanny dodgings. There was nothing amiss in every motion of those irrational beasts. There was clearly another Reason controlling everything from on high, down to the universal law of victor and vanquished. The first crowed in triumph and puffed its feathers in a clear sign of superiority. The other had ended up with a featherless neck, voiceless, and crippled. I don't know how, but everything was a hymn to the beauty and harmony of nature.[62]

The cock fight is an implicit parallel to Augustine's struggle between good and evil, beauty and ugliness. With the invocation of 'the universal law of victor and vanquished' and the vivid description of the violence of the fight, the Crucifixion is called to mind. There is an ambiguity here about which of the birds appears as beautiful and harmonious, or whether, akin to the Crucifixion, it is the violence and contrast between the two which gives rise to beauty and harmony. In his reconciliation of the voiceless, crippled, vanquished bird with 'the beauty and harmony of nature', Augustine articulates the 'perfection and overall beauty of the fight'. This paradox of terrible beauty, a delightful fight, implanted within Christianity at Calvary, is the same paradox which governs the violent reproduction of Jewish-Christian relations in medieval culture.

189

Conventions and Abbreviations

For medieval Christian literature, I have consulted the Latin Vulgate (*Vulgata Clementina*), and given quotations from the Douay-Rheims translation (via *vulsearch.sourceforge.net/*); the latter, using Migne's edition, has also been consulted for the *Glossa Ordinaria*. For Hebrew sources in chapter Seven, I used *The JPS Hebrew-English Tanakh* (Philadelphia, 2000). Books of the Bible are given their names as per the Vulgate, and glossed in square brackets where this might cause confusion (e.g. Paralipomenon [Chronicles]). References to Chaucer refer to Larry D. Benson, general editor, *The Riverside Chaucer* (Oxford, 1987); *The Canterbury Tales* are referred to by fragment and line number. Quotations from Shakespeare refer to *Complete Works*, ed. Stanley Wells and Gary Taylor (Oxford, 1988). Quotations in Middle English have been glossed or translated where they might present difficulty for the reader unfamiliar with Middle English. Otherwise, Middle English spelling has been modernized, except where translated: obsolete letters have been replaced with their modern equivalent (*thorn* as *th*, *yogh* as *y* or *gh* as appropriate); *i/j* and *u/v* have been regularized as in modern usage. Unless otherwise noted, translations are my own.

Ap. NT   ed. J. K. Elliott, *The Apocryphal New Testament. A Collection of Apocryphal Christian Literature in an English Translation* (Oxford, 1993)

CCKJ   Denys Pringle, *Churches of the Crusader Kingdom of Jerusalem: A Corpus*, 4 vols (Cambridge, 1993–2007)

EAN   Ann Eljenholm Nichols, *The Early Art of Norfolk: A Subject List of Extant and Lost Art Including Items Relevant to Early Drama* (Kalamazoo, MI, 2002)

GL   Jacobus de Voragine, *The Golden Legend: Readings on the Saints*, trans. William Granger Ryan, 2 vols (Princeton, NJ, 1993)

Gl. Ord. Glossa Ordinaria, ed. Steven Killings after Migne, via
vulsearch.sourceforge.net/

IE   Frederic Tübach, *Index Exemplorum* (Helsinki, 1969)

LMWN   Thomas of Monmouth, *Life and Miracles of St William of
Norwich*, ed. Augustus Jessopp and M. R. James (Cambridge,
1897)

MED   *Middle English Dictionary*, gen. ed. Hans Kurath (Ann Arbor, MI,
1946–2001)

MBLJC   Nicholas Love, *The Mirror of the Blessed Life of Jesus Christ*,
ed. Michael G. Sargent (Exeter, 2004)

ODNB   *Oxford Dictionary of National Biography*

OED   *Oxford English Dictionary*

PMLA   *Publications of the Modern Language Association of America*

References

1 'He Who is in Pain is Alive'

1 Simo Knuuttila, *Emotions in Ancient and Medieval Philosophy* (Oxford, 2004), p. 159.
2 The original title (*Märchen von einem, der auszog das Fürchten zu lernen*) makes clear the educative role of fear and terror; quotations are from Jacob and Wilhelm Grimm, *Complete Fairy Tales*, ed. Padraic Colum and Joseph Campbell (London, 1948). Medieval European analogues are given in Antti Aarne and Stith Thompson, *Types of the Folktale*, 2nd edn (Helsinki, 1964), no. 326.
3 Sigmund Freud, *The Uncanny*, ed. and trans. David McLintock (London, 2003), p. 124.
4 Judith Butler, *The Psychic Life of Power: Theories in Subjection* (Stanford, CA, 1999), pp. 6–10: 'a subject is not only formed in subordination, but . . . this subordination provides the subject's continuing condition of possibility' (p. 8).
5 Michel Foucault, *Discipline and Punish: The Birth of the Prison* (New York, 1975).
6 René Girard, *Violence and the Sacred*, trans. Patrick Gregory (Baltimore, MD, 1977).
7 Elaine Scarry, *The Body in Pain: The Making and Unmaking of the World* (Oxford, 1985); Talal Asad, *Formations of the Secular: Christianity, Islam, Modernity* (Stanford, CA, 2003), p. 80.
8 Raymond Scheindlin, *The Song of the Distant Dove: Judah Halevi's Pilgrimage* (Oxford, 2008), no. 20 (pp. 203–9).
9 See Mary Carruthers, *The Craft of Thought: Meditation, Rhetoric and the Making of Images* (Cambridge, 1998), p. 264; Rachel Fulton, *From Judgment to Passion: Devotion to Christ and the Virgin Mary 800–1200* (New York, 2002), pp. 174–5.
10 Richard of St Victor, *Benjamin Minor*, trans. S. V. Yankowski (Ansbach, 1960), pp. 23–4.
11 Tertullian, *De spectaculis*, ed. T. R. Grover and Gerald Rendall

(Cambridge, MA, 1931) §I (p. 233).

12 Tractate *Sotah*, ed. I. Epstein and trans. B. D. Klien (London, 1994), §31a (p. 151).

13 I am indebted to Corey Robin's study of fear as a political tool, *Fear: The History of a Political Idea* (Oxford, 2004), especially pp. 1–35 on Burke.

14 Søren Kierkegaard, *Fear and Trembling*, ed. and trans. Alastair Hannay (London, 1985), p. 57. Sherryll Mleynek, 'Abraham, Aristotle and God: The Poetics of Sacrifice', *Journal of the American Academy of Religion*, LXII (1994), pp. 107–21, reads the binding of Isaac as akin to Aristotelian tragedy.

15 Similar to the conception of pain proposed by Scarry, *Body in Pain*, that a medical feeling of pain parallels a separate cultural vocabulary and culture of pain which attempts to describe this pain.

16 See Anne Scott and Cynthia Kosso, 'Introduction', in *Fear and Its Representations in the Middle Ages and Renaisssance*, ed. Anne Scott and Cynthia Kosso (Leiden, 2002), pp. xi–xxxvii, esp. p. xxiii.

17 Terry Eagleton, *Sweet Violence: The Idea of the Tragic* (Oxford, 2003).

18 Aristotle, *The 'Art' of Rhetoric*, ed. John Henry Freese (London, 1926), §2:5:1 (p. 201). Thus this is a significant departure from (Lacanian) psychoanalysis, in which emotion is viewed as a coercive kind of 'disattachment'; see Butler, *Psychic Life*, pp. 88–95; Rei Terada, *Feeling in Theory: Emotion after the 'Death of the Subject'* (Cambridge, MA, 2001), p. 10.

19 Joanna Bourke, *Fear: A Cultural History* (London, 2005), pp. 3–6, connects such fears that we cannot avoid with those which humans have, in effect, invented.

20 Luttrell Psalter (London, British Library Add. MS 42130, f. 92v). The book was made for Sir Geoffrey Luttrell (d. 1345) in East Anglia in the 1320s or '30s. See Michael Camille, *Mirror in Parchment: The Luttrell Psalter and the Making of Medieval England* (London, 1998).

21 On the expulsion see Robin Mundill, *England's Jewish Solution: Experiment and Expulsion, 1262–1290* (Cambridge, 1998).

22 On the later medieval elaboration of the Passion narrative, see Anne Derbes, *Picturing the Passion in Late Medieval Italy: Narrative Painting, Franciscan Ideologies, and the Levant* (Cambridge, 1996); James Marrow, *Passion Iconography in Northern European Art of the Late Middle Ages and Early Renaissance* (Brussels, 1979); James Marrow, 'Inventing the Passion in the Late Middle Ages', in *The Passion Story: From Visual Representation to Social Drama*, ed. Marcia Kupfer (University Park, PA, 2008), pp. 23–51; Thomas Bestul, *Texts of the Passion: Latin Devotional Literature and Medieval Society* (Philadelphia, 1999), pp. 69–110.

23 Paula Fredriksen, 'No Pain, No Gain?', in *Mel Gibson's Bible: Religion, Popular Culture and 'The Passion of the Christ'*, ed. Timothy K. Beal

and Tod Linafelt (Chicago, 2006), pp. 91–8; see also Jeremy Cohen, *Christ Killers: The Jews and the Passion from the Bible to the Big Screen* (Oxford, 2007); Mitchell Merback, *The Thief, the Cross and the Wheel* (London, 1999); Robert Mills, *Suspended Animation: Pain, Pleasure and Punishment in Medieval Culture* (London, 2005); Ellen O. Ross, *The Grief of God: Images of the Suffering Jesus in Late Medieval England* (Oxford, 1999).

24 *MBLJC*, p. 168. The italicized passage quotes Psalm 44:5. On the convention of the Jews torturing in pairs see Marrow, *Passion Iconography*, p. 136.

25 Thomas Aquinas, 'Quæstio 159: de crudelitate', *Summa Theologiæ*, ed. and trans. Thomas Gilby (London, 1971), §2a2æ (vol. XLIV, pp. 76–81).

26 See L. F. Sandler, 'The Word in the Text and the Image in the Margin: The Case of the Luttell Psalter', *Journal of the Walters Art Gallery*, LIV (1996), pp. 87–99; Sandler comments, 'Verbs of aggressive action, such as "to pursue", "to trouble", "to destroy", "to kill" – so common in the psalms – were particularly prone to vivid visual translation' in the Luttrell Psalter.

27 From the psalm's headnote in the Douay-Rheims translation. 'Sicut oves' – like a sheep – recalls and reverses Isaiah 53:7 ('He shall be led as a sheep to the slaughter'), understood as the figure of the *ductio Christi*, the leading of Christ to Calvary through a rich range of ordeals (Marrow, *Passion Iconography*, pp. 95–7).

28 Augustine, 'Exposition 2 of Psalm 48', *The Works of Saint Augustine*, ed. and trans. Edmund Hill (Brooklyn, NY, 1996), vol. XVI, part 3, p. 374.

29 *Gl. Ord.*, Psalm 48:16.

30 Camille, *Mirror in Parchment*, p. 284.

31 Sandler, 'Word in the Text', p. 91.

32 Augustine's Latin quotes Colossians 3:3. Augustine, 'Exposition 2', *Works*, vol. XVI, part 3, p. 369.

33 *MBLJC*, p. 179.

34 See Janet Coleman, *Ancient and Medieval Memories: Studies in the Reconstruction of the Past* (Cambridge, 1992), pp. 448–9; also Knuuttila, *Emotions*, pp. 230–39, on different understandings of fear, anger and hate; Niklaus Largier, *In Praise of the Whip: A Cultural History of Arousal*, trans. Graham Harman (New York, 2007), pp. 35–41.

35 See Jeffrey Jerome Cohen, 'Monster Culture (seven theses)', in *Monster Theory: Reading Culture*, ed. Jeffrey Jerome Cohen (Minneapolis, 1996), pp. 3–25; Judith Halberstam, *Skin Shows: Gothic Horror and the Technology of Monsters* (Durham, NC, 1995); Matt Hills, *The Pleasures of Horror* (London, 2008); Tania Modleski , 'The Terror of Pleasure: The Contemporary Horror Film and Postmodern Theory', in *Studies in Entertainment: Critical Approaches to Mass Culture*, ed. Tania Modleski (Bloomington, IN, 1986), pp. 155–66.

36 Susan Sontag, 'The Artist as Exemplary Sufferer', in *Against Interpretation*, revd edn (London, 2009), pp. 39–51, p. 47.

37 Quoting Sarah Stanbury, *The Visual Object of Desire in Late Medieval England* (Philadelphia, 2007), p. 6 (pp. 5–9 for a discussion of affective piety).

38 See Anne Clark Bartlett and Thomas H. Bestul, eds, *Cultures of Piety* (Ithaca, NY, 1999); Sarah Beckwith, *Christ's Body: Identity, Culture and Society in Late Medieval Writings* (London, 1994), esp. pp. 42–6; Bestul, *Texts of the Passion*, pp. 1–26; Hans Belting, *Likeness and Presence: A History of the Image before the Era of Art,* trans. Edmund Jephcott (Chicago, 1996); Caroline Walker Bynum, *Holy Feast and Holy Fast: The Religious Significance of Food to Medieval Women* (Berkeley, CA, 1987); Esther Cohen, 'The Animated Pain of the Body', *American Historical Review*, CV (2000), pp. 36–68; Emily Richards, 'Writing and Silence: Transitions Between the Contemplative and Active Life', in *Pieties in Transition: Religious Practices and Experiences c. 1400–1640*, ed. Robert Lutton and Elisabeth Salter (Aldershot, 2007), pp. 163–79.

39 Caroline Walker Bynum, *Wonderful Blood: Theology and Practice in Late Medieval Northern Germany and Beyond* (Philadelphia, 2007), p. 121.

40 Miri Rubin, 'The Body, Whole and Vulnerable, in Fifteenth-Century England', in *Bodies and Disciplines: Intersections of Literature and History in Fifteenth-Century England*, ed. Barbara Hanawalt and David Wallace (Minneapolis, 1996), pp. 19–28; see too Bettina Bildhauer, *Medieval Blood* (Cardiff, 2006); Bildhauer comments that 'the body was not a self-evident entity in the Middle Ages, but one laboriously upheld by truth games and prohibitions against blood and bleeding, which were often discussed in disproportionate relation to what actual bodily harm they could cause' (p. 165).

41 See Scott E. Pincikowski, *Bodies of Pain: Suffering in the Works of Hartmann von Aue* (London, 2002), pp. 1–20, for a succinct summary of medieval and modern theories of pain; Bourke, *Fear*, pp. 73–6, on modern 'emotionology', pain and fear.

42 Graham Music, *Affect and Emotion* (Cambridge, 2001), pp. 4–8, defines feeling, emotion and affect, through a psychoanalytic lens.

43 The recent 'affective turn' in scholarship likewise tends to value the individual's experience over historical 'events'; however, this 'turn' is often also associated with conjectural interpretations of the past and a disregard for historical specificity. For a cogent discussion see Barbara H. Rosenwein, 'Worrying about Emotions in History', *American Historical Review*, CVII (2002), pp. 821–44.

44 Jesse Prinz, *The Emotional Construction of Morals* (Oxford, 2007).

45 MBLJC, pp. 171–4.

46 Mark Amsler, 'Affective Literacy: Gestures of Reading in the Later

Middle Ages', *Essays in Medieval Studies*, XVIII (2001), pp. 83–110; Mills, *Suspended Animation*.

47 Michael Camille, '"Seeing and Lecturing": Disputation from a Twelfth-Century Tympanum from Reims', in *Reading Medieval Images: The Art Historian and the Object*, ed. Elizabeth Sears, Thelma K. Thomas and Ilene H. Forsyth (Ann Arbor, MI, 2002), pp. 75–87, p. 78; Michael Camille, 'Seeing and Reading: Some Visual Implications of Medieval Literacy and Illiteracy', *Art History*, VIII (1985), pp. 26–32. See also Martha Dana Rust, *Imaginary Worlds in Medieval Books: Exploring the Manuscript Matrix* (New York, 2007), pp. 17–22.

48 These examples are taken from *MED*.

49 James Averill, 'Inner Feelings, Works of the Flesh, the Beast Within, Diseases of the Mind, Driving Force, and Putting on a Show: Six Metaphors of Emotion and their Theoretical Extensions', in *Metaphors in the History of Psychology*, ed. D. E. Leary (Cambridge, 1990), pp. 104–32 (pp. 106–7); on 'holy terror' in visual images see Jacques Rancière, *The Future of the Image*, trans. Gregory Elliott (London, 2008), pp. 135–7.

50 Jessica Brantley, *Reading in the Wilderness: Private Devotion and Public Performance in Late Medieval England* (Chicago, 2007), p. 2.

51 Camille, 'Seeing and Reading', p. 43.

52 Brantley, *Reading*, pp. 8–19.

53 Gilles Deleuze, *Cinema 1*, trans. Hugh Tomlinson and Barbara Habberjam (London, 1986), p. 42.

54 Wolfgang Iser, *The Act of Reading: A Theory of Aesthetic Response* (Baltimore, MD, 1978), p. 21.

55 Quoted in Michael Baxandall, *Painting and Experience in Renaissance Italy: A Primer in the Social History of Pictorial Style* (Harmondsworth, 1972), p. 41, emphases added; see too Hans Belting, *The Image and its Public in the Middle Ages: Form and Function in Early Paintings of the Passion*, trans. Mark Bartusis and Raymond Meyer (New Rochelle, NY, 1990), chap. 3.

56 Jill Bennett, 'Stigmata and Sense Memory: St Francis and the Affective Image', *Art History*, XXIV (2001), pp. 1–16, p. 6.

57 See Suzannah Biernoff, *Sight and Embodiment in the Middle Ages* (Basingstoke, 2002); Katherine Tachau, *Vision and Certitude in the Age of Ockham: Optics, Epistemology and the Foundations of Semantics 1250–1345* (Leiden, 1988), esp. pp. 6–16; Cynthia Hahn, '*Visio Dei*: Changes in Medieval Visuality', in *Visuality Before and Beyond the Renaissance*, ed. Robert S. Nelson (Cambridge, 2000), pp. 169–96.

58 Mary Carruthers, *The Book of Memory: A Study of Memory in Medieval Culture*, 2nd edn (Cambridge, 2008), p. 60.

59 Bennett, 'Stigmata', p. 4.

60 These examples are taken from *MED*.

61 Merback, *Thief*, p. 298.

62 Aristotle, *Rhetoric*, ed. Freese, §2:5:1 (p. 201).

63 Ibid., §2:5:1 (p. 209).

64 Knuuttila, *Emotions*, esp. p. 118 on classifying such emotions.

65 Aristotle, *Rhetoric*, ed. Freese, §2:8:12–14 (p. 229).

66 Asad, *Formations of the Secular*, p. 78.

67 Bynum, *Wonderful Blood*, p. 1.

68 See Carruthers, *Craft of Thought*, p. 104 and pp. 80–81, 113–14, 152; Merback, *Thief*, p. 16.

69 Psalm 116:15: 'Precious in the sight of the Lord is the death of His saints' (see David Biale, *Blood and Belief: The Circulation of a Symbol Between Christians and Jews* (Berkeley, CA, 2008), p. 74); on valorized bloodshedding see Biale, *Blood*; Bynum, *Wonderful Blood*; Peggy McCracken, *The Curse of Eve, the Wound of the Hero: Blood, Gender and Medieval Literature* (Philadelphia, 2003).

70 Eve Kosofsky Sedgwick, *Touching Feeling: Affect, Pedagogy, Performativity* (Durham, NC, 2003), pp. 130–31.

71 'Victim', from Latin *victima* (scapegoat, sacrificial offering), was not commonly used in the English language until the seventeenth century; 'martyr' (from the late Latin *martyr*, literally a 'witness', but used in Middle English to describe one who suffers for God or for love) is a more historically accurate term. Claire Sponsler has eloquently described the radical identification of the medieval self with the martyr's tortured body; see her *Drama and Resistance: Bodies, Goods and Theatricality in Late Medieval England* (Minneapolis, 1997), pp. 108–18.

72 Bernard of Clairvaux's sermon on the Last Beatitude contrasts the Christian shepherd and sheep with 'robbers', 'wolves' and 'hirelings', who 'do not suffer persecution for righteousness' sake so much as preferring to endure persecution rather than maintain righteousness . . .'. Bernard of Clairvaux, *Selected Writings*, ed. G. R. Evans (London, 1988), p. 96.

73 Augustine, *The City of God Against the Pagans*, ed. R. W. Dyson (Cambridge, 1998), §xiv:8 (p. 595).

74 Ibid., §xiv:8 (p. 596); Roger Bacon, *Opus Majus*, ed. and trans. Robert Belle Burke (London, 1928), vol. ii, p. 713.

75 Augustine, *City of God*, ed. Dyson, §xxi:3 (p. 1046).

76 Ibid., §xviii:51 (p. 899), §xix:27 (p. 964); Cohen, 'Animated Pain of the Body'.

77 See Cohen, 'Animated Pain of the Body', pp. 42–5, coining 'philo-passionism'.

78 Asad, *Formations of the Secular*, p. 79.

79 *The Jewish-Christian Debate in the High Middle Ages: A Critical Edition of the Nizzahon Vetus*, ed. and trans. David Berger (Philadelphia, 1979), p. 41.

80 Bernard of Clairvaux, *Selected Writings*, ed. Evans, p. 96.

81 Israel Jacob Yuval, *Two Nations in Your Womb: Perceptions of Jews and*

Christians in Late Antiquity and the Middle Ages, trans. Barbara Harshav and Jonathan Chipman (Berkeley, CA, 2006); Kenneth Stow,
Jewish Dogs: An Image and its Interpreters (Stanford, CA, 2006), p. 23.

82 Biale, *Blood*.

83 Jeremy Cohen, *Sanctifying the Name of God: Jewish Martyrs and Jewish
Memories of the First Crusade* (Philadelphia, 2004), pp. vii–viii; Susan
Einbinder, *No Place of Rest: Jewish Literature, Expulsion, and the
Memory of Medieval France* (Philadelphia, 2009); Steven Kruger,
The Spectral Jew: Conversion and Embodiment in Medieval Europe
(Minneapolis, 2006).

84 Augustine, *City of God*, ed. Dyson, §XXI:8 (p. 1063).

85 Seraphine Guerchberg, 'The Controversy over the Alleged Sowers of
the Black Death in the Contemporary Treatises on Plague', in *Change
in Medieval Society: Europe North of the Alps 1050–1500*, ed. Sylvia
Thrupp (New York, 1964), pp. 208–24.

86 Quoted in A. S. Abulafia, 'The Intellectual and Spiritual Quest for
Christ', in *Religious Violence Between Christians and Jews*, ed. A. S.
Abulafia (Basingstoke, 2002), pp. 61–85, p. 69. On 'overt antisemitism'
in Franciscan Passion devotion see Derbes, *Picturing the Passion*,
pp. 90–93; Colum Hourihane, *Pontius Pilate, Anti-Semitism, and the
Passion in Medieval Art* (Princeton, NJ, 2009).

87 References from MED s.v. 'wounde'.

88 Merback, *Thief*, p. 20.

89 Catherine of Siena, *The Dialogue*, ed. and trans. Suzanne Noffke
(New York, 1980), pp. 157, 217, 33, 27.

90 Anselm, 'Cur Deus Homo?', in *Basic Writings*, ed. and trans. Thomas
Williams (Indianapolis, 2007), §I:3–4 (p.248).

91 See Norman Cohn, *Pursuit of the Millennium* (Oxford, 1970), pp. 78–86;
also Largier, *In Praise of the Whip*, pp. 101–46.

92 Quoting and translated after Pavel Kalina, '*Cordium penetrativa*: An
Essay on Iconoclasm and Image Worship Around the Year 1400',
Umění, XLIII (1995), pp. 247–57, p. 248.

93 Merback, *Thief*, p. 47.

2 The Violence of Memory: Seven Kinds of
'Jewish' Torture

1 John Shinners, ed., *Medieval Popular Religion 1000–1500: A Reader*
(Peterborough, ON, 1997), p. 333. The regimen is pp. 332–4.

2 Harold Weinrich, *Lethe: The Art and Critique of Forgetting* (Ithaca,
NY, 2004), p. 9.

3 Rita Copeland, 'Introduction: Dissenting Critical Practices', in *Criticism
and Dissent in the Middle Ages*, ed. Rita Copeland (Cambridge, 1996),
pp. 6–15.

4 Anke Bernau, 'A Christian Corpus: Virginity, Violence and Knowledge

in the Life of St Katherine of Alexandria', in *St Katherine of Alexandria: Texts and Contexts in Medieval Europe*, ed. Jacqueline Jenkins and Katherine Lewis (Turnhout, 2003), pp. 109–30.

5 Conrad Rudolph, *Violence and Daily Life: Reading, Art, and Polemics in the Cîteaux Moralia in Job* (Princeton, NJ, 1997), pp. 42, 57.

6 Mary Carruthers, *The Book of Memory: A Study of Memory in Medieval Culture*, 2nd edn (Cambridge, 2008), pp. 166–8; Mary Carruthers, 'Reading with Attitude, Remembering the Book', in *The Book and the Body*, ed. D. W. Frese and K. O'Brien O'Keeffe (South Bend, IN, 1997), pp. 1–33, p. 2. See also Stephen Greenblatt, 'Mutilation and Meaning', in *The Body in Parts: Fantasies of Corporeality in Early Modern Europe*, ed. David Hillman and Carla Mazzio (London, 1997), pp. 221–41, on the 'engraving of the name of Jesus' as a bloody wound and 'sweet delight'.

7 Jody Enders, *The Medieval Theater of Cruelty* (Ithaca, NY, 1999), pp. 25–8.

8 Bruce Holsinger, 'Pedagogy, Violence, and the Subject of Music: Chaucer's "Prioress's Tale" and the Ideologies of "Song"', *New Medieval Literatures*, I (1997), pp. 157–92.

9 Suzannah Biernoff, *Sight and Embodiment in the Middle Ages* (Basingstoke, 2002), especially pp. 143–9.

10 See Thomas Bestul, *Texts of the Passion: Latin Devotional Literature and Medieval Society* (Philadelphia, 1999), pp. 147–64, on how 'methods of torture and experience of the spectacle of tortured victims may have conditioned the representations of the sufferings of Christ'; also Elizabeth Hanson, 'Torture and Truth in Renaissance England', *Representations*, XXXIV (1991), pp. 53–84

11 Robert Mills, *Suspended Animation: Pain, Pleasure and Punishment in Medieval Culture* (London, 2005), p. 54.

12 Indeed, many medieval thinkers – including Vincent of Beauvais, Geoffrey Chaucer, and the English friars John Bromyard and Robert Holcot – made clear that actual corporal punishment was to be avoided, but beating schoolchildren and criminals was approved of by many as a mode of reform; see Nicholas Orme, *Medieval Children* (New Haven, CT, 2001), pp. 83–5; Shulamith Shahar, 'The Boy Bishop's Feast: A Case Study in Church Attitudes Towards Children in the High and Late Middle Ages', *Studies in Church History*, XXXI (1994), pp. 243–60.

13 George Kennedy, *Classical Rhetoric and its Christian and Secular Tradition from Ancient to Modern Times* (London, 1980), p. 46; Janet Coleman, *Ancient and Medieval Memories: Studies in the Reconstruction of the Past* (Cambridge, 1992), pp. 39–59.

14 Quintilian, *The Orator's Education*, ed. and trans. Donald A. Russell (Cambridge, 2001), §6:2:7 (p. 49).

15 Donald Clark, *Rhetoric and Poetry in the Renaissance: A Study of Rhetorical Terms in English Renaissance Literary Criticism* (New York,

1922), pp. 66–9; Kennedy, *Classical Rhetoric*, pp. 198–9, describes the recovery of the complete Quintilian in the fifteenth century.

16 Quintilian, *Orator's Education*, §6:1:36 (p. 35); §6:1:44 (p. 39).

17 Ibid., §6:2:8–10 (p. 49).

18 Ibid., §6:2:20 (p. 55); §6:2:11–14 (p. 50).

19 Ibid., §6:2:24 (p. 57).

20 Ibid., §6:2:31 (p. 61).

21 Ibid., §6:2:29–30 (pp. 59–61).

22 *MBLJC*, p. 174.

23 Quintilian, *Orator's Education*, §6:2:34 (p. 63).

24 Ibid., §6:2:32 (p. 61).

25 [Cicero], *Ad Herennium*, ed. Harry Caplan (Cambridge, MA, 1954), §3:22:37 (p. 221).

26 See Coleman, *Ancient and Medieval Memories*, p. 448.

27 Bernard of Clairvaux, 'On Conversion', in *Selected Writings*, ed. G. R. Evans (London, 1988), §3:4 (p. 69).

28 A similar argument has recently been put forward, using Quintilian and *Ad Herennium*, by Theodore Lerud, *Memory, Images, and the English Corpus Christi Drama* (New York, 2008), pp. 7–13.

29 Emile Mâle, *The Gothic Image: Religious Art in France of the Thirteenth Century*, trans. Dora Nussey (New York, 1958), pp. 98–104; James Paxson, *The Poetics of Personification* (Cambridge, 1994), pp. 63–8; Mary Carruthers, *The Craft of Thought: Meditation, Rhetoric and the Making of Images* (Cambridge, 1998), pp. 143–50.

30 Prudentius, 'Psychomachia', in *Prudentius*, ed. and trans. H. J. Thomson (Cambridge, MA, 1959), vol. I, pp. 274–343, quoting pp. 329, 309.

31 On da Signa, see Mary Carruthers and Jan Ziolkowski, *The Medieval Craft of Memory: An Anthology of Texts and Pictures* (Philadelphia, 2002), pp. 103–18; on Bradwardine, see Carruthers, *Book of Memory*, pp. 361–8.

32 Enders, *Medieval Theater of Cruelty*, pp. 66, 70.

33 *GL*, vol. I, p. 203.

34 [Thomas a Kempis], *The First English Translation of the Imitatio Christi*, ed. Brendan Biggs (Oxford, 1997), p. 57.

35 Eckhart, 'Sermon 14: *In occisione gladii mortui sunt*', in *Selected Writings*, ed. and trans. Oliver Davies (London, 1994), p. 164.

36 Ibid., p. 165.

37 See Bernard of Clairvaux, *A Devotional Commentary on Psalm Ninety-One*, ed. and trans. anon. (London, 1953), p. 13.

38 Georges Duby, *The Age of the Cathedrals* (Chicago, 1981), p. 243.

39 Described and photographed in John Lowden and John Cherry, *Medieval Ivories and Works of Art: The Thomson Collection at the Art Gallery of Ontario* (Toronto, 2008), pp. 46–9.

40 Lee Patterson, 'Living Witnesses of our Redemption: Martyrdom and Imitation in Chaucer's Prioress's Tale', *Journal of Medieval and Early*

Modern Studies, XXXI (2001), pp. 507–60; see *GL*, vol. I, pp. 56–9. Medieval culture consistently made the connection with Rachel.

41 M. P. Hamilton, 'Echoes of Childermas in the Tale of the Prioress', *Modern Language Review*, XXXIV (1939), pp. 1–8; Clifford Davidson, *Festivals and Plays in Late Medieval Britain* (Aldershot, 2007), pp. 8–12.

42 *GL*, vol. I, p. 58 notes sceptically 'some of the Holy Innocents' bones have been preserved' but 'are so large that they could not have come from two-ycar-olds'.

43 See Shahar, 'Boy Bishop's Feast'; Eve Salisbury, '"Spare the Rod and Spoil the Child": Proverbial Speech Acts, Boy Bishop Sermons, and Pedagogical Violence', in *Speculum Sermonis: Interdisciplinary Reflections on the Medieval Sermon*, ed. Georgiana Donavin, Cary Nederman and Richard Utz (Turnhout, 2004), pp. 141–55, p. 141, noting these ceremonies 'disclose a mode of corporal discipline harsh even by medieval standards'; Richard DeMolen, '*Puer Christi imitatio*: the festival of the boy-bishops in Tudor England', *Moreana*, XXI (1975), pp. 17–28.

44 *GL*, vol. I, p. 58; Leah Sinanoglou, 'The Christ Child as Sacrifice: A Medieval Tradition and the Corpus Christi Plays', *Speculum*, XLVIII (1973), pp. 491–509, p. 501.

45 See F. David Martin, *Sculpture and Enlivened Space* (Lexington, KY, 1981), on how 'carnal' sculpture reveals our 'withness with things' (p. 171), a 'kinaesthetic reinforcement' of 'tactual' sensations.

46 See Jeremy Cohen, *Sanctifying the Name of God: Jewish Martyrs and Jewish Memories of the First Crusade* (Philadelphia, 2004), p. 120. Cohen analyses the Jewish victim of the Crusaders, Rachel of Mainz, as a semi-literary character, drawn from Jewish and Christian understandings of the biblical Rachel's mourning.

47 On liturgical elements, see Hamilton, 'Echoes'.

48 Enders, *Medieval Theater of Cruelty*, p. 27.

49 Published with a brief discussion in *Medieval English Lyrics*, ed. R. T. Davies (London, 1963), no. 183 (pp. 292–3).

50 For a conventional lullaby to the infant Christ see 'Lullay, myn lykyng', in ibid., no. 77. On the genre of 'sentimentally evocative' lyrics 'mingling grim warning with melancholy' see Rosemary Woolf, *The English Religious Lyric in the Middle Ages* (Oxford, 1968), pp. 154–7.

51 This, and subsequent, quotations from *Medieval English Lyrics*, ed. Theodore Silverstein (London, 1971), pp. 107–9. An early example in English, from *c.* 1330, is the homiletic poem 'Lollai, lollai, litil child' (see *Medieval English Lyrics*, ed. Silverstein, pp. 54–6). This poem appears in both English and Latin ('*Lolla, lolla, parvule . . .* ') in its manuscript (London, British Library Harley MS 913, ff. 32r–v, 63v), probably written by Franciscans in or around Waterford, Ireland (Neil Cartlidge, 'Festivity, Order, and Community in Fourteenth-century Ireland: The Composition and Contexts of BL MS Harley 913', *Yearbook*

of English Studies, XXXIII (2003), pp. 33–52). This poem is not addressed to the Christ-Child but by a mother to her 'litil child' as she meditates on the 'wikidnes' and 'sorow' that he will encounter in his life. The Franciscan background of this poem is unsurprising, given this order's sponsorship of the image of Christ's broken body in medieval devotion.

52 Bernard of Clairvaux, 'Sermons on the Song of Songs', in *Selected Works*, p. 220.

53 Edinburgh, National Library of Scotland Advocates' MS 18.7.21; see E. Wilson, *A Descriptive Index of the English Lyrics in John of Grimestone's Preaching Book* (Oxford, 1973); the poem is quoted here from *Middle English Lyrics*, ed. Maxwell Luria and Richard Hoffman (New York, 1974), no. 201.

54 Marina Warner, *No Go the Bogeyman: Scaring, Lulling and Making Mock* (London, 1998).

55 GL, vol. I, p. 71.

56 Leo Steinberg, *The Sexuality of Christ in Renaissance Art and in Modern Oblivion*, 2nd edn (Chicago, 1996), p. 51. Thus Jacobus de Voragine states unequivocally that Christ 'chose to be circumcised and to shed blood, because no phantasm can bleed' (GL, vol. I, p. 74), i.e., the circumcision is proof of Christ's humanity.

57 Anthony Bale, *The Jew in the Medieval Book: English Antisemitisms 1350–1500* (Cambridge, 2006), p. 132; Steven Kruger, *The Spectral Jew: Conversion and Embodiment in Medieval Europe* (Minneapolis, 2006), pp. 82–5; Simon of Trent (d. 1475) was represented as having his genitals mutilated (see Lionello Puppi, *Torment in Art: Pain, Violence and Martyrdom* (New York, 1991), p. 71).

58 MBLJC, pp. 41–3.

59 Contra Kathleen Biddick, *The Typological Imaginary: Circumcision, Technology, History* (Philadelphia, 2003).

60 Quotations are from John Lydgate, *Life of Our Lady*, ed. Joseph Lauritis (Pittsburgh, 1961).

61 See Steinberg, *Sexuality of Christ*, pp. 112–15; Lydgate borrowed directly from MBLJC, p. 42 (Jesus 'put his litel hande to hire face, als he wold that she shold not wepe . . .').

62 See J. Huizinga, *The Waning of the Middle Ages*, trans. F. Hopman (London, 1955), p. 10.

63 On the tiles' background and narrative sources see M. R. James and R. L. Hobson, 'Rare Mediaeval Tiles and their Story', *Burlington Magazine*, LII (1923), pp. 32–7. The main sources for the tiles are the 'infancy gospels', apocryphal accounts of the childhood of Jesus, but, by the fourteenth century, these had informed a huge number of *exempla* and preaching stories (see Sinanoglou, 'The Christ Child').

64 There is no firm evidence that the tiles were displayed at Tring's parish church.

65 See *Ap. NT*, pp. 88–99 (at §30–31 (p. 90), derived from Greek and Syriac).

66 *Ap. NT*, §31 (p. 90). This reverses Ecclesiasticus 30:1, 'He that loveth his son, frequently chastiseth him...'

67 *Enfaunces de Jesu Crist* or *Evangile de l'enfance* (Oxford, Bodleian Library MS Selden Supra 38). See James and Hobson, 'Rare Mediaeval Tiles'; Maureen Boulton, '"Evangile de l'enfance": Text and Illustration in Oxford, Bodleian Library, MS Selden Supra 38', *Scriptorium*, XXXVII (1983), pp. 54–65. Mary Dzon, 'Joseph and the Amazing Christ-Child of Late-Medieval Legend', in *Childhood in the Middle Ages and Renaissance*, ed. Albrecht Classen (Grand Rapids, MI, 2005), pp. 135–58, focuses on the representation of Joseph but includes a brief discussion (pp. 146–9) of the Middle English version of the miracles, noting (p. 148, n. 48) that 'the Middle English poets exaggerate the Jews' malice by having these characters threaten to make mincemeat out of Joseph and Mary, and to crucify Jesus'.

68 See Maureen Boulton, ed., *Les Enfaunces de Jesu Crist* (London, 1985), lines 853–956.

69 For Middle English versions, which are not as close to the Tring tile narrative as the Anglo-Norman text, see Roscoe Parker, ed., *The Middle English Stanzaic Version of the Life of St Anne* (London, 1928), lines 2083–227; *Altenglische Legenden*, ed. Carl Horstmann (Heilbronn, 1881), pp. 44–7; on a parallel, see C. M. Kauffmann, 'Art and Popular Culture: New Themes in the Holkham Library Picture Book', in *Studies in Medieval Art and Architecture*, ed. D. Buckton and T. A. Heslop (London, 1994), pp. 46–69.

70 E.g. *IE* 4715 (the Christ-Child drinks a nun's tears and then washes himself and her with them); *IE* 2689 (the Host transforms into the Christ-Child or bleeding flesh, an extremely common story); *IE* 3216 (the Christ-Child is laid upon the altar); *IE* 5207 (the Christ-Child's bathwater stints a child's crying).

71 Boulton, ed., *Enfaunces de Jesu Crist*, lines 495–8; 506–15; 1016–17; 1536–7.

72 See Holsinger, 'Violence', pp. 164–7.

73 'A Child is Being Beaten', in Sigmund Freud, *The Psychology of Love*, ed. Jeri Johnson (London, 2006), pp. 279–305, (pp. 281–2). See Largier, *In Praise of the Whip*, for a reading of medieval flagellation concerned with its eroticism.

74 Freud, 'Child', p. 286.

75 On the origins and early development of William's cult see John McCulloh, 'Jewish Ritual Murder: William of Norwich, Thomas of Monmouth and the Early Dissemination of the Myth', *Speculum*, LXXII (1997), pp. 698–740.

76 Bale, *Jew in the Medieval Book*, p. 125, including further details about the Loddon rood screen.

77 E.g. LMWN, pp. 88–9.

78 Ibid., p. 11.

79 Nigel Hiscock, *The Symbol at Your Door: Number and Geometry in Religious Architecture of the Greek and Latin Middle Ages* (Aldershot, 2007), pp. 154–5, 191–2.

80 Steven Kruger, *Dreaming in the Middle Ages* (Cambridge, 1992), p. 65.

81 Thus Albertus Magnus (d. 1280), in his commentary on Aristotle's *De divinatione per somnum*, suggests three types of visionary experience akin to Thomas's account of Elviva's dream: 'the dream's import is shown in appropriate metaphors that can be reliably interpreted'; 'the dream is not metaphorical, but rather expresses its meaning in image what will actually occur . . .'; dream images are presented and explained by someone who appears in the dream; the explanations, however, are not explicit but rather made "in verbis et figuris" [in words and figures].' Kruger, *Dreaming*, p. 120.

82 LMWN, p. 12. These features of William's cult are borrowed from that of St Lucy, whose attribute was a lamp and who was venerated with candles. The English *luce* for pike comes from Latin (*Esox Lucius*), via Old French *lus*.

83 Ibid., pp. 20, 192.

84 Ibid., p. xci.

85 Ibid., pp. 40–41. See Hannah Johnson, 'Rhetoric's Work: Thomas of Monmouth and the History of Forgetting', *New Medieval Literatures*, IX (2007), pp. 63–91, p. 91, on how the later parts of Thomas's work 'are premised on a kind of forgetting of the originary crime, allowing it to recede into the background as toothaches and fluxes, paralyzed limbs, and painful swellings come to the fore.'

86 LMWN, p. 101.

87 Ibid., pp. 7; 99; 110. Thomas's account has been used as a factual source by many scholars; e.g. Robert Chazan, *Church, State and Jew in the Middle Ages* (Springfield, NJ, 1979), p. 152; James Given, *Society and Homicide in Thirteenth-Century England* (Stanford, CA, 1977), pp. 51–2; Edmund King, *The Anarchy of King Stephen's Reign* (Oxford, 1994), p. 131. Gavin Langmuir, *Toward a Definition of Antisemitism* (Berkeley, CA, 1990), p. 233, notes the 'avowedly fictional' nature of this section but says that without it 'we would not have known about the case of Simon de Novers.'

88 LMWN, p. 97.

89 Ibid., p. 99.

90 Ibid., p. 111; James's polite translation is 'internal haemorrhage'; the Latin, 'per posteriora eius sanguis guttatim profluere inchoauit', 'drop by drop blood began to flow forth from his backside', is more graphic.

91 On Norwich, and the outplaying of the allegation, see McCulloh, 'Jewish Ritual Murder'; on Lincoln, see Gavin Langmuir, 'The Knight's Tale of Young Hugh of Lincoln', *Speculum*, XLII (1972), pp. 459–82; on

Trent, see Ronnie Po-Chia Hsia, *Trent 1475: Stories of a Ritual Murder Trial* (New Haven, CT, 1996).

92 On the background and devotional context of the Broughton image see Miriam Gill, 'From Urban Myth to Didactic Image: The Warning to Swearers', in *The Hands of the Tongue: Essays on Deviant Speech*, ed. Edwin D. Craun (Kalamazoo, MI, 2007), pp. 137–60.

93 William Shakespeare, *Henry IV Part 1*, III.1.242–51 (p. 470).

94 On the Five Wounds see Adelaide Bennett, 'Christ's Five Wounds in the Aves of the Vita Christi in a Book of Hours about 1300', in *Tributes in Honor of James H. Marrow*, ed. Jeffrey Hamburger and Anne Korteweg (London, 2006), pp. 75–84; Eamon Duffy, *The Stripping of the Altars: Traditional Religion in England 1400–1580* (New Haven, NJ, 1992), pp. 243–8; on the sacred heart, Andreas Bräm, 'Von Herzen: Ein Beitrag zur systematischen Ikopnographie', *Micrologus*, XI (2003), pp. 159–92; on capital punishment see Mills, *Suspended Animation*, pp. 22–4.

95 Martin Stevens and A. C. Cawley, eds, 'Judgement', in *The Towneley Plays* (Oxford, 1994), play 30, lines 526–33 (vol. I, p. 416).

96 Ruth Mellinkoff, *Outcasts: Signs of Otherness in Northern European Art of the Late Middle Ages* (Berkeley, CA, 1993), vol. I, p. 246; Gill, 'From Urban Myth', p. 140, observes that in some of the written sources the swearer is a Lombard merchant or rich man.

97 *RC*, VII:472–6.

98 Translated in Woolf, *English Religious Lyric*, p. 395.

99 Quoted from John Mirk, *Mirk's Festial*, ed. Theodor Erbe (London, 1905), pp. 113–14. The Latin source is the *Gesta Romanorum* (a popular pan-European *exempla* collection).

100 Caesarius of Heisterbach, *Dialogus Miraculorum*, ed. Joseph Strange (Cologne, 1851), Libri VIII:II:6 (vol. I, p. 95).

101 See Athene Reiss, *The Sunday Christ: Sabbatarianism in English Medieval Wall Painting* (Oxford, 2000), esp. pp. 33–5 on the 'interactive relationship' and 'individual implication' of the Sunday Christ. This is not dissimilar to the well-known Charters of Christ; see Martha Dana Rust, *Imaginary Worlds in Medieval Books: Exploring the Manuscript Matrix* (New York, 2007), pp. 19–21; on other analogues, Duffy, *Stripping*, pp. 238–48.

102 Michael Camille, *Mirror in Parchment: The Luttrell Psalter and the Making of Medieval England* (London, 1998), pp. 284–90.

3 The Jewish Profile and the History of Ugliness

1 See Todd Samuel Presner, '"Clear Heads, Solid Stomachs, and Hard Muscles": Max Nordau and the Aesthetics of Jewish Regeneration', *Modernism/modernity*, x (2003), pp. 269–96, esp. pp. 270–74 on the competing modes of depictions of Jews; also Eric Michaud, *The Cult*

of Art in Nazi Germany, trans. Janet Lloyd (Stanford, CA, 2004). See too Sander Gilman, *Health and Illness: Images of Difference* (London, 1995), pp. 51–67 (on Jews as 'the very model of the ugly and diseased', p. 55); Umberto Eco, *On Ugliness*, trans. Alastair McEwen (London, 2007), pp. 263–9. Michael Camille, *The Gargoyles of Notre Dame* (Chicago, 2009), chap. 4 ('Monsters of Race') describes the nineteenth-century rebuilding of Notre-Dame and its indebtedness to that century's racist concerns.

2 Maurice Kriegel, 'Un trait de psychologie sociale dans les pays méditerranéens du bas Moyen Age: le juif comme intouchable', *Annales, économies, sociétés, civilisations*, XXXI (1976), pp. 326–30; also Alexandra Cuffel, *Gendering Disgust in Medieval Religious Polemic* (Notre Dame, IN, 2007), pp. 160–82. On reading the body in medieval culture see John Burrow's concise survey, *Looks and Gestures in Medieval English Literature* (Cambridge, 2004); Jole Agrimi, 'Fisognomica e scolastica', *Micrologus*, I (1993), pp. 235–71.

3 Moshe Barasch, *Giotto and the Language of Gesture* (Cambridge, 1987), pp. 159–62.

4 Ibid., p. 160.

5 See Moshe Zimmermann, *Wilhelm Marr: The Patriarch of Anti-Semitism* (New York, 1986).

6 Casper Lavater, *The Physiognomist's Own Book: An Introduction to Physiognomy Drawn from the Writings of Lavater* (Pittsburgh, PA, 1841).

7 See Lynn Thorndike, *Michael Scot* (London, 1965); Martin Porter, *Windows of the Soul: Physiognomy in European Culture 1470–1780* (Oxford, 2005).

8 John Lydgate and Benedict Burgh, *Secrees of old Philisoffres: A Version of the 'Secreta Secretorum'*, ed. Robert Steele (London, 1894).

9 Ibid., lines 2530, 2607, 2628, 2656, 2717–18.

10 For the relevant images see Ruth Mellinkoff, *Antisemitic Hate Signs in Hebrew Illuminated Manuscripts from Medieval Germany* (Jerusalem, 1999), pp. 19–21; Ruth Mellinkoff, *Outcasts: Signs of Otherness in the Northern European Art of the Later Middle Ages* (Berkeley, CA, 1994), vol. I, pp. 122–33, 211–26. Mellinkoff notes the Jew in profile as signifier of 'evil' but goes little further. My reading is specific to Christian images; in Classical art, for instance, profile positioning indicates elevated or detached nobility; in Egyptian art it is used to give xpressive detail. I should include a significant caveat: profile view does not always relate to Jews, and Jews are not always depicted in profile.

11 W.J.T. Mitchell, *What Do Pictures Want? The Lives and Loves of Images* (Chicago, 2005), pp. 37–42, describing a medieval image of Christ in frontal position, now worn and effaced as a consequence of its own expressive and communicative power.

12 See Richard Brilliant, *Portraiture* (London, 1991), pp. 7–21; see too the provocative and stimulating comments on portraiture in Harry Berger, *Fictions of the Pose* (Stanford, CA, 2000), pp. 1–31, on the 'fabricated' nature of portraiture.

13 Examples are legion, but three outstanding ones from medieval England are: London, British Library Arundel MS 157, f. 8v (English psalter, c. 1200); Royal MS I.D.X, f. 5r (psalter, ?Oxford, c. 1210); the Luttrell Psalter (f. 90v).

14 See Mellinkoff, *Outcasts*, for a survey of these marks and traits.

15 See Cecil Roth, *Essays and Portraits in Anglo-Jewish History* (Philadelphia, 1962), pp. 22–5; Anthony Bale, *The Jew in the Medieval Book: English Antisemitisms 1350–1500* (Cambridge, 2006), pp. 3–5 (with reproduction).

16 See further Bale, *Jew in the Medieval Book*, pp. 145–58.

17 See Hannah Arendt, *The Origins of Totalitarianism*, revd edn (New York, 1973), pp. 3–10; also Richard H. King, *Race, Culture and the Intellectuals, 1940–1970* (Baltimore, 2004), pp. 58–70.

18 See Daniel Arasse, 'Fonctions de l'image religieuse au XVe siècle' in *Faire Croire: modalités de la diffusion et de la reception des messages religieux du XIIe au XVe siècle* (Rome, 1981), pp. 132–46; Jill Bennett, 'Stigmata and Sense Memory: St Francis and the Affective Image', *Art History*, XXIV (2001), pp. 1–16.

19 Hans Belting, *Likeness and Presence: A History of the Image before the Era of Art*, trans. Edmund Jephcott (Chicago, 1996), p. 9; see too David Freedberg, *The Power of Images: Studies in the History and Theory of Response* (Chicago, 1989); Biernoff, *Sight and Embodiment*, p. 145; Mills, *Suspended Animation*, p. 19; Norris Kelly Smith, *Here I Stand: Perspective from Another Point of View* (New York, 1994), pp. 21–34.

20 See Suzannah Biernoff, *Sight and Embodiment in the Middle Ages* (Basingstoke, 2002); David C. Lindberg, *Theories of Vision from Al-Kindi to Kepler* (Chicago, 1996), esp. p. 100; Erwin Panofsky, *The Codex Huygens and Leonardo da Vinci's Art Theory* (London, 1940); James Elkins, *The Poetics of Perspective* (Ithaca, NY, 1994), p. 270.

21 Frances Yates, *The Art of Memory* (Chicago, 1966), pp. 82–93, 108; Mary Carruthers, *The Book of Memory: A Study of Memory in Medieval Culture*, 2nd edn (Cambridge, 2008), pp. 24–5.

22 On medieval ideas of 'race' see Lisa Lampert, 'Race, Periodicity, and the (neo-) Middle Ages', *Modern Languages Quarterly*, LXV (2004), pp. 391–421; Thomas Hahn, 'The Difference the Middle Ages Make: Color and Race Before the Modern World', *Journal of Medieval and Early Modern Studies*, XXXI (2001), pp. 1–37; Robert Bartlett, 'Medieval and Modern Concepts of Race and Ethnicity', *Journal of Medieval and Early Modern Studies*, XXXI (2001), pp. 39–56.

23 Aquinas, 'Quæstio 145: de honestate', *Summa Theologiæ*, ed. and trans Thomas Gilby (London, 1971), vol. XLIII, p. 75.

24 The *Ad Herennium* says 'facial expression should show modesty and animation, and the gestures should not be conspicuous for either elegance or grossness, lest we give the impression that we are either actors or day labourers' ([Cicero], *Ad Herennium*, ed. Harry Caplan (Cambridge, MA, 1954), §xv:26 (p. 203)).

25 See Jan Ziolkowski, 'Avatars of Ugliness in Medieval Literature', *Modern Language Review*, LXXIX (1984), pp. 1–20, noting descriptions of ugliness developed from burlesques of beautiful women, allowing writers 'to indulge in the medieval passion for the outlandish' (p. 5).

26 Augustine, *On Order*, ed. and trans. Silvano Barruso (South Bend, IN, 2007), §2:IV:13, (p. 67).

27 *MBLJC*, pp. 159–60.

28 London, British Library MS Add. 49999, ff. 70r–80v.

29 London, British Library MS Add. 48985. The manuscript is described in N. F. Morgan, *Early Gothic Manuscripts (2) 1250–1285* (London, 1988), no. 158 (pp. 150–52).

30 Ibid., p. 151.

31 Bernhard Blumenkranz, *Le juif médiéval au miroir de l'art Chrétien* (Paris, 1966), p. 94; Mellinkoff, *Outcasts*, pp. 128–30; Debra Higgs Strickland, *Saracens, Demons and Jews. Making Monsters in Medieval Art* (Princeton, NJ, 2003), p. 111. Morgan, *Early Gothic Manuscripts*, p. 151, states that '[t]he first artist uses dramatic facial expressions to heighten the drama of the Passion and uses Jewish facial types and dark faces for the tormentors of Christ . . . The hostility towards the Jews in England during this period eventually resulted in their expulsion from the country in 1290'. Artist II uses similar exaggeration and caricature, although less distinctively.

32 The biblical sources are Matthew 26:3–5, 26:57–68 and Mark 14:53–65.

33 See Jeremy Cohen, *Living Letters of the Law: Ideas of the Jew in Medieval Christianity* (Berkeley, CA, 1999), pp. 35–7.

34 Bennett, 'Stigmata'.

35 See Lew Andrews, *Story and Space in Renaissance Art: The Rebirth of Continuous Narrative* (Cambridge, 1995), pp. 4–7, quoting and translating (p. 5) Frey's *Gotik und Renaissance* (1928).

36 Mary Carruthers and Jan Ziolkowski, *The Medieval Craft of Memory: An Anthology of Texts and Pictures* (Philadelphia, 2002), p. 116; the marginal wyverns are depicted in profile, whereas the human faces are drawn in three-quarter view, suggesting further visual/moral modes via position.

37 On these terms see Umberto Eco, *Art and Beauty in the Middle Ages*, trans. Hugh Bredin (New Haven, CT, 1986), p. 43.

38 The term 'scopic regime', borrowed from film theory, suggests the constructed and regulatory nature of the viewer's gaze; long before the advent of vanishing-point perspective, medieval ideas of *perspectiva naturalis* were configured around regulatory lines of vision.

39 Rita Copeland, *Pedagogy, Intellectuals, and Dissent in the Later Middle Ages: Lollardy and Ideas of Learning* (Cambridge, 2001), pp. 99–140, on how hermeneutics and 'the "same" literal sense can be prized in one context and debased in another' (p. 101). Roland Barthes, *Image, Music, Text*, ed. and trans. Stephen Heath (London, 1977), pp. 55–8, discusses the features of the 'obvious' and 'obtuse' meanings of gesture-images; Barthes notes a 'somewhat low language, the language of a rather pitiful disguise' in grotesques, showing the character's 'fissure and its suture', and in doing so 'carries a certain *emotion*'.

40 Janet Coleman, *Ancient and Medieval Memories: Studies in the Reconstruction of the Past* (Cambridge, 1992), pp. 448–9; Biernoff, *Sight and Embodiment*, p. 138. Likewise, Ziolkowski notes, in courtly literature, descriptive 'diptychs, with their facing panels of the sublimely beautiful and the nauseatingly repugnant' ('Avatars of Ugliness', p. 7).

41 The lyric is in Worcester Cathedral MS F.10, f. 25r and Oxford, Balliol College MS 149, f. 12v; edited in *Catalogue of Manuscripts Preserved in the Chapter Library of Worcester Cathedral*, ed. John Kestell Floyer (Oxford, 1906), pp. 5–7, and *Middle English Marian Lyrics*, ed. Karen Saupe (Kalamazoo, MI, 1998), no. 35, via www.lib.rochester.edu/camelot/TEAMS/saupe.htm; only Floyer gives the full version (*Catalogue*, p. 6). The Worcester manuscript is a Latin sermon collection owned by two Worcester priors in the period 1499–1518. The second part of the lyric, a dialogue between the Virgin and Christ, is printed by Carleton Brown, *Religious Lyrics of the XIVth Century* (Oxford, 1924), no. 128. The source for this dialogue is the verses attributed to Bernard of Clairvaux, 'Liber de Passione Christi et doloribus et planctibus matris ejus' (see Migne, *Patrologia Latina*, 182 (col. 1136)), although the Worcester manuscript gives 'Chrisostomus' as the source. The relation between the first part of 'The angell saide to thee' and Bernard's verses is questionable.

42 See Daniel Arasse, *L'annonciation italienne: une histoire de perspective* (Paris, 1999). See too John F. Moffitt, *Painterly Perspective and Piety: Religious Uses of the Vanishing Point, from the Fifteenth to the Eighteenth Century* (Jefferson, NC, 2008), pp. 24–9, on 'the carefully contrived perspective effect' which had a specific 'ecclesiastical' and 'liturgical' purposes.

43 Very much akin to the moment of literal suspense – liminality, hanging – described by Robert Mills as a point of religious desire and excess (*Suspended Animation: Pain, Pleasure and Punishment in Medieval Culture* (London, 2005), esp. pp. 53–8).

44 Thomas Wilson, *Arte of Rhetorique*, ed. G. H. Mair (Oxford, 1909), p. 199; in Puttenham's 1589 *Arte* the device ('antitheton' or 'the recounter') is nicknamed, appropriately, 'the Quareller'; see George Puttenham, *The Arte of English Poesie*, ed. Gladys Doidge Willcock

and Alice Walker (repr. Cambridge, 1970), pp. 210–11. It was much used in medieval rhetoric, notably and to great effect by Chaucer (see, for example, the 'dredful joye' of *Parliament of Fowls* (line 3), repeated in *Troilus & Criseyde*, 2:2776).

45 *Antitheton* is a juxtaposition of ideas, whereas *antithesis* is the juxtaposition of terms. Isidore of Seville, *Etymologies*, ed. and trans. Stephen Barney et al. (Cambridge, 2006), §i.xxxvi.21 (p. 60).

46 *Ad Herrenium*, ed. and trans. Caplan, §iv.xlv.58 (p. 377).

47 Isidore of Seville, *Etymologies*, §ii.xxi.5 (p. 76); see too Geoffrey of Vinsauf, *Poetria Nova*, trans. Margaret Nims (Toronto, 1967), line 1103 (p. 56).

48 Constance Brittain Bouchard, *'Every Valley Shall Be Exalted': The Discourse of Opposites in Twelfth-Century Thought* (Ithaca, NY, 2003).

49 Ibid., p. 5.

50 Biernoff, *Sight and Embodiment*, p. 96.

51 Carruthers, *Book of Memory*, pp. 97–8, 173–4.

52 Augustine, *On Order*, ed. and trans. Barruso, 1.7.19, p. 25.

53 Christ occupies the space which, on a 'T and O' map, is usually given to the Mediterranean; Longinus is in Europe (Japeth) and Stephaton in Africa (Ham). The 'T' on such maps represents waterways dividing Asia, Africa and Europe. See Keith D. Lilley, *City and Cosmos: The Medieval World in Urban Form* (London, 2009), pp. 16–18.

54 The biblical source is John 19:31–7.

55 On Stephaton see W. C. Jordan, 'Stephaton: The Origin of the Name', *Classical Folia*, xxxiii (1979), pp. 83–6, and Leopold Kretzenbacher, 'Zum kaum noch bekannten Namen des Kreuzigungszeugen Stephaton', *Österreichische Zeitschrift für Volkskunde*, lv (2001), pp. 1–22. See too the cognate Crucifixion scene with Longinus and Stephaton in the Huth Psalter (London, British Library Add. ms 38116, f. 11v) of *c.* 1280–1300, with a similarly defined sense of the Jew in profile.

56 *Gl. Ord.* follows Bede in explicating the story as a fulfilment of Isaiah 5, the destruction of the winepress of Israel and the admonition to the Israelites that 'hath hell enlarged her soul, and opened her mouth without any bounds' (5:14), that 'the Lord of hosts shall be exalted in judgment, and the holy God shall be sanctified in justice' (5:17). Mitchell Merback, *The Thief, the Cross and the Wheel* (London, 1999), pp. 52–4, explores an image of Longinus and Stephaton in the sixth-century Syriac *Rabbula Gospels* showing Longinus in three-quarter view and Stephaton in profile.

57 Celia Chazelle, *The Crucified God in the Carolingian Era: Theology and Art of Christ's Passion* (Cambridge, 2001), pp. 147–8.

58 Ibid., p. 148.

59 See Miriam Bunim, *Space in Medieval Painting and the Forerunners of Perspective* (New York, 1940), p. 17.

60 Merback, *Thief*, p. 221.

61 Ibid.

62 Michael Camille, *The Gothic Idol: Ideology and Image-Making in Medieval Art* (Cambridge, 1989), p. 180.

63 Sarah Beckwith, *Christ's Body: Identity, Culture and Society in Late Medieval Writings* (London, 1994), p. 42.

64 Walter Sauer, ed., *The Metrical Life of Christ* (Heidelberg, 1977), lines 826–9 (p. 63).

65 On 'excessive' corporeality see Steven Kruger, *The Spectral Jew: Conversion and Embodiment in Medieval Europe* (Minneapolis, 2006), p. xxiv.

66 Susan Gubar, *Judas: A Biography* (New York, 2009), pp. xxi, xxii, 5.

67 The 'frenzy of the visible' is Linda Williams' term; see *Hard Core: Power, Pleasure, and the "Frenzy of the Visible"*, 2nd edn (Berkeley, CA, 1999), pp. 35–7.

68 Gubar, *Judas*, pp. 92–4

69 Cambridge, Trinity College MS 323 (unique manuscript). My modern English translation modifies that given by Donald E. Schueler, 'The Middle English *Judas*: An Interpretation', PMLA, XCI (1976), 840–45, pp. 840–41. On other Judas legends see Paul Baum, 'The Mediaeval Legend of Judas Iscariot', PMLA, XXXI (1916), pp. 481–585.

70 This woman is read as a version of Mary Magdalene by Mary-Ann Stouck, 'A Reading of the Middle English *Judas*', *Journal of English and Germanic Philology*, LXXX (1981), pp. 188–98.

71 Stouck, 'A Reading'; R. Axton, 'Interpretations of Judas in Middle English Literature', in *Religion in the Poetry and Drama of the Late Middle Ages in England*, ed. Piero Boitani and Anna Torti (Cambridge, 1990), pp. 179–97; Kim Paffenroth, *Judas: Images of the Lost Disciple* (London, 2001), pp. 76–7.

72 'Brown' suggests the mixing of orange and black, a composite of colours. OED refers to 'the mediæval belief that Judas Iscariot had red hair and beard' (s.v. 'Judas').

73 Paffenroth, *Judas*, p. 50; Hilary Wayment, *Corpus Vitrearum Medii Aevi: King's College Chapel, Cambridge* (London, 1972), p. 70, describes the 'most unusual sanguine paint . . . used to render Judas's hair' in the Cambridge window.

74 These and other examples are in Wayland D. Hand, 'A Dictionary of Words and Idioms Associated with Judas Iscariot', *University of California Publications in Modern Philology*, XXIV (1942), pp. 289–356 [no. 3].

75 Ruth Mellinkoff, 'Cain and the Jews', *Journal of Jewish Art*, VI (1979), pp. 16–38; Israel Knohl, 'Cain; Son of God or Son of Satan?' in *Jewish Biblical Interpretation and Cultural Exchange*, ed. Natalie Dohrmann and David Stern (Philadelphia, 2008), pp. 37–50.

76 Archer Taylor, 'The Gallows of Judas Iscariot', *Washington University*

Studies, IX (1922), pp. 135–56; examples include the German *Judaskirschen* (the English Winter Cherry), known in French as the *cerise de juif* (Jews' cherry).

77 See Irit Kleiman, 'The Life and Times of Judas Iscariot: Form and Function', *Medievalia et Humanistica*, XXIII (2007), pp. 15–40, pp. 16–18.

78 Lydgate and Burgh, *Secrees*, lines 2577–81.

79 Hugh of St Victor, quoted in Emile Mâle, *Religious Art from the Twelfth to the Eighteenth Century* (London, 1949), p. 65; the Wilton Diptych is London, National Gallery, NG4451.

80 Bale, *Jew in the Medieval Book*, p. 123.

81 See David Biale, *Blood and Belief: The Circulation of a Symbol between Christians and Jews* (Berkeley, CA, 2008), p. 78, for cognate medieval Jewish uses of the colour red to denote blood.

82 John Lydgate, 'Praier to St Edmund', in *Minor Poems of John Lydgate*, ed. H. N. McCracken (London, 1911), vol. I, pp. 124–7.

83 John Lydgate, 'Praier to St George', in ibid., vol. I, pp. 145–54.

84 See Alexander Murray, *Suicide in the Middle Ages*, II: *The Curse on Self-Murder* (Oxford, 2001).

85 Annette Weber, 'The Hanged Judas of Freiburg Cathedral: Sources and Documents', in *Imagining the Self, Imagining the Other: Visual Representation and Jewish-Christian Dynamics in the Middle Ages and Early Modern Period*, ed. Eva Frojmovic (Leiden, 2002), pp. 165–88.

86 Chantilly, Musée Condé MS 65. Jean Longnon and Raymond Chazelles, ed., *Les Très Riches Heures du Duc de Berry* (London, 1969), p. 213. This image was added to the book by Jean Colombe in the 1480s, filling a folio which had been left incomplete.

87 Jerome had first connected Judas with Psalm 108, a connection repeated by Ambrose, Bede, Augustine, Gregory the Great; see David L. Jeffrey, ed., *A Dictionary of Biblical Tradition in English Literature* (Grand Rapids, MI, 1993), p. 418.

88 Judas's dramatic prop was his coat, which cost two shillings for canvas, and ten pence for the making of it, in the Coventry Corpus Christi drama. See Hardin Craig, ed., *Two Coventry Corpus Christi Plays* (London, 1902), p. 87. For an analysis of Judas, his usury and the 'startling juxtaposition' of Mary with Judas ('thesis with antithesis') at the Padua Arena Chapel, see Anne Derbes and Mark Sandona, *The Usurer's Heart: Giotto, Enrico Scrovegni, and the Arena Chapel in Padua* (University Park, PA, 2008), pp. 45–83. Derbes and Sandona note that late medieval devotional tracts state that 'Satan entered Judas's *ventro* – a word meaning both belly and womb' (p. 62), further drawing out the implicit parallel in the *Très Riches Heures* between Judas and Mary.

89 See Roger Luckhurst, *The Trauma Question* (London, 2008), pp. 148–9.

4 The Jew's Hand and the Virgin's Bier: Tangible Interruption.

1 London, British Library Yates Thompson MS 13, f. 133v. On this manuscript (which is connected to the Luttrell Psalter) see L. F. Sandler, *Gothic Manuscripts*, no. 98, vol. II, pp. 107–9, who identifies the artist with one *fl. c.* 1330; on royal patronage, see Anne Rudloff Stanton, 'Isabelle of France and her Manuscripts', in *Capetian Women*, ed. Kathleen Nolan (New York, 2003), pp. 225–52.

2 See John Burrow, *Gestures and Looks in Medieval Narrative* (Cambridge, 2002); also, Jean-Claude Schmitt, *La raison des gestes dans l'Occident medieval* (Paris, 1990).

3 So says Guy de Chauliac, author of the pre-eminent late medieval medical treatise; see *The Middle English Translation of Guy de Chauliac*, ed. Björn Wallner (Lund, 1964), vol. I, p. 39.

4 See Schmitt, *Raison des gestes*, pp. 122–33.

5 Margaret E. Owens, *Stages of Dismemberment: The Fragmented Body in Late Medieval and Early Modern Drama* (Wilmington, DE, 2005).

6 See Carol Berger, 'The Hand and the Art of Memory', *Musica Disciplina*, XXXV (1981), 87–121.

7 Mary Carruthers, *The Book of Memory: A Study of Memory in Medieval Culture*, 2nd edn (Cambridge, 2008), pp. 166–7; Carruthers is here discussing Bradwardine, on whom see above, p. 35.

8 Carruthers, *Book of Memory*, p. 167.

9 See Rachel Fulton, 'Quae est ista quae ascendit sicut aurora consurgens?' The Song of Songs as the *historia* for the Office of the Assumption', *Mediaeval Studies*, LX (1998), pp. 55–122, on how 'evidence' for the Assumption was generated in the Middle Ages.

10 Louis Réau, *Iconographie de l'art chrétien* (Paris 1955–9), vol. II, p. 604.

11 *Ap. NT*, pp. 708–14; on Pseudo-Melito see I. Ortiz de Urbina, *Patrologia Syrica*, 2nd edn (Rome, 1965), p. 41.

12 See *Ap. NT*, pp. 695–723.

13 Similarly, the apocryphal *Gospel of Pseudo-Matthew* provided an account of the Virgin's life and added details to Christ's infancy, in particular foregrounding the Circumcision.

14 See Stephen J. Shoemaker, '"Let us go and burn her body": The Image of the Jews in the Early Dormition Traditions', *Church History*, LXVI (1999), pp. 775–823; examples are collected in *On the Dormition of Mary: Early Patristic Homilies*, ed. Brian J. Daley (Crestwood, NY, 1998), esp. p. 176, 'his hands were cut off'. James Marrow, *Passion Iconography in Northern European Art of the Late Middle Ages and Early Renaissance* (Brussels, 1979), pp. 117–23, describes later medieval traditions of Jews seeking to burn Christ's body.

15 St John Damascene, *On Holy Images and Three Sermons on the Assumption*, trans. Mary H. Allies (London, 1898), pp. 189–90.

16 *GL*, vol. II, pp. 77–88. On the influence of this version see Ruth Evans, 'When a Body Meets a Body: Fergus and Mary in the York Cycle', *New Medieval Literatures*, I (1997), pp. 193–212.

17 *GL*, vol. II, p. 81.

18 The image of the Jew with his hands cut can be seen in the glass at Gresford (Denbighshire), although, in general, Western European images show the Jew stuck to the bier. The English printed version of *GL*, Caxton's *Legenda aurea* (London, 1483) contains both versions: that 'his hands clevyd to the bere and were departed fro the body, like as two staves had been sawed off, and soo he was like a tronke til that feith changed his thought' (p. cclxi) and the hands 'cleved to the bere / so that he henge by the handes on the bere / and was sore tormented / and wepte and brayed' (p. cclix).

19 The withering of Moses' hand was explicitly understood in *Gl. Or.*, following Isidore of Seville, as a figure of the Jews who, alienated from their God, go forth in filth; when they acknowledge the Saviour they will regain their pristine colour. Réau, *Iconographie*, vol. II, p. 611 overstates the relationship between the Dormition legend and the story of Oza, arguing that 'l'origine de cette légende est transparent – empruntée purement et simplement au récit [of Oza] de l'Ancien Testament'.

20 In the now-destroyed *Death of the Virgin* image at Susegana by the Collalto Master, Thomas appeared under the litter with his hands gesturing towards the Virgin's body whereas Jephonius is at the back of the bier, but Thomas occupied the space usually given to the Jew (reproduced in Daniele Ferrara, *Giovanni Baronzio e la pittura a Rimini nel Trecento* (Milan 2008), p. 80). In the medieval Paris pageant of the Assumption the story of Thomas's doubt at the Assumption is elaborated from the *Golden Legend* of Jacobus de Voragine, with Mary throwing her gage to Thomas from Heaven (see *Histoire du Théâtre en France: Les Mystères*, ed. Louis Petit de Julleville (Paris, 1880), vol. II, p. 470–71).

21 Richard Rambuss, 'Devotion and Defilement: The Blessed Virgin Mary and the Corporeal Hagiographics of Chaucer's Prioress's Tales', in *Textual Bodies: Changing Boundaries of Literary Representation*, ed. L. H. Lefkovitz (Albany, NY, 1997), pp. 75–100.

22 Sarah Stanbury, *The Visual Object of Desire in Late Medieval England* (Philadelphia, 2007), pp. 165–8.

23 Some other English examples include the window at St Peter Mancroft, Norwich (window 4G), in which the Virgin's bier is attacked by a soldier bearing the arms of the Duke of Suffolk, on which see Rebecca Pinner, 'Medieval Images of St Edmund in Norfolk Churches', in *St Edmund, King and Martyr: Changing Images of a Medieval Saint*, ed. Anthony Bale (Woodbridge, 2009), pp. 111–32, pp. 126–7; Cambridge, St John's College MS 262, f. 64r; Cambridge, Fitzwilliam

Museum MS 48, ff. 78r–82v (Carew-Poyntz Hours); Cambridge, Fitzwilliam Museum MS 370, f. 1r; London, British Library Add. MS 49999, f. 61r (De Brailes Hours) and Royal MS 2.B.vii, f. 298r (Queen Mary Psalter); London, Victoria and Albert Museum 83–1864, Syon Cope; New York, Pierpont Morgan Library MS M.302, f. 4r; Norwich, Castle Museum MS 158.926.4f, f. 70v; Oxford, Bodleian Library MS Barlow 22, f. 14v, Barlow Hours; Oxford, Bodleian Library MS Douce 231, f. 61r.

24 On the Barantyn family, see ODNB, 'Drew Barantyn'; R. W. Heath-Whyte, *The Medieval Wall-Paintings of St Mary's Church, Chalgrove* (Chalgrove, 1991). On Chalgrove, see E. W. Tristram, *English Wall Painting of the Fourteenth Century* (London, 1955), pp. 70–71, describing 'the vivid incident'; Tristram comments that 'in this picture, as in many of the period, Jews are immediately recognisable by their caricatured noses'; A. Caiger-Smith, *English Medieval Mural Painting* (Oxford, 1963), pp. 153–4; Ellen O. Ross, *The Grief of God: Images of the Suffering Jesus in Late Medieval England* (Oxford, 1999), pp. 56–8.

25 Ross, *Grief of God*, p. 57.

26 Heath-Whyte, *Medieval Wall-Paintings*, p. 50.

27 For similar use of *oppositio* see Alyce A. Jordan, *Visualizing Kingship in the Windows of the Sainte-Chapelle* (New York, 2002), p. 25.

28 Marilyn Aronberg Lavin, *The Place of Narrative: Mural Decoration in Italian Churches, 431–1600* (Chicago, 1990), p. 166, notes comparable Italian examples, based on 'the concept of progress toward a final goal'; Lavin also covers various 'choreographed' architectural settings.

29 See John Baldovin, *The Urban Character of Christian Worship: The Origins, Development, and Meaning of Stational Liturgy* (Rome, 1987); Richard McCall, *Do This: Liturgy as Performance* (Notre Dame, IN, 2007).

30 Quotation from Carruthers, *Craft of Thought*, p. 266, who describes how at the Carolingian abbey of Centula-St. Riquier 'a locational memory [was] woven into the very fabric of monastic buildings' (p. 268).

31 See David Kunzle, *The Early Comic Strip: Narrative Strips and Picture Stories in the European Broadsheet from c. 1450 to 1825* (Berkeley, CA, 1973), p. 14; Anthony Bale, *The Jew in the Medieval Book: English Antisemitisms 1350–1500*, p. 158.

32 Pamela Patton describes similar anti-Jewish imagery in a medieval Spanish cloister in which, 'reminiscent of a modern cinematographer's back-and-forth cutting between simultaneous events . . . a dramatic effect, overshadowing the peaceful, liturgically significant communion of Christ and his disciples with a forceful reminder of the downfall to come and of the Jewish agency implicitly behind it'; 'The cloister as cultural mirror: anti-Jewish imagery at Santa María la Mayor in Tudela', in *Der Mittelalterliche Kreuzgang: Architektur, Funktion und*

Programm, ed. Peter Klein (Regensburg, 2003), pp. 317–31, pp. 321–2.

33 See Alan Fletcher, 'The N-Town Plays', in *The Cambridge Companion to Medieval English Theatre*, ed. Richard Beadle (Cambridge, 1994), pp. 163–88.

34 Theresa Coletti, 'Devotional Iconography in the *N-Town* Marian Plays', *Comparative Drama*, XI (1977), pp. 22–44; Patrick J. Collins, *The N-Town Plays and Medieval Picture Cycles* (Kalamazoo, MI, 1979).

35 See J. A. Tasioulas, 'Between Doctrine and Domesticity: The Portrayal of Mary in the N-Town Plays', in *Medieval Women in their Communities*, ed. Diane Watt (Cardiff, 1997), pp. 222–45; Seeta Chaganti, *The Medieval Poetics of the Reliquary: Enshrinement, Inscription, Performance* (New York, 2008), pp. 73–94, on 'the problem of the Marian body' in the N-Town plays.

36 For a fuller discussion see Emma Lipton, *Affections of the Mind: The Politics of Sacramental Marriage in Late Medieval English Literature* (Notre Dame, IN, 2007), pp. 89–127; see too Merrall Llewelyn Price, 'Re-Membering the Jews: Theatrical Violence in the N-Town Marian Plays', *Comparative Drama*, XLI (2007), pp. 439–63, focusing on the vengeful Mary.

37 See Lipton, *Affections of the Mind*, p. 121.

38 Rosemary Woolf, *The English Mystery Plays* (London, 1972), p. 287, described the play as 'wooden, stilted and lifelessly aureate in diction' but qualified this, adding that '[t]he impact of this play was clearly to the eye and to the musical ear: spectacle and music are essential to it'.

39 Quotations are taken from *The N-Town Plays*, ed. Stephen Spector (Oxford, 1991).

40 *Feretrum* literally means 'shrine' but also 'a beere, wheron deed bodies are borne; somtyme a thinge, wheron ymages, relikes, or iewelles are borne', as described by Thomas Elyot in 1538 (see *Lexicons of Early Modern English*, s. v. 'feretrum'), a definition which succinctly shows Mary's body as a relic.

41 See Joanna Dutka, *Music in the English Mystery Plays* (Kalamazoo, MI, 1980), p. 68.

42 Matthew 26:69; Mark 14:66; Luke 22:56.

43 Anselm, *Prayers and Meditations*, ed. and trans. Benedicta Ward (Harmondsworth, 1973), p. 112 (The Second Prayer to St Mary).

44 Matthew Kinservik, 'The Struggle over Mary's Body', *Journal of English and Germanic Philology*, XCV (1996), pp. 190–203, comments 'Only after the sanctity of Mary's body is ensured through her death and assumption . . . are the struggles between the Jews and the followers of Christ ended and the mechanism of Christian salvation finally established in N-Town. To understand this movement we need to examine Mary as the vessel of the New Law, the importance attached to the inviolability of her body, and the functions she serves as intercessor and relic'. Evans, 'When a Body', p. 208, notes that the

play 'represents Mary as an object to be alternately revered and hated'. The stage direction at the point of Assumption reads '*Et hic assendent in celum cantantibus organis*'.

45 Margaret Raftery, '(Type)Casting the Other: The Representation of Jews and Devils in Two Plays of the Assumption', *European Medieval Drama*, IX (2005), pp. 35–60; Rachel Fulton, *From Judgment to Passion: Devotion to Christ and the Virgin Mary 800–1200* (New York, 2002), pp. 272–5.

46 David Ward, 'Spirited Away', *The Guardian* (London), 27 April 2004.

47 William Wey, *The Itineraries of William Wey*, ed. Francis Davey (London, 1857), p. 16; Seigneur de Caumont, *Voyaige d'oultremer en Jhérusalem*, ed. Marquis de la Grange (Paris, 1858), p. 49; the tradition apparently mirrored those of 'The Hill of Evil Counsel', where the Jews were said to have resolved to put Jesus to death.

48 This information is based on *Records of Early English Drama: York*, ed. and trans. Alexandra F. Johnston and Margaret Rogerson (Manchester, 1979), vol. II, p. 682. At York, the song 'Surge proxima mea, columba mea' (Arise now, my neighbour, my dove) was sung at the Virgin's funeral, an allusion to Canticles 2:10 which appears in the very earliest versions of the Dormition story (Dutka, p. 38). This is sung at the end of the play when Mary appears to Thomas, but in its injunction it answers or opposes to Jew 'jumping', surging, close to the Virgin's body. The song at York was actually a translation of the song in the N-Town play, *Arys now, my dowe, my nehebor, and my swete frende! / Tabernacle of joye, vessel of lyf, hefnely temple to reyn*, as noted by Rambuss, 'Devotion', p. 84; see too Fulton, *Judgment to Passion*, pp. 273–4.

49 See Evans, 'When a Body', pp. 201–4.

50 *Records: York*, ed. and trans. Johnston and Rogerson, vol. II, p. 732.

51 Woolf, *English Mystery Plays*, pp. 287, 290; see also Evans, 'When a Body', p. 203.

52 Quintilian, *The Orator's Education*, ed. and trans. Donald A. Russell (Cambridge, 2001), §6:3:8, (p. 67)

53 See Jody Enders, *Murder by Accident* (Chicago, 2009), p. xix. Enders describes a Parisian Passion play of 1380 in which an actor was mortally wounded in a 'special effect gone wrong' (pp. 1–9).

54 The poem is published in *King Horn, Floriz and Blauncheflur, The Assumption of Our Lady*, ed. George H. McKnight (London, 1901), pp. 111–36. The detail of the privy is an anti-Jewish commonplace: late medieval Passion accounts subject Christ to a similar degradation (Marrow, *Passion Iconography*, pp. 104–9); on similar scatological narratives, see Bale, *Jew in the Medieval Book*, pp. 28, 48.

55 Quoted from Carruthers, *Book of Memory*, pp. 362–3.

56 For recent critical discussion of the Croxton *Play* see Michael Jones, 'Theatrical History in the Croxton Play of the Sacrament', *English*

Literary History, LXVI (1999), pp. 223–60; David Lawton, 'Sacrilege and Theatricality: the Croxton *Play of the Sacrament*', *Journal of Medieval and Early Modern Studies*, XXXIII (2003), pp. 281–309; Greg Walker, 'Medieval Drama: The Corpus Christi in York and Croxton', in *Readings in Medieval Texts: Interpreting Old and Middle English Texts*, ed. David Johnson and Elaine Treharne (Oxford, 2005), 370–86.

57 The text consulted is from Greg Walker, ed., *Medieval Drama: An Anthology* (Oxford, 1996).

58 Ann Nichols, 'The Hierosphthitic Topos: Or, The Fate of Fergus: Notes on the N-Town Assumption', *Comparative Drama*, XXV (1991), pp. 29–41; Owens, *Stages of Dismemberment*, p. 74.

59 Richard Homan, 'Devotional Themes in the Violence and Humor of the Play of the Sacrament', *Comparative Drama*, XX (1986), pp. 327–40, notes the intense visuality of the Croxton *Play* at these moments.

60 Quoting Lawton, 'Sacrilege and Theatricality', pp. 295–6.

61 Jones, 'Theatrical History', p. 228.

62 Jill Bennett, 'Stigmata and Sense Memory: St Francis and the Affective Image', *Art History*, XXIV (2001), p. 9.

63 See Lisa Lampert, *Gender and Jewish Difference from Paul to Shakespeare* (Philadelphia, PA, 2004), p. 107; Richard Homan, 'Mixed Feelings about Violence in the Corpus Christi Plays', *Themes in Drama*, XIII (1985), pp. 92–100, p. 99, comments that 'in English plays from the fifteenth century violence frequently inspires conflicting emotions within a single scene'.

64 The Jews' obstinacy towards Christianity is suggested in Mark 4:12, 'that seeing they may see, and not perceive' etc.; see too Acts 7:51. On the image's durability see Ronald Schechter, *Obstinate Hebrews: Representations of Jews in France, 1715–1815* (Berkeley, CA, 2003).

65 Schechter, *Obstinate Hebrews*, p. 8.

66 Enders, *Medieval Theater of Cruelty*, p. 23

67 Augustine, *The City of God Against the Pagans*, ed. R. W. Dyson (Cambridge, 1998), §XVI:8 (p. 708).

68 Augustine, *City of God*, §XXI:9 (p. 1064). 'Hierosphthitic' is the term used by Nichols, 'Hierosphthitic Topos', describing incidents in medieval culture when 'a sacred object . . . is touched for unholy reasons' (p. 30); Nichols suggests Oza as the archetype.

69 Sarah Beckwith, *Christ's Body: Identity, Culture and Society in Late Medieval Writings* (London, 1994), p. 52.

70 *IE*, 2413.

71 *IE*, 2419.

72 *IE*, 4784.

73 See Beverly Boyd, *Middle English Miracles of the Virgin* (San Marino, CA, 1964), p. 133.

74 *IE*, 4135C.

75 *IE*, 2416.

76 *IE*, 2420.

77 *IE*, 2420, 3704.

78 See Theodore Andersson, 'The Thief in *Beowulf*', *Speculum*, XXIX (1984), pp. 493–508, p. 508.

79 Mary Carruthers, *The Craft of Thought: Meditation, Rhetoric and the Making of Images* (Cambridge, 1998), p. 117.

80 There are many examples, but some potent ones are reproduced and discussed, particularly in terms of beatitudes and maledictions, in Schmitt, *Raison des gestes*, pp. 156–72.

81 See Berger, 'The Hand'.

82 Burrow, *Gestures and Looks*, p. 27

83 See Burrow, *Gestures and Looks*, pp. 14–16; Schmitt, *Raison des gestes*, p. 17.

5 Visiting Calvary: Contrition, Intimacy and Virtual Persecution

1 J. Field, *Kingdom, Power and Glory: A Historical Guide to Westminster Abbey* (London, 1996), pp. 47–53.

2 M. J. Pragai, *Faith and Fulfilment: Christians and the Return to the Promised Land* (London, 1985), p. 68.

3 William Shakespeare, *Richard II*, V:6:49–50 (p. 395).

4 Joseph Dacier, ed., *The Chronicles of Enguerrand de Monstrelet*, trans. Thomas Johnes (London, 1867), vol. I, p. 483.

5 Robert Fabyan, *Prima pars cronicarum* (London, 1516), p. 174v.

6 Abraham Millgram, *Jerusalem Curiosities* (Philadelphia, 1990), p. 325.

7 This story comes from John Barbour, *Bruce*, ed. Walter Skeat (London, 1874), book IV, lines 206–10 (vol. I, pp. 83–4).

8 See William Shakespeare, *Henry IV Part 2*, ed. Matthias Shaaber (Harmondsworth, 1970), p. 132.

9 John Lydgate, *The Lives of SS Edmund and Fremund and the Extra Miracles of St Edmund*, ed. Anthony Bale and A.S.G. Edwards (Heidelberg, 2009), line 493 (p. 49; also p. 153).

10 A commonplace of Christian and Jewish thought, becoming increasingly central from the thirteenth century; see Marcia Kupfer, 'Mappaemundi: Image, Artefact, Social Practice', in *The Hereford World Map: Medieval World Maps and Their Context*, ed. P.D.A. Harvey (London, 2006), pp. 253–68; P. S. Alexander, 'Jerusalem as the Omphalos of the World: On the History of a Geographical Concept', in *Jerusalem: Its Sanctity and Centrality to Judaism, Christianity and Islam*, ed. Lee I. Levine (New York, 1999), pp. 104–19; Kathy Lavezzo, *Angels on the Edge of the World: Geography, Literature and English Community, 1000–1534* (Ithaca, NY, 2006), pp. 108–9; Ora Limor, 'The Place of the End of Days": Eschatological Geography in Jerusalem', in *The Real and Ideal Jerusalem in Jewish, Christian and Islamic Art:*

Studies in Honor of Bezalel Narkiss on the Occasion of His 70th Birthday, ed. Bianca Kühnel (Jerusalem, 1998), pp. 13–22.

11 Mary Carruthers, *The Craft of Thought: Meditation, Rhetoric and the Making of Images* (Cambridge, 1998), p. 42.

12 June L. Mecham, 'A Northern Jerusalem: Transforming the Spatial Geography of the Convent of Wienhausen', in *Defining the Holy: Sacred Space in Medieval and Early Modern Europe*, ed. Andrew Spicer and Sarah Hamilton (Aldershot, 2005), pp. 139–60, quoting p. 139.

13 For an overview of medieval pilgrims' accounts of Jerusalem and its hinterland, see Nicole Chareyron, *Pilgrims to Jerusalem in the Middle Ages* (New York, 2000); a more sophisticated approach is taken by Annabel Wharton, *Selling Jerusalem: Relics, Replicas, Theme Parks* (Chicago, 2006), pp. 49–97, on medieval and Franciscan mediations of Jerusalem; see too Ora Limor, '"Holy Journey: Pilgrimage and Christian Sacred Landscape', in *Christians and Christianity in the Holy Land*, ed. Ora Limor and Guy Stroumsa (Turnhout, 2006), pp. 321–53, and the illuminating comments of Merback, *Thief*, pp. 48–57.

14 Wharton, *Selling Jerusalem*, p. 18.

15 Carruthers, *Craft of Thought*, p. 41; Mitchell Merback, *The Thief, the Cross and the Wheel* (London, 1999), p. 49.

16 Simon Coleman and John Elsner, *Pilgrimage Past and Present: Sacred Travel and Sacred Space in the World Religions* (London, 1995), pp. 83–9, gives a useful summary account (quotation from pp. 84–5).

17 Carruthers, *Craft of Thought*, p. 40.

18 Blake Leyerle, 'Landscape as Cartography in Early Christian Pilgrim Narratives', *Journal of the American Academy of Religion*, LXIV (1996), pp. 119–43.

19 Catherine Delano-Smith, 'The Intelligent Pilgrim: Maps and Medieval Pilgrimage to the Holy Land', in *Eastward Bound: Travels and Travellers 1050–1500*, ed. Rosamund Allen (Manchester, 2004), pp. 107–30, pp. 108–13.

20 Coleman and Elsner, *Pilgrimage*, p. 88; see too Sabine MacCormack, '*Loca Sancta*: The Organization of Sacred Topography in Late Antiquity', in *The Blessing of Pilgrimage*, ed. Robert Ousterhout (Urbana, IL, 1990), pp. 7–40. On the medieval concept of *duratio* (God's time, in which Christian history is replayed in the present) see Mecham, 'A Northern Jerusalem', p. 153.

21 See Aubrey Stewart, ed. and trans., *John Poloner's Description of the Holy Land* (London, 1894).

22 John Wilkinson, ed. and trans., *Jerusalem Pilgrims before the Crusades* (Warminster, 2002), p. 83

23 Ibid., p. 139

24 The poem was recently edited by George Shuffelton, *Codex Ashmole 61: A Compilation of Popular Middle English Verse* (via www.lib. rochester.edu/camelot/teams/sgas34frm.htm), item 34, from which

quotations are taken. As Shuffelton, *Codex*, notes, there are similarities with William Wey's late fifteenth-century text. As Suffelton suggests, the poem was written in later fifteenth-century England and, on account of its many mistakes and infelicities, is likely a translation, or corrupt version, of another text.

25 An indulgence, 'from guilt and punishment', a spiritual pardon; see R. N. Swanson, *Indulgences in Late Medieval England: Passports to Paradise?* (Cambridge, 2007).

26 Later on in his pilgrimage, the narrator of *The Stasyons of Jerusalem* retells the story of St Helena, albeit in a garbled way, maintaining and repeating the adversarial and interruptive depiction of Jewry (267–86).

27 See Rosalind Field, 'The Heavenly Jerusalem in *Pearl*', *Modern Language Review*, LXXXI (1986), pp. 7–17; also Muriel A. Whitaker, '*Pearl* and some Illustrated Apocalypse Manuscripts', *Viator*, XII (1981), pp. 183–96.

28 J. J. Anderson, ed., *Sir Gawain and the Green Knight, Pearl, Cleanness, Patience* (London, 1996), p. 38 (my translation).

29 On the symbolism of the dodecahedron see Edward I. Condren, *The Numerical Universe of the Gawain-Pearl Poet* (Gainesville, FL, 2002), pp. 64–73; also Nigel Hiscock, *The Symbol at Your Door: Number and Geometry in Religious Architecture of the Greek and Latin Middle Ages* (Aldershot, 2007).

30 As Kathleen Scott points out, the patron probably dictated what he/she wanted the content of the pictures to be, possibly some time after the accompanying poems had been finished. See *Later Gothic Manuscripts*, no. 12, vol. II, pp. 66–8.

31 See John Baldovin, *The Urban Character of Christian Worship: The Origins, Development, and Meaning of Stational Liturgy* (Rome, 1987); Julie Ann Smith, '"My Lord's Native Land": Mapping the Christian Holy Land', *Church History*, LXXVI (2007), pp. 1–31.

32 See *CCKJ*, vol. III, pp. 132–7 on the House of Caiaphas and the Chapel of the Repose and the legends associated with these sites. The 'Prison' at the Convent of the Sisters of Zion is a twentieth-century legend.

33 See M. R. Savignac, 'A New Holy Place', *Revue Biblique*, XIV (1907), pp. 113–28.

34 Although, confusingly, often *via dolorosa* processions now start at one of the other Prisons, at the Convent.

35 *Ap. NT*, pp. 172–3. The Latin *Gospel of Nicodemus* says there was no gap between Pilate's sentence and the beginning of the mocking of Christ (*Ap. NT*, p. 176) but that the Jews imprisoned Joseph of Arimathea for a week 'in a windowless house' (*Ap. NT*, p. 178).

36 James Marrow, *Passion Iconography in Northern European Art of the Late Middle Ages and Early Renaissance* (Brussels, 1979), pp. 110–11.

37 Joanna Summers, *Late-Medieval Prison Writing and the Politics of Autobiography* (Oxford, 2004).

38 See Guy Geltner, *The Medieval Prison: A Social History* (Princeton, NJ, 2008), pp. 88–9, 100–3. Medieval Jerusalem also featured a Prison of St Peter (*CCKJ*, vol. III, no. 353).

39 For a reproduction of this capital see *CCKJ*, vol. III, p.51.

40 On these sites see, respectively, *CCKJ*, vol. III, pp. 89, 93, 319 and vol. II, p. 257. Pringle (*CCKJ*, vol. III, p. 89) remarks laconically of the 'Condemnation' chapel, 'it is difficult to determine which particular event it was intended to recall'. Likewise, medieval pilgrims 'invented' the site of the Church of Dominus Flevit ('the master wept') on the Mount of Olives. Entirely an invention of tenth-century pilgrims, Dominus Flevit became identified with the place where Jesus wept over Jerusalem (Luke 19:41).

41 Seigneur de Caumont, *Voyaige d'oultremer en Jhérusalem*, ed. Marquis de la Grange (Paris, 1858), pp. 49–50.

42 John of Würzburg, *Description of the Holy Land*, ed. and trans. Aubrey Stewart (London, 1897), p. 31.

43 Felix Fabri, *Wanderings in the Holy Land*, ed. and trans. Aubrey Stewart (London, 1892–3), §112a, vol. I, pp. 352–3.

44 Suggested by Wharton, *Selling Jerusalem*, with chapters on 'Mechanically Reproduced Jerusalem' (as in modern travel guides) and 'Spectacularized Jerusalem' (including 'The Holy Land Experience' theme park in Florida).

45 See Kathryne Beebe, 'Knights, Cooks, Monks and Tourists: Elite and Popular Experience of the Late-medieval Jerusalem Pilgrimage', *Studies in Church History*, XLII (2006), pp. 99–109, exploring social mixing which occurred on pilgrimages to Jerusalem.

46 For a provocative and productive reading see Peter Phipps, 'Tourism and Terrorism: An Intimate Equivalence', in *Tourists and Tourism: A Reader*, ed. Sharon Gmelch (Long Grove, IL, 2004), pp. 71–90.

47 See Nine Miedema, 'Following in the Footsteps of Christ: Pilgrimage and Passion Devotion', in *The Broken Body: Passion Devotion in Late-Medieval Culture*, ed. A. A. MacDonald, H.N.B. Ridderbos and R. M Schlusemann (Groningen, 1998), pp. 73–92; Jonathan Sumption, *Pilgrimage: An Image of Medieval Religion* (London, 1975), pp. 104–13.

48 See Suzanne Yaeger, *Jerusalem in Medieval Narrative* (Cambridge, 2008), p. 139.

49 Robert Mills, *Suspended Animation: Pain, Pleasure and Punishment in Medieval Culture* (London, 2005), p. 159.

50 Phipps, 'Tourism and Terrorism', p. 74; on the Franciscans in the Holy Land see Sylvia Schein, 'La *Custodia Terrae Sanctae* franciscaine et les Juifs de Jérusalem à la fin du moyen-age', *Revue des études juives*, CXLI (1982), pp. 369–77, noting the particular anti-Jewish tenor of the Franciscan enterprise.

51 See Chareyron, *Pilgrims to Jerusalem*, p. 72

52 Caumont, *Voyaige*, p. 46. For amusingly despondent medieval

responses to 'Jaffa the desolate' see Chareyron, *Pilgrims to Jerusalem*, pp. 70–74.

53 See Anthony Goodman, *Margery Kempe and her World* (Oxford, 2002), pp. 186–7 on aristocratic English victims; Reinhold Roericht, *Deutsche Pilgerreisen nach dem Heiligen Lande* (Berlin, 1880), includes numerous examples of pilgrims dying at Ramle.

54 On this remarkable building see *CCKJ*, vol. II, pp. 187–92, including photographs of the building's wonderful interior.

55 See Thomas Renna, 'Jerusalem in Late Medieval Itineraria', in *Pilgrims and Travelers to the Holy Land*, ed. Bryan Le Beau and Menachem Mor (Omaha, NE, 1996), pp. 119–31 (esp. at pp. 122–3)

56 Fabri, *Wanderings*, ed. and trans. Stewart, p. 246.

57 Ibid., p. 246.

58 In *Early Travels in Palestine*, ed. and trans. Thomas Wright (London, 1848), pp. 290–91.

59 See Fabri, *Wanderings*, ed. and trans. Stewart, pp. 248–55.

60 Ibid., p. 255.

61 Ibid., p. 258.

62 William Wey, *The Itineraries of William Wey* (London, 1857), p. 95.

63 'est tamen rebus necessariis vacua'; 'ut ita loquar tanquam ex carcere . . .'; *Itinéraire d'Anselme Adorno*, ed. Jacques Heers et al. (Paris, 1978), pp. 304–6.

64 Richard Torkington, *Ye Oldest Diarie of Englysshe Travell*, ed. W. J. Loftie (London, 1884), p. 24.

65 Ibid.

66 Fabri, *Wanderings*, pp. 72, 305; Roericht, *Deutsche Pilgerreisen*, gives many pilgrims the soubriquet 'Bärfußer', barefoot.

67 On 'invented tradition' and space see Edward Said, 'Invention, Memory and Place', *Critical Enquiry*, XXVI (2000), pp. 175–92. Said comments of Jerusalem (p. 180) that 'symbolic associations' of Jerusalem obscure the 'existential reality of what as a city and real place Jerusalem is'.

68 *CCKJ*, vol. II, pp. 68–71, vol. III, p. 170, also Caumont, *Voyaige*, p. 47.

69 Wey, *Itineraries*, p. 8.

70 M. C. Seymour, ed., *The Defective Version of Mandeville's Travels* (Oxford, 2002), no. 10 (p. 52).

71 Caumont, *Voyaige*, pp. 47–8.

72 *Itinéraire*, p. 306.

73 'Ramle, where you still find walls erected by our forefathers; this is evident from the inscriptions upon the stones . . .'; Sandra Benjamin, ed., *The World of Benjamin of Tudela* (Madison, WI, 1995), p. 183.

74 From *Jewish Travellers*, ed. Elkan Adler and Judah Eisenstein, revd edn (London, 2004), p. 138. Yitzhak Hilo of Larissa (fl. 1330) also connected Ramle with Timna (Genesis 36:40, Deuteronomy 8:9). I am grateful to Shimon Gat for sharing parts of his thesis, 'The City of Ramla in the Middle Ages' (PhD, Bar Ilan University, 2003; in Hebrew) with me.

6 Making Calvary

1 Thomas Renna, *Jerusalem in Medieval Thought, 400–1300* (Lewiston, NY, 2002), p. 200.

2 See S. de Blaauw, 'Jerusalem in Rome and the Cult of the Cross', in *Pratum Romanum: Richard Krautheimer zum 100. Geburtstag*, ed. R. L. Colella (Wiesbaden, 1997), pp. 55–73.

3 See the remarkable list, from St Cyril (*c.* 348) to late nineteenth-century Prussia, of 'True Cross' artefacts in A. Frolow, *La relique de la Vraie Croix: Recherches sur le développement d'un cult* (Paris, 1961), pp. 155–661.

4 E.g. S.A.J. Bradley, 'The Norman Door of St Helen, Stillingfleet, and the Legend of the Holy Rood Tree', in *Archaeological Papers from York Presented to M. W. Barley*, ed. P. V. Addyman and V. E. Black (York, 1984), pp. 84–100.

5 Kelly Holbert, 'Relics and Reliquaries of the True Cross', in *Art and Architecture of Late Medieval Pilgrimage in Northern Europe and the British Isles*, ed. Sarah Blick and Rita Tekippe (Leiden, 2005), pp. 337–63.

6 A. Grabar, *Ampoules de Terre Sainte* (Paris, 1958); Dan Barag, 'Glass Pilgrim Vessels from Jerusalem', *Journal of Glass Studies*, XIII (1971), pp. 45–63; C. Hahn, '*Loca sancta* Souvenirs: Sealing the Pilgrim's Experience', in *The Blessings of Pilgrimage*, ed. R. Ousterhout (Urbana, IL, 1990), pp. 85–96.

7 Susan Stewart, *On Longing: Narratives of the Miniature, the Gigantic, the Souvenir, the Collection* (Baltimore, 1984), p. 134.

8 Dean MacCannell, *The Tourist*, 2nd edn (New York, 1989), pp. 91–107.

9 Annabel Wharton, *Selling Jerusalem: Relics, Replicas, Theme Parks* (Chicago, 2006), p. 9.

10 Scholars of Jerusalem have discussed the city in terms of the accuracy of its sacred geography, but the imagination does not demand that what is felt most ardently be justified to truth or fact. S. Borgehammar, *How The Holy Cross Was Found* (Stockholm, 1991), pp. 85–143, seeks to show how 'the cross could well have been uncovered while Helena was in Jerusalem'; D. Hunt, *Holy Land Pilgrimage in the Later Roman Empire AD 312–460* (Oxford, 1982), pp. 28–33, argues for a specific historical context in Jerusalem, *c.* 325, in which stories concerning Helena emerged.

11 L. J. Tixeront, *Les Origines de l'Église d'Édesse et la Légende d'Abgar* (Paris, 1888), pp. 170–75;

12 See H.J.W. Drijvers and J. W. Drijvers, *The Finding of the True Cross: The Judas Kyriakos Legend in Syriac* (Leuven, 1997); also *Cynewulf's Elene*, ed. P.O.E. Gradon (Exeter, 1977); Andrew Scheil, *The Footsteps of Israel: Understanding Jews in Anglo-Saxon England* (Ann Arbor, MI, 2004), pp. 204–40; N. Pigoulewsky, 'Le martyre de Saint Cyriaque de Jérusalem', *Revue de l'Orient Chrétien*, XXVI (1928), pp. 305–49; Borgehammar, *How the Holy Cross Was Found*. Two similar legends

circulated: one in which Macarius, bishop of Jerusalem, takes the place of Judas and another, the *Protonike* legend which circulated in Syriac and Armenian, replaces Helena with Protonike ('first victory [of the Cross]'), a convert to Christianity whose daughter is brought back to life upon the discovery of the True Cross (see Drijvers and Drijvers, *Finding of the True Cross*, pp. 14–16).

13 See Barbara Baert, *A Heritage of Holy Wood: The Legend of the True Cross in Text and Image* (Leiden, 2004), pp. 392–3.

14 St Stephen, protomartyr (Acts 7), lived at the time of Christ, not, as Helena, in the fourth century.

15 Cynewulf's *Elene*, ed. Pamela Gradon (Exeter, 1996), lines 194–275, describing the Viking-like seafaring to the East of Helena's armoured heroes.

16 [L'abbé] Manceaux, *Histoire de l'Abbaye d'Hautvillers* (Epernay, 1880), vol. III, p. 322–32.

17 Baert, *Heritage*, pp. 133–41.

18 Graham Jones, 'Holy Wells and the Cult of St Helen', *Landscape History*, VIII (1986), pp. 59–75

19 On these wells see Robert Charles Hope, *The Legendary Lore of the Holy Wells of England* (London, 1893), pp. 83–4; *The Victoria County History of the County of Lancaster*, ed. William Farrer and J. Brownbill (London, 1907–12), vol. III, pp. 58–60, vol. VI, p. 75.

20 Mike Haigh, 'St Helen's Well, Stainland', *Source: The Holy Wells Journal*, IV (1986).

21 Scheil, *Footsteps of Israel*, pp. 219–27, notes the importance of 'the blindness/ ignorance motif' (p. 224) in the Anglo-Saxon *Elene*.

22 T. W. Norwood, *Account of the Ancient Chapel of Rushton* (Leek, 1856).

23 Toulmin Smith, ed., *English Gilds* (London, 1870), p. 148.

24 See *ODNB*, 'Helena'.

25 Jones, 'Holy Wells', p. 65.

26 On the development of the imagery *anastasis* see A. D. Kartsonis, *Anastasis: The Making of an Image* (Princeton, NJ, 1986).

27 E.g. Aquileia, Bologna, Brindisi, Cambridge, Constance, Fulda, Garway (Herefordshire), Le Liget, Neuvy-St-Sépulchre, Northampton, Orphir (Orkney), Østerlar (Denmark), Paderborn, Pisa; Robert Ousterhout, '*Loca sancta* and the Architectural Response to Pilgrimage', in *Blessings of Pilgrimage*, ed. Ousterhout, pp. 108–24, especially pp. 110–14 (quotation from p. 111); the classic survey is Richard Krautheimer, 'Introduction to an Iconography of Medieval Architecture', *Journal of the Courtauld and Warburg Institutes*, V (1942), pp. 1–33; see too C. Andrault-Schmitt, 'Les églises des templiers de la Creuse et l'architecture religieuse au XIIIe siècle en Limousin', *Bulletin de la Société des antiquaires de l'Ouest et des musées de Poitiers*, x (1996), pp. 73–141; *La Gerusalemme di San Vivaldo e i Sacri Monti in Europa*, ed. S. Gensini, (Montaine, 1989); John Elsner, 'Replicating Palestine

and Reversing the Reformation: Pilgrimage and Collecting at Bobbio, Monza and Walsingham', *Journal of the History of Collections*, IX (1997), pp. 117–30; D. Jacoby, 'Pèlerinage médiéval et sanctuaires de terre sainte: La perspective vénitienne', *Ateneo Veneto*, XXIV (1986), pp. 27–58; Colin Morris, *The Sepulchre of Christ and the Medieval West: From the Beginning to 1600* (Oxford, 2005), pp. 341–62.

28 See Robert Ousterhout, 'The Church of Santo Stefano: A "Jerusalem" in Bologna', *Gesta* XX (1981), pp. 311–21.

29 Ousterhout, 'Loca sancta', p. 118.

30 Jaroslav Folda, *Crusader Art in the Holy Land: From the Third Crusade to the Fall of Acre, 1187–1291* (Cambridge, 2005), p. 131.

31 See Morris, *The Sepulchre of Christ*, pp. 361–6; Wharton, *Selling Jerusalem*, pp. 118–31; Mitchell Merback, *The Thief, the Cross and the Wheel* (London, 1999), pp. 41–4.

32 See Ariel Toaff, 'Jews, Franciscans, and the First *Monti di Pietà*', in *Friars and Jews in the Middle Ages and Renaissance*, ed. Steven J. McMichael and Susan E. Myers (Leiden, 2004), pp. 239–54.

33 Wharton, *Selling Jerusalem*, p. 101.

34 See George Kubler, 'Sacred Mountains in Europe and America', in *Christianity and the Renaissance*, ed. Timothy Verdon and John Henderson (Syracuse, NJ, 1990), pp. 413–41.

35 Held at Thetford's Priory of the Holy Sepulchre (Norfolk), *EAN*, p. 96.

36 Yves-Pascal Castel, 'La lente procession des croix et calvaires du pays bigouden', *Cahiers de l'Iroise*, XXIX (1982), pp. 134–40.

37 Especially as many relics of the Passion had been brought to Rome, a similar experience could be had to pilgrimage to Jerusalem. See Nine Miedema, 'Following in the Footsteps of Christ: Pilgrimage and Passion Devotion', in *The Broken Body: Passion Devotion in Late-Medieval Culture*, ed. A. A. MacDonald, H.N.B. Ridderbos and R. M. Schlusemann (Groningen, 1998), pp. 82–3.

38 A further storey in grey stone was added in the early sixteenth century. The red brick may give the chapel its name, or the name may corrupt 'Rood Mount'. A summary history and these etymologies are given in Paul Richards, 'The Red Mount Chapel, King's Lynn' in *Walsingham: Pilgrimage and History* (Walsingham, 1999), pp. 133–7.

39 On fifteenth-century Lynn see Anthony Goodman, *Margery Kempe and her World* (Oxford, 2002).

40 Richards, 'Red Mount Chapel', p. 134; Terence Paul Smith, 'The Medieval Town Defences of King's Lynn', *Journal of the British Archaeological Association*, II/33 (1970), pp. 57–88, p. 79.

41 Identified by Richard Marks, *Image and Devotion in Late Medieval England* (Stroud, 2004), p. 203.

42 As Bartlett describes, such landscapes were, following Calvary, the conventional medieval location for gallows, as at Swansea, London's Tyburn, Paris and Vienna; see Robert Bartlett, *The Hanged Man*

(Princeton, NJ, 2004), p. 44.

43 Eighteenth-century etchings show such a wall; see David Higgins, *The Antiquities of King's Lynn: From the Sketchbooks of Edwards Edwards* (King's Lynn, 2001).

44 St Margaret's at Lynn, the town's main church which founded the Red Mount chapel, did own a silver processional cross (showing Christ, the Virgin and St John), made in 1476 (see EAN, p. 78). Walsingham's shrine was at the height of its popularity in the period 1475–1529. The Holy House at Walsingham is represented in medieval pilgrim badges (see Brian Spencer, *Pilgrim Souvenirs and Secular Badges* (London, 1998). Pamela Sheingorn, *The Easter Sepulchre in England* (Kalamazoo, MI, 1987), pp. 249–50 assesses the evidence of Walsingham drama. There was a Guild of the Holy Cross (patron: St Helena) at Lynn, and the Lynn Shipman's Guild was dedicated to the Exaltation of the Cross; see *English Gilds*, ed. Smith, pp. 54–6, 83–5.

45 Joan Evans and Norman Cook, 'A Statue of Christ from the Ruins of Mercers' Hall', *Archaeological Journal*, CXI (1954–5), pp. 168–80.

46 See J. C. Dickinson, *The Shrine of Our Lady of Walsingham* (Cambridge, 1956), pp. 94–105, for the most complete account of the building's nature. The revelation of this building through vision mirrors the transformative acts of seeing found in many pilgrimage accounts of the Holy Land (see Georgia Frank, *Memory of the Eyes: Pilgrims to Living Saints in Christian Late Antiquity* (Berkeley, CA, 2000), p. 103).

47 In fact, Richeldis de Favereches was a twelfth-century Norman noblewoman (Morris, *The Sepulchre of Christ*, p. 346); Geoffrey, Richeldis' son and the founder of Walsingham Priory, had been in the Holy Land in the early twelfth century and the Holy House can be seen as a provincial counterpart to the Templar churches being built in London and Paris around the same time in which an aesthetic memory of the Holy Land begat a souvenir replica. See too Christopher Harper-Bill, 'The Foundation and Later History of the Medieval Shrine', in *Walsingham*, pp. 63–79.

48 [Anon.], *Of this chapel se here the fundacyon...* (London, 1496).

49 William Wey, *The Itineraries of William Wey*, ed. Francis Davey (London, 1857) pp. xxviii–xxx. Wey retired to Edington upon his return from the Holy Land; Edington was an anomalous institution, a house of *Bonhommes*, a community of religious brethren (neither enclosed nor an abbey) which followed the Augustinian rule. See Suzanne Yeager, *Jerusalem in Medieval Narrative* (Cambridge, 2009), pp. 20–21, and p. 179, n. 16 and 17.

50 Oxford, Bodleian Library MS Bodley 565, ff. 2r–v; *c.* 1470. The *ex libris* inscriptions on the book's rear flyleaves show that the book once belonged to the monastery at Edington. Another manuscript (Oxford, Bodleian Library MS Douce 389) was probably written by Wey.

51 Wey, *Itineraries*, p. xxx.

52 On the 'measurement' of Christ see David Areford, 'The Passion Measured: A Late Medieval Diagram of the Body of Christ', in *The Broken Body: Passion Devotion in Late Medieval Culture*, ed. A. A. MacDonald, H.N.B. Ridderbos and R. M. Schlusemann (Groningen, 1998), pp. 213–38.

53 See H. E. Salter and Mary Lobel, ed., *The Victoria County History of the County of Oxford: The University of Oxford* (London, 1954), p. 319.

54 See Morris, *The Sepulchre of Christ*, pp. 352–3, who connects the Church with Wey's project at Edington; Jean-Paul Esther, 'Monumentenbeschrijving en bouwgeschiedenis van den Jeruzalemkapel', in *Adornes en Jeruzalem*, ed. N. Geirnaert and A. Vendewalle (Bruges, 1983), pp. 51–81, p. 62.

55 The octagon suggests salvation which follows circumcision and resurrection on the eighth day; so baptisteries and chapter houses were generally octagonal: see Hiscock, *Symbol at Your Door*, pp. 256–7.

56 *Itinéraire d'Anselme Adorno*, ed. Jacques Heers et al. (Paris, 1978), pp. 266–7.

57 Ibid., pp. 266–9.

58 Kathryn Beebe, 'Reading Mental Pilgrimage in Context: The Imaginary Pilgrims and Real Travels of Felix Fabri's "Die Sionpilger"', *Essays in Medieval Studies*, xxv (2008), pp. 39–70; Kathryn Rudy, 'A Guide to Mental Pilgrimage: Paris, Bibliothèque de l'Arsenal ms.212', *Zeitschrift für Kunstgeschichte*, lxiii/lxiv (2000), pp. 494–515. Also, for another comparison, Horst Wenzel, *Georg Emmerich und das Heilige Grab in Görlitz* (Görlitz, 1994).

59 Sabine MacCormack, '*Loca Sancta*: The Organization of Sacred Topography in Late Antiquity', in *The Blessing of Pilgrimage*, ed. Robert Ousterhout (Urbana, il, 1990), p. 7.

60 Stijn Bossuyt, 'The Liturgical Use of Space in Thirteenth-Century Flanders', in *Defining the Holy: Sacred Space in Medieval and Early Modern Europe*, ed. Andrew Spicer and Sarah Hamilton (Aldershot, 2005), pp. 187–203, includes material on Saint Omer and Lille and urban processions in which the city became the Heavenly Jerusalem.

61 Hillel Schwartz, *The Culture of the Copy: Striking Likenesses, Unreasonable Facsimiles* (New York, 1996), p. 212.

62 Yeager, *Jerusalem*, p. 132.

63 Ibid., pp. 150–51, notes 'interiorized pilgrimage was a focal point of the Cistercian heritage', but the evidence suggests that, by the later Middle Ages, expressions of an interiorized pilgrimage were very widespread across clerical and secular realms.

64 Schwartz, *Culture of the Copy*, p. 378.

65 The terms of this discussion are taken from Wharton, *Selling Jerusalem*, p. 50, on the differences between relics, souvenirs and replicas.

66 Morris, *Sepulchre of Christ*, p. 341.

67 On Kempe's travels in context see Goodman, *Margery Kempe*, pp. 152–74.

68 References to *The Book of Margery Kempe* are by line number and refer to *The Book of Margery Kempe*, ed. Barry Windeatt (Woodbridge, 2004).

69 See Leviticus 15:8; Numbers 12:14; Deuteronomy 25:9; Job 7:19; Isaiah 50:6. These references, so close to those in the Gospels, provide the template for this part of the Passion narrative. Conversely, Jesus uses spittle for healing (Mark 7:33); Augustine says in his 'Second Discourse on Psalm 133', reading the story of David's spittle running down his beard as an allegory of Christ's Passion, that 'spittle is a sign of weakness, the beard is a symbol of strength'; spittle represents, says Augustine, 'external weakness'; see too James Marrow, *Passion Iconography in Northern European Art of the Late Middle Ages and Early Renaissance* (Brussels, 1979), p. 132.

70 Lynn Staley notes how Jacques de Vitry, in his life of Marie d'Oignies which was known to Kempe and/or her amanuensis, compared heretics to mad dogs or Jews, 'since they do not comprehend the nature of the holy within their midst'. See Lynn Staley, *Margery Kempe's Dissenting Fictions* (University Park, PA, 1994), pp. 44–5.

71 As Scherb notes, Kempe's rebuking of authority figures is self-authorizing, as Kempe sets the parameters of blasphemy. See Victor Scherb, 'Blasphemy and the Grotesque in the Digby Mary Magdalene', *Studies in Philology*, XCVI (1999), pp. 225–40, p. 231. Jeffrey Jerome Cohen, 'Was Margery Kempe Jewish?', in *Medieval Identity Machines* (Minneapolis, 2003), pp. 185–8, notes how, although Kempe's most frequent description of Jews is as 'cruel', she also repeatedly describes both Jews and herself as 'boystows' – boisterous – as Kempe seeks, like the boisterous 'Jew' she describes, to have her 'exorbitant voice' heard.

72 Paul Strohm, *Theory and the Premodern Text* (Minneapolis, 2001), pp. 27–30.

73 See www.paintedchurch.org/passcon.htm (accessed 7 August 2009), for examples of Passion cycles.

74 Suzannah Biernoff, *Sight and Embodiment in the Middle Ages* (Basingstoke, 2002), pp. 138–9.

75 As Beckwith comments, 'Kempe's *imitatio Christi* . . . consists in her willing assumption of suffering, and the way she functions as an object of scorn to those around her . . . Thus, in an irritating, albeit Christ-like fashion, she thanks people for the abuse they heap on her head, and the book comes to read more and more like a trial, a test of her sanctity where sanctity is proved by the act of testing itself' (Sarah Beckwith, *Christ's Body: Identity, Culture and Society in Late Medieval Writings* (London, 1994), p. 78). Clarissa Atkinson, *Mystic and Pilgrim: The Book and the World of Margery Kempe* (Ithaca, NY, 1983), pp. 114–15, notes how many of Kempe's ordeals took place on a Friday, the day on which Christ's Passion was commemorated.

76 *The Book of Margery Kempe*, p. 104 (n.).

77 Mark 11:11; Luke 24:50.

78 MBLJC, p. 173.

79 The 'helpful cripple' is a motif of saints' lives (SS Basil, Fremund, Giles) and vernacular literature.

80 Avraham David, 'The Jewish Settlement in Palestine in the Mameluke Period (1260–1516)', in *The Jewish Settlement in Palestine 634–1881*, ed. Alex Carmel, Peter Schäfer and Yossi Ben-Artzi (Wiesbaden, 1990), pp. 40–85, p. 66; see too Schein, 'La *Custodia*', pp. 372–3; Schein also describes the anti-Jewish animus of the Franciscans, in particular how the Jewish community was presented by the Franciscans as a menace to their work in the Holy Land.

81 The fifteenth-century Suffolk poet John Lydgate (close to Kempe in location and date) uses 'Sarseyne' for the heathen Danes in his *Lives of SS Edmund and Fremund*. This example is given, along with several other relevant etymological citations, in the *Oxford English Dictionary*, s.v. 'Saracen'; see *The Book of Margery Kempe*, p. 173.

82 Similarly, writing in the 1470s Anselmo Adorno notes the handsome Mameluks ('alios egregios mamalucos'), who are excellent warriors ('bonos armigeros') who ride with the pilgrims with gaiety and good humour ('qui in itinere hilariter ac jocunde more satellitum equitarunt'). *Itinéraire*, p. 306.

83 Like the memorable conflict at Constance, where the other pilgrims gang up against Kempe (lines 1991–2021).

84 Sylvia Schein, 'Bridget of Sweden, Margery Kempe and Women's Jerusalem Pilgrimages in the Middle Ages', *Mediterranean Historical Review*, XIV (1999), pp. 44–58. Similarly, but from a much earlier period, Jerome's description of Paula's visits to Golgotha and Bethlehem has been described as 'strikingly empty' whilst Athanasius' account is comprised largely of biblical allusions. See Frank, *Memory of the Eyes*, pp. 105–110.

85 These are standard mystical terms, cognate with Kempe's 'ghostly' or spiritual eye through which she sees.

86 Rosalynn Voaden, 'Travels with Margery: Pilgrimage in Context', in *Eastword Bound: Travel in the Middle Ages 1050–1550*, ed. R. Allen (Manchester, 2004), pp. 177–95, p. 185. Against Voaden, one might note that *The Book of Margery Kempe* is not shy of describing Kempe's *curiositas* elsewhere!

87 Wharton, *Selling Jerusalem*, p. 101

88 Ibid., p. 126

89 Translation from Carolyn Malone, *Façade as Spectacle: Ritual and Ideology at Wells Cathedral* (Leiden, 2004), pp. 134–7; see also Allan Doig, *Liturgy and Architecture: From the Early Church to the Middle Ages* (Aldershot, 2008), pp. 183–7.

90 Merback, *Thief*, p. 19.

7 Cultures in Pain

1 Avraham Yaakov Finkel, ed. and trans., *Sefer Chasidim* (Northvale, NJ, 1997), pp. 365–6. For accessibility, quotations are from Finkel's informal translation.

2 Ibid., p. 366; however, see Talya Fishman, 'The Rhineland Pietists' Sacralization of Oral Torah', *Jewish Quarterly Review*, XCVI (2005), pp. 9–16, pp. 10–12, on the meaning of *sefarim* in this context, which would, Fishman suggests, have included only sacred Torah books and scrolls.

3 See Anthony Bale, 'Fictions of Judaism in Medieval England', in *The Jews in Medieval Britain*, ed. Patricia Skinner (Woodbridge, 2003), pp. 129–44, pp. 143–4 on Cambridge, Pembroke College MS 59; Judith Olszowy-Schlanger, *Les manuscrits hébreux dans l'Angleterre médiévale: étude historique et paléographique* (Paris, 2003); conversely, *Sefer Chasidim*, p. 369, forbids using Christian ecclesiastical books to bind Jewish books.

4 *Sefer Chasidim*, pp. 54–67.

5 Thus the *Sefer Chasidim* includes the striking story of a helpful apostate: 'It happened that on a Shabbat a fire broke out in the house of a Jew. An apostate who saw the blaze said the Jew, "Hand me your *sefarim*. I want to carry them outside and save them from the fire." When the Jew did not hand him the books, the apostate took the books himself and rescued them.' *Sefer Chasidim*, p. 359.

6 Averroës, *Three Short Commentaries on Aristotle's 'Topics', 'Rhetoric', and 'Poetics'*, ed. and trans. Charles E. Butterworth (Albany, NY, 1977), p. 73.

7 Ibid., pp. 73–4.

8 The term 'sensory underpinnings' is taken from Kalman P. Bland, 'Medieval Jewish Aesthetics: Maimonides, Body, and Scripture in Profiat Duran', *Journal of the History of Ideas*, LIV (1993), pp. 533–59, p. 536; on the interpenetration of Jewish and Latin models of reading and writing in medieval Spain, see Eleazar Gutwirth, 'A Song and Dance: Transcultural Practices of Daily Life in Medieval Spain', in *Jews, Muslims and Christians in and around the Crown of Aragon*, ed. Elena Lourie and Harvey J. Hames (Leiden, 2004), pp. 207–27; Katrin Kogman-Appel, 'Hebrew Manuscript Painting in Late Medieval Spain: Signs of a Culture in Transition', *Art Bulletin*, LXXXIV (2002), pp. 247–72.

9 Barrie Dobson, *The Jews of Medieval York and the Massacre of March 1190* (York, 1974).

10 Quotations from William's Latin account are from Richard Howlett, ed., *Historia rerum Anglicarum* (London, 1884–5), vol. I, pp. 312–23. Howlett here (vol. I, p. 318) notes an allusion to Ecclesiastes 8:4.

11 Migne, *Patrologia Latina*, gives a dozen references, including from Augustine, Gregory and Anselm.

12 Dobson, *Jews of Medieval York*, p. 27; Yom Tov was a leading Tosafist, a group of scholars engaged in commentary on Rashi; see C. Roth, *The Intellectual Activities of Medieval English Jewry* (London, 1949), pp. 21–2; Susan L. Einbinder, *Beautiful Death: Jewish Poetry and Martyrdom in Medieval France* (Princeton, NJ, 2002), pp. 29–30.

13 Newburgh, *Historia*, ed. Howlett, vol. I, p. 320; Rachel Fulton, *From Judgment to Passion: Devotion to Christ and the Virgin Mary 800–1200* (New York, 2002), p. 441, comments of this passage that 'the underlying (if unstated) historiographical premise being that in order to make clear the motivations of the agents in the narrative, something of their speech must be imagined along with the particulars of their actions. Accordingly, historical reality – indeed, historical truth – is here defined not only as that which may be corroborated "objectively", as it were, by the testimony of "credible witnesses", but also that which is most subjectively read: the expectations, emotions, and reasoning of the persons described by the historian in his narrative.'

14 Dobson, *Jews of Medieval York*, p. 24.

15 Nancy F. Partner, *Serious Entertainments: The Writing of History in Twelfth-Century England* (Chicago, 1977), p. 226.

16 Einbinder, *Beautiful Death*, p. 31.

17 On *Kiddush ha-Shem* in medieval Europe see Simha Goldin, 'The Socialisation for *Kiddush ha-Shem* among Medieval Jews', *Journal of Medieval History*, XXIII (1997), pp. 117–38; Daniel Boyarin, *Dying for God: Martyrdom and the Making of Christianity and Judaism* (Berkeley, CA, 1999); Jeremy Cohen, *Sanctifying the Name of God: Jewish Martyrs and Jewish Memories of the First Crusade* (Philadelphia, 2006).

18 For Menahem of Worms's Hebrew account see *Sefer Gezerot Ashkenaz ve-Tsarefat*, ed. Abraham Habermann (Jerusalem, 1945), p. 150; Joseph of Chartres' account is *Sefer Gezerot*, ed. Habermann, pp. 152–3, and is translated by Cecil Roth, 'A Hebrew Elegy on the York Martyrs of 1190', *Transactions of the Jewish Historical Society of England*, XVI (1945/51), pp. 212–20; Ephraim of Bonn's account is *Sefer Gezerot*, ed. Habermann, pp. 127–8; parts of Ephraim's *Sefer Zekhirah* dealing with the assaults on the Jews in 1146–7 are translated in Shlomo Eidelberg, *The Jews and the Crusaders: The Hebrew Chronicles of the First and Second Crusades* (Madison, WI, 1977), pp. 121–33.

19 Dobson, *Jews of Medieval York*, p. 21, calling it 'unquestionably the most valuable of all the Hebrew sources to survive'.

20 This same section of Deuteronomy was frequently used in Jewish stories of women who died of hunger or ate their children during the Roman siege of Jerusalem. See Yuval, *Two Nations*, pp. 53–5; the Middle English account of the siege, the fourteenth-century alliterative poem *The Siege of Jerusalem*, has frequently been seen as indebted to ritual-murder narratives in its portrait of Jewish women's infant cannibalism; however, the poet's use of this image could also be drawn

from Eusebius' Latin version of Talmudic and rabbinic accounts, which were themselves fulfilments of, or resonant with, Deuteronomy 28:53–7.

21 Gabrielle Spiegel, 'History, Historicism and The Social Logic of the Text in the Middle Ages', *Speculum*, LXV (1990), pp. 59–86; Monika Otter, *Inventiones: Fiction and Referentiality in Twelfth-Century English Historical Writing* (Chapel Hill, NC, 1996); Janet Coleman, *Ancient and Medieval Memories: Studies in the Reconstruction of the Past* (Cambridge, 1982).

22 Susan Einbinder, *No Place to Rest: Jewish Literature, Expulsion and the Memory of Medieval France* (Philadelphia, 2009), p. 83; Cohen, *Sanctifying*; likewise, Dobson notes that 'it would be wise to remember that Ephraim's purpose was the commemoration of martyrs rather than an explanation of the reasons for martyrdom' (*Jews of Medieval York*, p. 22).

23 See Lillian Randall, *Images in the Margins of Gothic Manuscripts* (Berkeley, CA, 1966); Michael Camille, *Image on the Edge: The Margins of Medieval Art* (London, 1992); Laura Kendrick, *Animating the Letter: The Figurative Embodiment of Writing from Late Antiquity to the Renaissance* (Columbus, OH, 1999); Mary Carruthers, *The Craft of Thought: Meditation, Rhetoric and the Making of Images 400–1200* (Cambridge, 2000), pp. 161–5.

24 See Marc Michael Epstein, *Dreams of Subversion in Medieval Jewish Art and Literature* (University Park, PA, 1997), p. 19.

25 Evelyn Cohen, 'Decoration', in *Barcelona Haggadah: Facsimile* (London, 1992), remarks that the 'hunting motif, popular in fourteenth-century *haggadot*, seems to have been purely decorative and without iconographic significance, just as in Latin manuscripts of the time'.

26 Camille, *Image*, pp. 9–10; Jody Enders, *The Medieval Theater of Cruelty* (Ithaca, NY, 1999), pp. 85–7, suggests that marginal penises represent *testes*, i.e. testicles *and* witnesses.

27 Kendrick, *Animating the Letter*; Carruthers, *Craft*, pp. 163–4

28 Epstein, *Dreams of Subversion*, p. 11. Epstein invokes the common Hebrew mnemonic 'YaKiNeHaZ', through which medieval Jews recalled the various constituent elements of the Passover *seder* meal should it fall on a Sabbath (*Yayin, Kiddush, Ner, Havdalah, Zeman*: wine, the Kiddush prayer, candle, the blessing, the thanksgiving for the season). This mnemonic, Epstein suggests, 'called to mind' the Judeo-German phrase '*jag den Has*' (the hare hunt) and so Passover *haggadah* books were illustrated with a hare hunt; this strand of imagery intersects at once with depictions of Esau as hunter (hunting Israel-as-quarry), with the hare as a symbol for Israel, and with strategies of subversion which show the Jews evading the 'snares' of their enemies. According to Epstein, the 'Jewish appropriation of the symbol of the hare is effected in an atmosphere charged with

theological polemic', and the 'original' 'YaKiNeHaZ' mnemonic stemmed from 'a confluence of symbolic and linguistic associations' rooted in Jewish self-identity and resistance. The hunt answers Christian persecution and, in many Hebrew manuscript illustrations, the hare jumps out of the decoration, away from its pursuer, as the 'Jewish' hare triumphs over its 'Christian' hunter. Epstein's seductive reading demands qualification, at least in terms of the Prato Haggadah, as the Judeo-German '*jag den Has*' pun would be meaningless for both a Sephardi/Iberian audience and/or a Spanish-speaking illustrator. Epstein (pp. 28–35) describes the use of the image in Spain.

29 This text appears in the Prato Haggadah on ff. 12–12v.

30 The *Midrash Mekhilta* (*Parashat Bo*, chapter 5), a commentary on the book of Exodus, connects the exodus with both sacrifice and circumcision. Whilst in the Christian tradition the deer is 'timid' and 'unwarlike' (Isidore, *Etymologies*, ed. and trans. Barney *et al*, §xii:i:21, p. 248), it should not be considered either weak or feminine for its name in Hebrew (*eyal*) is cognate with the Hebrew words for 'ram', 'chief' and 'strength'. Some Jewish tradition use the deer to represent the *shekinah* (God's presence), especially in its exile. See I. Tishby, *The Wisdom of the Zohar: An Anthology* (Oxford, 1989), vol. i, pp. 359–85. On controversial but symbolically central questions of blood, see David Biale, *Blood and Belief: The Circulation of a Symbol between Christians and Jews* (Berkeley, ca, 2008).

31 Augustine, 'Exposition of Psalm 41', ed. John Rotelle, trans. Maria Boulding, *Expositions of the Psalms 33–50*, in *The Works of Saint Augustine* (New York, 2000), vol. xvi, part 3, pp. 242–3, emphases added.

32 Ibid.

33 This quotation is taken from the Aberdeen Bestiary (via www.abdn.ac.uk/bestiary/), and standard bestiary lore; the description is given in Isidore, *Etymologies*, ed. and trans. Barney et al., §xxi:i:18–19 (p. 248).

34 Quoting Isidore, *Etymologies*, ed. and trans. Barney et al., §xii:i:23 (p. 248).

35 Augustine, 'Exposition of Psalm 117', §2, *Expositions*, vol. xix, part 3, pp. 334–5.

36 Biale, *Blood and Belief*, pp. 46–71.

37 See Carruthers, *Book of Memory*, pp. 78–9, 323–4, describing hunting and fishing *topoi* in memory-aids, starting with Aristotle's use of the imagery of hunting and 'tracking down' for recollecting from a starting-point and Quintilian's assertion that 'just you would not find a particular bird or animal if you did not know its birthplace or its haunts. . . we have therefore to be selective in our search'. Carruthers quotes Richard de Bury's *Philobiblon* which describes researchers as being 'like keen hunters after rabbits' (*Book of Memory*, p. 201); Geoffrey of Vinsauf's *Poetria Nova* uses language of hunting, searching, and the following of pathways to describe textual composition.

38 See Adriana Fisch Hartley, 'La chasse inversé dans les marges à droller des manuscrits gothiques', in *La Chasse au Moyen Age*, ed. Agostino Paravicini Bagliani and Baudouin Van den Abeele (Florence, 2000), pp. 111–28; Marcelle Thiébaux, *The Stag of Love: The Chase in Medieval Literature* (Ithaca, NY, 1974); such imagery informs *Sir Gawain and the Green Knight*, the late fourteenth-century English poem, in which Sir Gawain's three days of hunting (described in technical language) are used to suggest a range of parallels in his sexual, ethical and religious trials. Likewise, Dante's *De vulgarii eloquentia* is suffused with hunting imagery to describe the pursuit of linguistic meaning.

39 Thiébaux, *Stag of Love*, p. 35; E. R. Rogers, *The Perilous Hunt: Symbolism in Hispanic and European Balladry* (Lexington, KY, 1980), pp. 6–40, on 'ominous' and 'love-pursuit' hunting in medieval European ballads.

40 As discussed by Epstein, *Dreams of Subversion*, p. 31; this image is cognate with those found in Christian books as described in Randall, *Images*.

41 Nicholas Mirzoeff, 'The Multiple Viewpoint: Diaspora and Visual Culture', in *Diaspora and Visual Culture: Representing Africans and Jews*, ed. Nicholas Mirzoeff (London, 2000), pp. 1–18, p. 7.

42 Avicenna, *A Compendium on the Soul*, ed. and trans. Edward van Dyck (Verona, 1906), p. 63.

43 Or 'knowing that some image is an image of something previously sensed' (Coleman, *Ancient and Medieval Memories*, p. 450).

44 These terms are taken from the exercise of 'sorouful compassion thorh fervent inward affection' of the 'peynful passion of Jesu' in the Passion meditation of MBLJC, p. 159.

45 See Ramie Targoff, *Common Prayer: The Language of Public Devotion in Early Modern England* (Chicago, 2001), pp. 6–12.

46 Bale, *Jew in the Medieval Book*, pp. 105–111.

47 See especially William C. Jordan, *Unceasing Strife, Unending Fear: Jacques de Thérines and the Freedom of the Church in the Age of the Last Capetians* (Princeton, NJ, 2005), a microportrait of the circumstances surrounding the expulsion of the French Jews in 1306; Robin Mundill, *England's Jewish Solution: Experiment and Expulsion* (Cambridge, 1998) on the economic factors involved in the 1290 expulsion from England.

48 'The longest hatred' and 'the generic hatred' describe 'antisemitism'; see Robert Wistrich, *Antisemitism: The Longest Hatred* (London, 1991) and *Antisemitism: The Generic Hatred. Essays in Honor of Simon Wiesenthal* (London, 2007). I have found the following helpful in thinking about the contemporary issues involved: Idith Zertal, *Israel's Holocaust and the Politics of Nationhood* (Cambridge, 2005), chapters 5 and 6; Oren Baruch Stier, *Committed to Memory: Cultural Mediations of the Holocaust* (Amherst, MA, 2003); Martin S. Jaffee, 'The Victim-Community in Myth and History: Holocaust Ritual, the Question of Palestine, and the Rhetoric of Christian Witness', *Journal of Ecumenical*

Studies, 28 (1991), pp. 223–38, especially the description of Jewish 'self-understanding as a community of suffering' and how the 'redemptive possibilities of victimization are played out historically through political power'; Shoshana Felman, 'Theaters of Justice: Arendt in Jerusalem, the Eichmann Trial, and the Redefinition of Legal Meaning in the Wake of the Holocaust', *Critical Inquiry* XXVII (2001), pp. 201–38; Dan Stone, *Constructing the Holocaust*, chapter 6, 'Narrative Theory and Holocaust Historiography', pp. 211–38, especially Stone's description of how Holocaust accounts '[narrate] the events in ways that render them compatible with existing storyforms' (p. 223). Norman Finkelstein, *The Holocaust Industry: Reflections on the Exploitation of Jewish Suffering*, 2nd edn (London, 2003), esp. pp. 49–55, discusses 'the Holocaust dogma of eternal Gentile hatred', marking 'the climax of a millennial Gentile hatred of Jews', which, he argues, serves 'the exploitation of Jewish suffering' largely for the profit of (American) Jewry.

49 Sarah Beckwith, *Christ's Body: Identity, Culture and Society in Late Medieval Writings* (London, 1984), p. 2.

50 R. I. Moore, *The Formation of a Persecuting Society. Power and Deviance in Western Europe, 950–1250* (Oxford, 1987), p. 4.

51 Marc Andre Bernstein, *Foregone Conclusions: Against Apocalyptic History* (Berkeley, CA, 1994); George Eliot, *Daniel Deronda*, ed. John Rignall (London, 1999), p. 618.

52 An example is James Carroll's review of Jeremy Cohen's *Christ Killers*, 'Jeremy Cohen shows exactly how the Christ-killer charge lodged, like a killer-virus, in the imagination of the West. Alas, he shows, also, how it remains a mortal problem for Christians, a threat to Jews – a germ of further hatred. Meticulous truth-telling like Cohen's is the only antidote to this ancient plague', quoted on the book's website at www.oup.com.

53 David Nirenberg, *Communities of Violence: Persecution of Minorities in the Middle Ages* (Princeton, NJ, 1998), p. 215.

54 Ibid., p. 228.

55 For an intelligent consideration of these issues see Jody Enders, *Murder by Accident* (Chicago, 2009), pp. xvi–xviii.

56 Dan Cohn-Sherbok, *The Crucified Jew: Twenty Centuries of Christian Anti-Semitism* (Grand Rapids, MI, 1997), pp. xiv–xvi.

57 Marvin Perry and Frederick M. Schweitzer, *Jewish-Christian Encounters Over the Centuries: Symbiosis, Prejudice, Holocaust, Dialogue* (New York, 1994); *Antisemitism: Myth and Hate From Antiquity to the Present* (New York, 2002).

58 Hannah Arendt, *The Origins of Totalitarianism* (New York, 1951), p. 3.

59 See Peter Novick, *The Holocaust in American Life* (New York, 2000), p. 8; see also above p. 236 n. 48.

60 See Eve Kosofsky Sedgwick, *Touching Feeling: Affect, Pedagogy, Perfomativity* (Durham, NC, 2003), p. 124.

61 See Jacqueline Rose, *The Last Resistance* (London, 2007), p. 69.
62 Augustine, *On Order*, ed. and trans. Silvano Borruso (Chicago, 2006), §1.8.25 (p. 33).

Select Bibliography

Amsler, Mark, 'Affective Literacy: Gestures of Reading in the Later Middle Ages', *Essays in Medieval Studies*, XVIII (2001), pp. 83–110

Arasse, Daniel, *L'annonciation italienne: une histoire de perspective* (Paris, 1999)

Arendt, Hannah, *The Origins of Totalitarianism*, revd edn (New York, 1973)

Asad, Talal, *Formations of the Secular: Christianity, Islam, Modernity* (Palo Alto, CA, 2003)

Bale, Anthony, *The Jew in the Medieval Book: English Antisemitisms 1350–1500* (Cambridge, 2006)

Baum, Paul, 'The Mediaeval Legend of Judas Iscariot', PMLA, XXXI (1916), pp. 481–585

Baxendall, Michael, *Painting and Experience in Renaissance Italy* (Oxford, 1972)

Beckwith, Sarah, *Christ's Body: Identity, Culture and Society in Late Medieval Writings* (London, 1994)

Belting, Hans, *Likeness and Presence: A History of the Image before the Era of Art*, trans. Edmund Jephcott (Chicago, 1996)

Bennett, Jill, 'Stigmata and Sense Memory: The Topographic Body of St Francis as Affective Image', *Art History*, XXIV (2001), pp. 1–16

Bernstein, Marc André, *Foregone Conclusions: Against Apocalyptic History* (Berkeley, CA, 1994)

Bestul, Thomas, *Texts of the Passion: Latin Devotional Literature and Medieval Society* (Philadelphia, 1996)

Biale, David, *Blood and Belief: The Circulation of a Symbol between Christians and Jews* (Berkeley, 2008)

Biernoff, Suzannah, *Sight and Embodiment in the Middle Ages* (London, 2002)

Bildhauer, Bettina, *Medieval Blood* (Cardiff, 2006)

Bland, Kalman, *The Artless Jew: Medieval and Modern Affirmations and Denials of the Visual* (Princeton, NJ, 2001)

Brantley, Jessica, *Reading in the Wilderness: Private Devotion and Public Performance in Late Medieval England* (Chicago, 2007)

Bynum, Caroline Walker, *Holy Feast and Holy Fast. The Religious Significance of Food to Medieval Women* (Berkeley, CA, 1987)

—, *Wonderful Blood: Theology and Practice in Late Medieval Northern Germany and Beyond* (Philadelphia, 2007)

Camille, Michael, 'Seeing and Reading: Some Visual Implications of Medieval Literacy and Illiteracy', *Art History*, VIII (1985), pp. 26–32

—, '"Seeing and Lecturing": Disputation from a Twelfth-Century Tympanum from Reims', in *Reading Medieval Images: The Art Historian and the Object*, ed. Elizabeth Sears, Thelma K. Thomas and Ilene H. Forsyth (Ann Arbor, MI, 2002), pp. 75–87

Carruthers, Mary, *The Book of Memory: A Study of Memory in Medieval Culture*, 2nd edn (Cambridge, 2008)

—, *The Craft of Thought: Meditation, Rhetoric and the Making of Images 400–1200* (Cambridge, 2000)

—, 'Reading with Attitude, Remembering the Book', in *The Book and the Body*, ed. D. W. Frese and K. O'Brien O'Keeffe (South Bend, IN, 1997), pp. 1–33

Chazelle, Celia, *The Crucified God in the Carolingian Era: Theology and Art of Christ's Passion* (Cambridge, 2001)

Cohen, Esther, 'The Animated Pain of the Body', *American Historical Review*, CV (2000), pp. 36–68

Cohen, Jeffrey Jerome, ed., *Monster Theory: Reading Culture* (Minneapolis, MN, 1996)

Cohen, Jeremy, *Christ Killers: The Jews and the Passion from the Bible to the Big Screen* (Oxford, 2007)

—, *Sanctifying the Name of God: Jewish Martyrs and Jewish Memories of the First Crusade* (Princeton, NJ, 2004)

—, *Living Letters of the Law: Ideas of the Jew in Medieval Christianity* (Berkeley, CA, 1999)

Coleman, Janet, *Ancient and Medieval Memories: Studies in the Reconstruction of the Past* (Cambridge, 1992)

Coleman, Simon, and John Elsner, *Pilgrimage Past and Present: Sacred Travel and Sacred Space in the World Religions* (London, 1995)

Derbes, Anne, *Picturing the Passion in Late Medieval Italy: Narrative Painting, Franciscan Ideologies, and the Levant* (Cambridge, 1996)

—, and Mark Sandona, *The Usurer's Heart: Giotto, Enrico Scrovegni, and the Arena Chapel in Padua* (University Park, PA, 2008)

Dobson, Barrie, *The Jews of Medieval York and the Massacre of March 1190* (York, 1974)

Duffy, Eamon, *The Stripping of the Altars: Traditional Religion in England 1400–1580* (New Haven, CT, 1992)

Eco, Umberto, *On Ugliness*, trans. Alastair McEwen (London, 2007)

Einbinder, Susan, *No Place of Rest: Jewish Literature, Expulsion, and the*

Memory of Medieval France (Philadelphia, 2009)

Enders, Jody, *The Medieval Theater of Cruelty* (Ithaca, NY, 1999)

—, *Murder by Accident* (Chicago, 2009)

Epstein, Marc Michael, *Dreams of Subversion in Medieval Jewish Art and Literature* (University Park, PA, 1997)

Frojmovic, Eva, ed., *Imagining the Self, Imagining the Other: Visual Representation and Jewish-Christian Dynamics in the Middle Ages and Early Modern Period* (Leiden, 2002)

Fulton, Rachel, *From Judgment to Passion: Devotion to Christ and the Virgin Mary 800–1200* (New York, 2002)

Gubar, Susan, *Judas: A Biography* (New York, 2009)

Harvey, P.D.A., ed., *The Hereford World Map: Medieval World Maps and Their Context* (London, 2006)

Hills, Matt, *The Pleasures of Horror* (London, 2008)

Holsinger, Bruce, 'Pedagogy, Violence, and the Subject of Music: Chaucer's "Prioress's Tale" and the Ideologies of "song"', *New Medieval Literatures*, I (1997), pp. 157–92

Jones, Michael, 'Theatrical History in the Croxton Play of the Sacrament', *English Literary History*, LXVI (1999), pp. 223–60

Kalina, Pavel, '*Cordium penetrativa*: An Essay on Iconoclasm and Image Worship around the Year 1400', *Umění*, XLIII (1995), pp. 247–57

Kendrick, Laura, *Animating the Letter: The Figurative Embodiment of Writing from Late Antiquity to the Renaissance* (Columbus, OH, 1999)

Kinservik, Matthew, 'The Struggle over Mary's Body', *Journal of English and Germanic Philology*, XCV (1996), pp. 190–203

Kruger, Steven, *The Spectral Jew: Conversion and Embodiment in Medieval Europe* (Minneapolis, 2006)

Lampert, Lisa, 'Race, Periodicity, and the (Neo-) Middle Ages', *Modern Languages Quarterly*, LXV (2004), pp. 391–421

—, *Gender and Jewish Difference from Paul to Shakespeare* (Philadelphia, 2004)

Largier, Niklaus, *In Praise of the Whip: A Culture History of Arousal*, trans. Graham Harman (New York, 2007)

Lawton, David, 'Sacrilege and Theatricality: the Croxton *Play of the Sacrament*', *Journal of Medieval and Early Modern Studies*, XXXIII (2003), pp. 281–309

Marrow, James, *Passion Iconography in Northern European Art of the Late Middle Ages and Early Renaissance* (Brussels, 1979)

McCulloh, John, 'Jewish Ritual Murder: William of Norwich, Thomas of Monmouth and the Early Dissemination of the Myth', *Speculum*, LXXII (1997), pp. 698–740

Mellinkoff, Ruth, *Outcasts: Signs of Otherness in Northern European Art of the Late Middle Ages* (Berkeley, CA, 1993)

—, *Antisemitic Hate Signs in Hebrew Illuminated Manuscripts from Medieval Germany* (Jerusalem, 1999)

Merback, Mitchell, *The Thief, the Cross and the Wheel: Pain and the Spectacle of Punishment in Medieval and Renaissance Europe* (London, 1999)

Mills, Robert, *Suspended Animation: Pain, Pleasure and Punishment in Medieval Culture* (London, 2005)

Mitchell, W.J.T., *What Do Pictures Want? The Lives and Loves of Images* (Chicago, 2005)

Moore, R. I., *The Formation of a Persecuting Society. Power and Deviance in Western Europe, 950–1250* (Oxford, 1987)

Nirenberg, David, *Communities of Violence: Persecution of Minorities in the Middle Ages* (Princeton, NJ, 1998)

Ousterhout, Robert, 'The Church of Santo Stefano: A "Jerusalem" in Bologna', *Gesta*, xx (1981), pp. 311–21

Owens, Margaret E., *Stages of Dismemberment: The Fragmented Body in Late Medieval and Early Modern Drama* (Wilmington, DE, 2005)

Porter, Martin, *Windows of the Soul: Physiognomy in European Culture 1470–1780* (Oxford, 2005)

Renna, Thomas, *Jerusalem in Medieval Thought, 400-1300* (Lewiston, NY, 2002)

Richards, Emily, 'Writing and Silence: Transitions Between the Contemplative and Active Life', in *Pieties in Transition: Religious Practices and Experiences c. 1400–1640*, ed. Robert Lutton and Elisabeth Salter (Aldershot, 2007), pp. 163–79

Ross, Ellen, *The Grief of God: Images of the Suffering Jesus in Late Medieval England* (Oxford, 1999)

Rudolph, Conrad, *Violence and Daily Life: Reading, Art, and Polemics in the Cîteaux Moralia in Job* (Princeton, NJ, 1997)

Scarry, Elaine, *The Body in Pain: The Making and Unmaking of the World* (Oxford, 1985)

Scheil, Andrew, *The Footsteps of Israel: Understanding Jews in Anglo-Saxon England* (Ann Arbor, MI, 2004)

Scherb, Victor, 'Blasphemy and the Grotesque in the Digby Mary Magdalene', *Studies in Philology*, XCVI (1999), pp. 225–40

Schwartz, Hillel, *The Culture of the Copy: Striking Likenesses, Unreasonable Facsimiles* (New York, 1996)

Scott, A., and C. Kosso, ed., *Fear and its Representations in the Middle Ages and Renaissance* (Leiden, 2003)

Shoemaker, Stephen J., '"Let us Go and Burn her Body": The Image of the Jews in the Early Dormition Traditions', *Church History*, LXVI (1999), pp. 775–823

Sinanoglou, Leah, 'The Christ Child as Sacrifice: A Medieval Tradition and the Corpus Christi Plays', *Speculum*, XLVIII (1973), pp. 491–509

Stanbury, Sarah, *The Visual Object of Desire in Late Medieval England* (Philadelphia, 2007)

Steinberg, Leo, *The Sexuality of Christ in Renaissance Art and in Modern*

Oblivion, 2nd edn (Chicago, 1996)

Strickland, Debra Higgs, *Saracens, Demons and Jews: Making Monsters in Medieval Art* (Princeton, NJ, 2003)

Wharton, Annabel, *Selling Jerusalem: Relics, Replicas, Theme Parks* (Chicago, 2006)

Woolf, Rosemary, *The English Religious Lyric in the Middle Ages* (Oxford, 1968)

Yuval, Israel, *Two Nations in Your Womb: Perceptions of Jews and Christians in Late Antiquity and the Middle Ages*, trans. Barbara Harshav and Jonathan Chipman (Berkeley, CA, 2006)

Ziolkowski, Jan, 'Avatars of Ugliness in Medieval Literature', *Modern Language Review*, LXXIX (1984), pp. 1–20

Acknowledgements

It is a pleasure to record the generous support I have received for this project. The Leverhulme Trust awarded me a Research Fellowship; The University of Michigan, Ann Arbor, awarded me a Frankel Fellowship; and Birkbeck, University of London, provided a congenial, supportive academic home. The book could not have been written without two superb libraries: The British Library and the University of Michigan University Library.

Parts of chapter Two were rehearsed as 'The Jew in Profile', *New Medieval Literatures*, 8 (2006), and I am very grateful to Simon Forde at Brepols for permission to republish a reworked version here.

Audiences at lectures and conferences have given me so much constructive feedback, at the universities of Cambridge, Cardiff, Exeter, Iowa, Oxford (*Imagining Jerusalem in the Medieval West* conference), Pennsylvania, Manchester, Michigan, Sussex (*Religions of the Book* conference), Tel Aviv (*Jewish Art in Context* conference), Toronto, Warwick, and also at the New Chaucer Society congress at Swansea and London Medieval Society. I am also very grateful to those who organized these occasions, specifically to Kate Ash, Anke Bernau, Helen Cooper, Rita Copeland, Matthew Dimmock, Lucy Donkin, Todd Endelmann, Alexandra Gillespie, Simha Goldin, Diane Heath, Elliot Kendall, Kathy Lavezzo, Kathy Mair, Emma Mason, Deborah Dash Moore, Helen Phillips, Miri Rubin, Fiona Somerset, and David Stern. Many colleagues and friends have discussed this work with me and helped me with points of information, often challenging me and causing me to think again: thanks to Amir Banbaji, Tomer Condon-Siegal, Tony Edwards, David Feldman, Shimon Gat, Steven Kruger, Lisa Lampert-Weissig, Megan MacNamee, Vivian Mann, Tim Phillips, Danna Piroyansky, Gervase Rosser, Miri Rubin, Paul Strohm, Barry Trachtenberg, Hal Weitzman and Lorna Campbell. Annie Crombie, Agatha Crombie, Tammy Reynolds, Alex Barker, and Ben Wright asked all the right questions. I'm very grateful to my parents, Ruth and John, for all their encouragement and support. Isabel Davis, Kathy Lavezzo, Michael Leaman, Martha Jay, Molly Murray and Anat Pick read, and gave especially helpful feedback on, parts of the text. Mika Ahuvia provided superb and crucial research assistance during my time in Michigan, and BeagleBrain of Ann Arbor saved my data when my laptop died at a particularly inopportune moment. Any errors and shortcomings in these pages are, of course, my own.

This book is dedicated with love to Tim, for everything, and to Percy, for playing while I worked.

Photo Acknowledgements

The author and publishers wish to express their thanks to the following sources of illustrative material and/or permission to reproduce it:

Anthony Bale: p. 119, 131, 136, 137, 148, 155, 156, 157; Bodleian Library, University of Oxford: pp. 47, 48; All Rights Reserved © The British Library Board: pp. 13, 63, 71, 74, 75, 80, 91, 100, 102, 129, 146, 181; © The Trustees of the British Museum: p. 46 (1922.4-12); © The Courtauld Institute of Art, London: p. 151; Item Reproduced by Permission of the Huntington Library, San Marino, California: p. 67; Courtesy of The Library of the Jewish Theological Seminary: pp. 175, 176 top and bottom; Katherine Lewis: p. 51; John Lowden: p. 37; Anne Marshall: p. 60; © RMN/René-Gabriel Ojéda: p. 89; Timothy Phillips: p. 152; Photo © Victoria and Albert Museum, London: p. 86; Reproduced by kind permission of the Dean and Chapter of York: p. 108.

Index

Medieval names are entered under their common forms, e.g. 'Chaucer, Geoffrey' but 'Anselm of Canterbury'. References to modern scholars are given when integral to evidence or argument. Manuscripts discussed in details are listed under 'Manuscripts'. English place-names (other than county-towns) are followed by their medieval county; European place-names are given, where appropriate, with their modern name and current country.

Acta Cyriaci 144
Acta Pilati, see Gospel of Nicodemus
Ad Herennium 31, 33–4, 77, 82, 209 n.24
Adorno, Anselmo 139–40, 156–8, 231 n.82
Adorno, Jacopo 158
Adorno, Pietro 158
aequalitas 73
affect (*adfectus, affectio*) 14, 17–22, 29, 32–3, 40, 44, 57, 65, 68, 81, 111–12, 114, 122, 133, 170
Albertus Magnus 66, 205 n.81
al-Idrīsī 132
amor 27
Andrew, St 74, 140
Annas 161
Anselm of Canterbury 10, 28, 106, 155
antithesis 73, 77, 211 n.45, 213 n.88
antitheton 77, 210 n.44, 211 n.45
Aquinas, Thomas 14–15, 17, 69, 85
Arasse, Daniel 77
Arendt, Hannah 68, 187
Arezzo (Italy) 144
Aristotle 12, 22–3, 28, 169, 205 n.81, 235 n.37
Asad, Talal 10, 25
Augustine of Hippo 7, 10–11, 15–16, 24–5, 26, 31, 69, 78, 114, 177–8, 179, 189, 230 n.69

Augustinians 29, 167, 228 n.49
Averroës 169–70
Avicenna 183–4

Bacon, Roger 24
Barasch, Moshe 65
Bartholomew, St 74
Belting, Hans 68
Benedictines 51
Benjamin of Tudela 140
Bennett, Jill 21
Bernard of Clairvaux 26, 33, 36, 42, 198 n.72
Bernstein, Michael André 185
Bertrandon de la Brocquière 138
Beverley (Yorkshire) 148–9
Black Death 27
Boethius 131
Bologna (Italy) 130, 150
Boncompagno da Signa 35, 73
Bradwardine, Thomas 35, 92, 111
Bridget of Sweden 165
Brindle (Lancashire) 147
Bromyard, John 59–60
Broughton (Buckinghamshire) 58–60
Bruges [Brugge] (Belgium) 139, 156–9
Brussels 107
Burgh, Benedict 66
Burgh-by-Sands (Cumberland) 120

Burke, Edmund 11
Burnsall (Yorkshire) 149
Bury St Edmunds (Suffolk) 51, 52, 102, 184

Caiaphas 71–3, 106, 130, 161
Cambrai (France) 150
Camille, Michael 16, 19–20, 81, 176–7
Candia [Heraklion] (Greece) 137
Canterbury (Kent) 51, 165
Carmelites 133
Carruthers, Mary 23, 31, 68, 121, 122, 216 n.30, 235 n.37
Catherine of Alexandria, St 30
Catherine of Siena 28
Caumont, seigneur de 132, 137, 140
Centula-St Riquier (France) 216 n.30
Chalgrove (Oxfordshire) 96–9, 101, 105
Chastiau Pélerin ['Atlit] (Israel) 150
Chaucer, Geoffrey 200 n.12:
    'Pardoner's Tale' 59; 'Prioress's
    Tale' 31, 39–40, 85
Christ, see Jesus Christ
Christopher, St 124
Church of the Holy Sepulchre 118, 119–20, 123, 125, 127, 130–32, 135–6, 138–9, 142, 149–53, 158
Cicero 24, 30, 33, 77, 78, 110
circumcision 39, 43–5, 49, 52, 214 n.13, 229 n.55
Clement IV, pope 27
Clement, St 115
clementia 14, 25
Cohn-Sherbok, Dan 187
Colchester (Essex) 149
Colombe, Jean 86
compunctus, compunctio cordis 31, 76, 79
Constance [Konstanz] (Germany) 163
Constantine the Great 142
contentio 17, 77, 112

contrapositum 77
contrarium 17
Copeland, Rita 74, 210 n.39
Croxton Play of the Sacrament 111–14
crudelitas 14
curiositas 165
Currance, Robert 153
Cynewulf 144–5
Cyprus 124

Daniel 131–2
David, Gerard 158
De physiognomia libellus 66
disciplina 17
Dobson, Barrie 170
Dominicans 21, 133
dreams 52–3, 54–5, 127
Duby, Georges 36
ductus 96, 98, 101, 158
Dysmas 80, 130–31

Eckhart von Hochheim 35–6
Edington (Wiltshire) 155–7
Edmund, St 54, 74, 85, 120
Edward I, king 120
Egeria 121
Elche [Elx] (Spain) 107
Eliot, George 185
Emmaus 124, 135
Enders, Jody 35
Enfaunces de Jesu Crist 46–8
Enguerrand de Monstrelet 119
Enlightenment 9–11
Ephraim of Bonn 171–4
Epstein, Marc Michael 177, 234 n.28
Eriugena 30
ethos 32

Fabri, Felix 133–4, 138–9
Fabyan, Robert 119–20
Fetullus 132
Finn, Elizabeth 118
Foucault, Michel 9–10, 112

Franciscans 42, 115, 132–4, 136, 138,
    151, 163, 199 n.86, 202 n.51, 221
    n.13, 223 n.50, 231 n.80
Freud, Sigmund 8–9, 49–50, 188
Frey, Dagobert 73

Gargrave (Yorkshire) 148
Gaza 138
Geoffrey of Monmouth 149
George, St 85, 124, 139–40
Gestas 130–31
gestus, gesture 44, 48, 54, 65, 79,
    81, 84, 90–92, 209 n.24, 210
    n.39
Giotto di Bondone 65
Girard, René 10
Glossa Ordinaria 15
Gloucester 51
Golden Legend, see Jacobus de
    Voragine
Gospel of Nicodemus 130–31, 222
    n.35
Gospel of Pseudo-Matthew 45–6
Gothic 9
Gregory of Tours 93, 144
Gregory the Great 30
Grimestone, John 42
Grimm [brothers], Jacob and
    Wilhelm 7, 24, 188
Gubar, Susan 82

Halevi, Judah 10
Hautvillers (France) 145
Hawes, Stephen 31
Helena, St 124, 136, 142–9, 222 n.26,
    225 n.12
Henry IV, king 118–20, 135
Henry of Huntingdon 149
Herod the Great 36–8, 41
Holy Innocents 38–9, 49, 62–3
horror 8, 11, 17–18, 86, 188
Hugh of Lincoln, St 184
Hugh of St Victor 85, 180
Huizinga, Johan 45

illustratio 77
imitatio Christi 24, 27, 35–6, 75, 80,
    134, 151, 161–3, 165, 230 n.75
inventio 142
Isidore of Seville 77–8

Jacobus de Voragine 35, 94–5, 99,
    103, 144
Jaffa (Israel) 124, 137, 140
James, St 140
Jean, duke of Berry 86
Jephonius 90–96
Jeroboam 115
Jerome, St 82, 123
Jerusalem 93, 98, 107, 118–36,
    138–40, 142–67
Jesus Christ 12–17, 18–20, 24–30, 32,
    36, 38–9, 50, 55, 57, 58–60, 62,
    75, 78–81, 82–4, 94–5, 113, 115,
    165; childhood of 38 41–3, 45–8,
    52, 61, 77; face of 67–8, 71–3;
    imprisonment of 129–34; *see
    also* circumcision; *imitatio
    Christi*, martyrdom
Jewish Boy of Bourges 47
John de Cheyney 56–7
John of Damascus 115
John of Genoa 21
John of Salisbury 19
John of Würzburg 132–3
John the Baptist, St 131
Joseph of Chartres 171–2
Josephus 170–71
Judas 57, 65, 67, 81–8
Judas Cyriacus 144–9

Kempe, Margery 160–65, 167
Kiddush ha-Shem 171–2
Kierkegaard, Søren 11
King's Lynn (Norfolk) 152–4
Knuuttila, Simo 7

Laurence, St 74
Lavater, Johann Caspar 66
Le Puy 184

Leonard, St 131

Limbourg, Herman, Paul and
　　Johan 86

Lincoln 51, 58, 184

Lisbon 39

Litlyngton, Nicholas 118

liturgy 10, 20, 39, 40, 53, 77, 88,
　　96–9, 104–5, 107, 121, 123, 128,
　　130, 150, 155 6, 158, 171–3

Loddon (Norfolk) 51–2

Longinus 79–81

Love, Nicholas 13–14, 17, 43, 70

Lucy, St 124

Luttrell Psalter, see Manuscripts

Luttrell, Geoffrey 13, 16–17, 31, 62

Lydda [Lod] (Israel) 140

Lydgate, John 43, 66, 85

Lynn, see King's Lynn

MacCormack, Sabine 159

Malory, Thomas 131

Mandeville, Sir John 140

mansuetudine 25

manuscripts: Chantilly, Musée
　　Condé MS 65 (Très Riches
　　Heures du Duc de Berry)
　　86–9; BL Add. MS 14761
　　(Barcelona Haggadah) 182;
　　BL Add. MS 42130 (Luttrell
　　Psalter) 12–16, 18, 22, 23–4,
　　62–4, 101–2; BL Add. MS 48985
　　(Salvin Hours) 70–75, 79–81;
　　BL Add. MS 70000 (Percy
　　Psalter) 180–81; BL Cotton MS
　　Nero A. X 128–9; BL Harley 616
　　180; BL Harley MS 2888 180;
　　BL Royal MS 6.E.VI 99–100;
　　BL Yates Thompson MS 13
　　(Taymouth Hours) 90–92, 101;
　　New York, Jewish Theological
　　Seminary MS 9478 (Prato
　　Haggadah) 174; Oxford,
　　Bodleian Library MS Bodley
　　565 154–7, 228 n.50; Oxford,
　　Bodleian Library MS Selden

Supra 38 46–7

mappa mundi 79, 80, 120, 155

Margaret, St 131

Mark, St 124

Marr, Wilhelm 66

Martial, St 140

martyrdom 14, 24, 27, 31, 36, 39, 42,
　　50–54, 57, 74–81, 85, 87, 124,
　　139–40, 145, 147, 170–72; see also
　　kiddush ha-Shem

Mary 36, 39, 41–5, 48, 53, 58, 61,
　　76–8, 87, 90–111, 115, 132, 145,
　　154–6

Masada (Israel) 170–71

Massacre of the Innocents, see Holy
　　Innocents

meditatio 122

Menahem of Worms 171–2

Merback, Mitchell 23

Meshullam of Volterra 141

Metrical Life of Christ 81

Milan [Milano] (Italy) 39

Mirk, John 60–61

Mirzoeff, Nicholas 183

Mohammed 105

Moore, R. I. 185

Neoplatonism 24–5

Nicholas, St 124

Nicholson, James 84

Nirenberg, David 186

Nizzahon Vetus 25–6

Norwich 51, 54–5, 57–8, 67

Nottingham 166–7

N-Town plays 101–7

Offa, king 120

oppositio 17, 98

optics 31

ostensio vulnerum 61

Oswald, king 115

Othmar 132

Oxford 70

Padua (Italy) 38

Paris 107, 145

Pascasius Radbertus 79

passio 17, 49, 52, 55, 59, 61–2, 70, 73, 75, 162

pathos 14, 26, 32, 40; *see also* affect, *adfectus*

Paul, St 74, 124, 131, 140

Paula, St 123

Pearl 127–9

Perry, Marvin 187

Perspective, perspective 21, 68, 70, 72, 77, 80, 209 n.38

Peter, St 140

Physiognomia Latina 66

Physiognominica 66

physiognomy 65–8, 81, 85

Piacenza (Italy) 150

Pierro della Francesca 144

Pietro d'Abano 66

Pilate 83, 130, 132, 222 n.35

Polo, Marco 131

Poloner, John 123

Prinz, Jesse 19

Prudentius 31, 34–5, 170

Pseudo-Bonaventure 13, 43, 84, 131

Pseudo-Cicero, *see Ad Herennium*

Pseudo-Melito of Sardis 93

pulchrum 73

punctus 31

Pynson, Richard 154

Quintilian 31–3, 110, 170

Rachel 38, 40, 201 n.40

Ramle (Israel) 135–41

relics 38, 93, 95, 105, 116, 122, 124, 126, 135, 140, 142–4, 147, 150, 152, 155–6, 160, 217 n.40, 217 n.44, 227 n.37, 229 n.65

Repyngdon, Philip 163

Rhodes (Greece) 124

Richard of St Victor 10

Ripoll (Spain) 107

Robert of Bury 52, 184

Roch, St 131

Rome 143, 159

Rushton Spencer (Staffordshire) 148

sacri monti 150–52

sado-masochism 25

Safed [Tzfat] (Israel) 150

Saladin 118

Salisbury (Wiltshire) 39

Santiago de Compostella (Spain) 159

Santo Toribio di Liébana (Spain) 159

sapientia 165

Saracens 70, 125, 132, 139, 140, 163, 165, 166

Scarry, Elaine 10

Schechter, Ronald 113

Schwartz, Hillel 159–60

Schweitzer, Frederick 187

scientia 165

Scot, Michael 66

Secreta secretorum 66

Sefer Chasidim 168–9

Sefer Minhagim 27

Sefton (Lancashire) 147

Seneca 14, 131

Shakespeare, William 58, 84, 118

Simeon, St 124

Simon de Nodariis 55

souvenirs 135, 143, 147

Stasyons of Jerusalem 124–6, 133

Stephaton 79–81

Stephen, king 52, 55

Stephen, St 144, 226 n.14

Stewart, Susan 143

Strasbourg 27

Sylvester II, pope 120

Tertullian 11

Theodoric 132

Thomas à Kempis 35, 50

Thomas Becket, St 74–5

Thomas of Monmouth 50, 52–7

Toaff, Ariel 151
Torkington, Richard 139–40
Towneley plays 58–9
Trent [Trento] (Italy) 58
Tring (Hertfordshire) 45
trivium 31
Turbe, William 50

uglincss 33 4, 65, 67, 69, 73, 88, 92,
     110, 189, 209 n.25

Valencia (Spain) 107
Valenciennes (France) 107
Varallo (Italy) 150–51, 165
Venice [Venezia] (Italy) 163
Virgin, *see* Mary

Walsingham (Norfolk) 154
Warner, Marina 43
Waterford (Ireland) 202 n.51
Weaver, William 164
Wells (Somerset) 166
Westminster Abbey 118–19, 160
Wey, William 154–7
Wharton, Annabel 165
William of Newburgh 170–72
William of Norwich 50–58, 81
William of St Thierry 27
Wilton Diptych 85
Winchester (Hampshire) 51
Wistrich, Robert 186
Woolf, Rosemary 110

Yates, Frances 68
Yehudah Ha-Chasid 168
Yom Tov of Joigny 172, 232 n.12
York 107–10, 149, 161, 170–74